THE HISTORICAL JESUS
A Continuing Quest

THE
HISTORICAL JESUS
A Continuing Quest

by

CHARLES C. ANDERSON

WILLIAM B. EERDMANS PUBLISHING COMPANY
Grand Rapids, Michigan

To
DOROTHY

Wife, Homemaker, Mother,
God's greatest human gift to us,
My choicest earthly treasure

Preface

The critical study of the life of Jesus has been a subject of intense investigation for almost two centuries now. The ways in which critics have dealt with the subject have been many and diverse. In the present study we join that investigation on the basis of six questions:

(1) Is it possible to write a biography (history) of Jesus?
(2) What is the place of miracle in the life of Jesus?
(3) How should the resurrection of Jesus be interpreted? Literally or in some other way?
(4) What is the nature and place of mythology in the New Testament?
(5) What is the historical value of John as compared with the Synoptics?
(6) What is the central significance of Jesus?

The first chapter presents in outline form the theological premises on which this study is based, along with the process by which the author arrived at those premises. This chapter has been included so that the rationale for the further treatment of the subject may be clearly before us.

The following chapters take up successively the six areas suggested by the six questions. Each chapter combines two approaches to the subject: (1) How should the question be answered from a biblical perspective? (2)

How well have modern critical movements done in answering the question in light of the biblical perspective?

It will become apparent that the author considers history, and the course of Jesus' life as a part of that history, of primary importance for the Christian faith; and that different critical positions take history with varying degrees of seriousness. Furthermore, the question of history is examined from both a quantitative and a qualitative perspective. That is, what is the nature of history?

This study gives particular attention to the philosophical orientation of each specific approach to the life of Jesus. The philosophical point of departure of the various critical movements has had a great deal to do with the amount and nature of history that each movement has found in the Gospels.

—C.C.A.

Contents

CHAPTER ONE

The Source of Authority

Introduction

In the final chapter of *The Quest of the Historical Jesus*, Albert Schweitzer came to grips with the question of the historical accuracy of the Gospel portrait of Jesus' life. He there contrasted his historical conclusions with those of Wilhelm Wrede. Schweitzer's final chapter bore the title "Thoroughgoing Scepticism and Thoroughgoing Eschatology."[1] His chief point was that if one followed the logic of Wrede's hypotheses he would land in skepticism, whereas if one followed Schweitzer's own hypotheses he would find Jesus as the complete messianic figure who is presented to us in the Gospels.

With the first of these two alternatives we find ourselves in complete agreement. We shall develop this further shortly, but it is sufficient here to affirm that if the kind of investigation pursued by Wrede and his many successors in the critical school is legitimate, the net result can only be that we must forever give up any attempt to know certainly anything of the life or character of that first-century personality, Jesus.

With the second element in Schweitzer's conclusion, however, we cannot agree. The Jesus whom he finally presents is little more than a deluded, apocalyptic fanatic.

[1] Albert Schweitzer, *The Quest of the Historical Jesus*, trans. W. Montgomery (New York: Macmillan, 1910), pp. 330-97.

While we may admire a man's resourcefulness and constancy in the face of danger and defeat, if that attitude is not coupled with truth but is rather only a product of delusion, he cannot command our respect and devotion. It is the contention of this chapter, therefore, that there must be some means of ascertaining the accuracy and truth of the picture of Jesus in the Gospels, or else we may as well discard the Gospels along with the rest of the Bible as worthless documents concerning human redemption, even though we may continue to admire them as ancient literary productions.

What we shall do here, therefore, is attempt to clear the ground for our analysis in the succeeding chapters. We feel that this is the best way to approach the subject, for then the background that accounts for this particular investigation will be clearly before us.

It must be admitted in the first place that none of us approaches the New Testament, or any other piece of literature, from a completely detached point of view. We all are born into a particular society at a particular time. We all share in the common store of our culture and its predecessors. We all develop a certain set of values. We all learn to separate truth and error according to the norms of the prevailing society or culture. We could draw up at great length those factors which condition us and have an effect on our analysis of the New Testament. Furthermore, we need to begin with a frank and honest admission of our thinking with respect to man's relationship to the Supreme Being and of our ability to communicate, have fellowship with, and please him.

This backlog of information is very important. None of us comes without it, but what is even more important, and what we are contending for here, is that whatever may be included in that backlog, it must not completely predetermine our response to the New Testament. If that be the case, the New Testament will have little more effect on us ultimately than a telephone book. What the writer has particularly in mind here is the *Vorverständnis* of Bultmann. If one approaches the New Testament with a preconception of what it means to live authentically, he has set himself up as a standard above the text he examines, and it is a foregone conclusion what he will find in it. If I know what is the true meaning of life, it is of no value to me to seek it in the Bible or elsewhere. At this point the remarks of Barth in reply to Bultmann are most apropos:

> Of course, everyone approaches the New Testament with some kind of preconception, as he does any other document. We all have our prior notions of possibility, truth and importance. We all know what we think is our capacity to understand. And, of course, as we seek to understand the New Testament, our first reaction is bound to be one of self-defence against its strangeness. We shall want to cling to our prior understanding and preconceptions. More than that, we shall always be trying to confine this strangeness within the strait jacket of our prior understandings and preconceptions. We shall always be trying to incorporate and domesticate its strange elements. But have we any right to elevate all this into a methodological principle? . . . What is the relevance here of idealism or positivism, to which our fathers were so attached? . . . How can we listen to the New Testament if we are always thrusting some *conditio sine qua non* between ourselves and the text? To do it is to invite all kinds of wrong exegesis, if nothing worse. Surely it would be better to cultivate as flexible and open-minded approach as we can, instead of donning the existentialist strait jacket? Better by far to wait and see if we can understand it first. Let the New Testament serve as the catalyst of our capacity to understand. Do not make our capacity to understand the catalyst of the New Testament! Accept the New Testament's understanding of ourselves before we take our own self-understanding too seriously and try to force it on the text. If we adopted this procedure, we should find our understanding of the text enhanced.[2]

There is, however, another danger from the opposite direction. In some circles it is considered almost sacrilegious to undertake the kind of investigation we are engaged in here. I am reminded of a young man concerning whom one of my college professors told me one day. After the professor had gone on for some time in class

[2] Karl Barth, "Rudolf Bultmann—an Attempt to Understand Him," *Kerygma and Myth*, II, ed. Hans Werner Bartsch, trans. Reginald H. Fuller (London: S. P. C. K., 1962), pp. 124-25.

regarding the Bible and its trustworthiness, the student raised his hand and commented, "I'd believe the Bible if it said that the moon was made out of green cheese." To this my professor in a clear display of wisdom replied, "You wouldn't either. You'd throw it in the nearest trash can!" This, I think, points out the other danger that lurks at the door of orthodoxy. To be sure, many theologians of the liberal and existentialist variety feel that the Bible abounds in statements that partake of the character of "the moon is made of green cheese," but the conservative theologian denies this. He has great confidence in the reliability of the New Testament because in every instance where he has been able to check it out, it has proved itself a reliable and trustworthy document. Therefore, while he makes no pretense of coming to the Scriptures with no presuppositions, he feels that his own presuppositions fit most adequately the facts of human existence *and* the Scriptures.

This leads us to a further area. What view of man is most adequate to explain both the fact of human existence and that of the Bible? If the twentieth century has done one thing, it has served to demonstrate shockingly and convincingly that the old liberal view of the nature of man was hopelessly naïve. One hesitates even to mention the evidence, for it is so horrifyingly obvious to us all: an economic depression the likes of which our world has never before seen; the most horrible wars conceivable in pre-twentieth-century man's imagination; a world that has become so used to sitting on the brink of thermonuclear annihilation that it does not even talk of it too openly. All this in a day when man was at last supposed to realize the great benefits of an age of scientific and technological progress.

We have had to learn that if you give a wicked man a spear he is dangerous, but if you give him a stockpile of hydrogen bombs he is terrifying; and in spite of our whistling in the dark there is no reason to believe that sooner or later, apart from the direct intervention of God, annihilation of the human race will not take place.

All this has been mentioned as an exhibit of the

depravity of mankind; and while we have been speaking primarily on the level of international politics, the evidence on the individual level is a thousand times more obvious. The most obvious and apparent fact of human existence, in our view, is the *total depravity* of human nature. This frequently misunderstood phrase means that every part of man's nature has been affected, and that there is in man a complete lack of spiritual good, or good in its essential relation to God. This concept does not mean that men are as bad as they can be, that they have no knowledge of God or of good or evil, that they are incapable either of seeing good in their fellow men or of performing charitable acts to them, or that every depraved man is a victim of every form of sin.[3] Simply put, it is the belief that man is improperly and adversely oriented toward God.

What makes all this so impressive to the conservative theologian is that the point of view he reaches from his examination of current human experience is precisely the same as what he sees portrayed in the Bible. The Bible does not tell about a "moon made of green cheese," which is directly contrary to fact. It talks about fallen men; and when the conservative theologian looks about him, that is precisely what he sees.

As we develop in this chapter the background and basis for the following chapters, we can and must do so only very briefly, for other capable scholars have treated these matters at length.[4] Moreover, some of the issues that will be raised here will be dealt with more completely in later chapters. We introduce them here merely to show how they fit into the entire system.

[3] Loraine Boettner, *Studies in Theology* (Grand Rapids: Eerdmans, 1947), pp. 246-47.

[4] While a long list could be given here, the reader is referred in particular to the following in addition to the works cited in this chapter: E. J. Carnell, *An Introduction to Christian Apologetics* (Grand Rapids: Eerdmans, 1948); James Orr, *Revelation and Inspiration* (New York: Scribner, 1910); and B. B. Warfield, *The Inspiration and Authority of the Bible* (Philadelphia: Presbyterian and Reformed, 1948).

Special Revelation

Of the various categories into which revelation has been and may be divided, two of the most constantly used are "general revelation" and "special revelation." Berkhof defines general revelation as "a revelation in nature round about us, in human consciousness, and in the providential government of the world"[5]; and special revelation as "a revelation embodied in the Bible as the Word of God."[6] More recently special revelation has been defined by some in a less specific sense so that it has the idea of the immediate or direct communication of truth. We shall return to a consideration of this shortly. To put the matter perhaps more simply, by general revelation we mean that knowledge of God which man can gain by the observation of nature and the use of his reason; by special revelation we mean that knowledge of God which is the result of God's immediate or direct action or which comes by the communication of words.

To an important degree we have centered in these two ideas of revelation the real substance of the theological debates that have characterized modern theology. Prior to the era of the Enlightenment, while the reality of general revelation was admitted by all, special revelation was taken very seriously and as being the determinative element in the relationship of God with man. The last two centuries, however, have been characterized by increased subjectivism in theological study. Man has set himself up as the final authority in matters of religion. In place of submission to Scripture, we find the assertion of the competence of man as the final authority for religious truth.

This great confidence in the ability of man to solve his problems unaided was one of the characteristic features of the theology of liberalism, and it remained unchallenged in the critical school until the time of Karl Barth. Although orthodoxy had long seen where such a dispro-

[5] Louis Berkhof, *Systematic Theology* (Grand Rapids: Eerdmans, 1959), p. 36.

[6] *Ibid.*

portionate emphasis on general revelation led, Barth was the first to expose its fallacy to critical scholars:

> It is not the right human thoughts about God which form the content of the Bible, but the right divine thoughts about men. The Bible tells us not how we should talk with God but what he says to us; not how we find the way to him, but how he has sought and found the way to us; not the right relation in which we must place ourselves to him, but the covenant which he has made with all who are Abraham's spiritual children and which he has sealed once and for all in Jesus Christ.[7]

The work of Barth signaled a return to an emphasis on special revelation; but as so often in theology, the return to a theological term does not necessarily mean a return to the former content of that term. The theological position generally designated neo-orthodoxy takes special revelation very seriously. It has not, however, returned to the idea of special revelation as it has been traditionally held in the Christian Church, but has given to the term a new meaning that we shall discuss shortly.

With Bultmann and his successors, and those critics to the left of Bultmann, there has returned an emphasis on general revelation and the attendant emphasis on the ability of man. Ogden has stated it most succinctly: "If the price for becoming a faithful follower of Jesus Christ is some form of self-destruction, whether of the body or of the mind—*sacrificium corporis, sacrificium intellectus*—then there is no alternative but that the price remain unpaid."[8]

In another context he pleads for what amounts to a doctrine of general revelation when he writes,

> One of the most pressing tasks of postliberal theology is to so formulate the doctrine of revelation that *this* point is made its controlling center. This means, of course, we will have to reject all the traditional attempts to distinguish sharply between "Old Testament and New Testament," "law and gos-

[7] Karl Barth, *The Word of God and the Word of Man*, trans. Douglas Horton (New York: Harper, 1957), p. 43.

[8] Schubert M. Ogden, *Christ Without Myth* (New York: Harper, 1961), p. 130.

pel," "nature and grace," "philosophy and theology," "general revelation and special revelation," "reason and faith," "question and answer," "prophecy and fulfillment." ... Faith has nothing to gain and much to lose if it is not made unmistakably clear that no other word is spoken in Jesus than is everywhere spoken in the actual events of nature and history and specifically witnessed to with more or less adequacy by "the law and the prophets."[9]

In any attempt to arrive at an adequate doctrine of revelation, the conservative theologian sees two inherent dangers. One is the danger of saying that either general revelation or special revelation is the proper conception. While the conservative puts great weight and emphasis on special revelation, general revelation does find an important place in his thinking. General revelation serves to illustrate the severity of the plight in which man finds himself, for instead of responding to it properly, man misunderstands and abuses it, and this only stands to underscore his guilt.

The second danger to the conservative theologian lies in placing general and special revelation on the same plane. While general revelation is of value, special revelation is absolutely essential. It therefore transcends general revelation in value and gives to it the place of importance it occupies. Man apart from special help from God is not able to reach the conclusions he needs to reach from examination of his sensory environment alone.

At this point it is of utmost importance that we understand from a biblical perspective the proper relationship of revelation to reason. It is not that the Bible or revelation sets itself up as opposed to or contrary to reason; it is rather that the biblical conception of revelation professes to contain material beyond reason or the unaided ability of man to know.

There are, therefore, two primary factors that make special revelation absolutely necessary: (1) Human depravity has caused man to misuse and pervert general revelation; and (2) general revelation does not contain enough of a witness to lead man to a meaningful relation-

[9] *Ibid.*, p. 156.

ship to God. Let us look at each of these factors briefly.

The misuse and perversion of general revelation is dealt with most systematically from a biblical perspective by Paul in the first part of Romans. In the section 1:18-3:20 he deals with the inadequacy of both the general revelation and the special revelation given to the Jews until the coming of Christ. Neither group has made adequate use of the revelation given to it. Of the Gentiles he writes, "For although they knew God they did not honor him as God or give thanks to him, but they became futile in their thinking and their senseless minds were darkened" (1:21). More primarily in reference to the Jews he writes, "For no human being will be justified in his sight by works of the law, since through the law comes knowledge of sin" (3:20). He summarizes his contention respecting both groups when he says, "I have already charged that all men, both Jews and Greeks, are under the power of sin" (3:9). It is human sinfulness, therefore, that renders general revelation inadequate, and as a matter of fact would make special revelation of little more value had it not culminated in Jesus Christ (3:21-26).

But there is a second reason for the necessity of special revelation. Not only does man abuse and misuse general revelation, but general revelation does not contain enough substance to give man what he needs to know about the nature and requirements of God. As Ramm has noted, it is necessary because of the transcendence and incomprehensibility of God.[10] Here liberalism and its successors have gone astray by overemphasizing the significance of man's religious experience. One need only look at religion in our contemporary world to see this. Concepts of God and religion are multitudinous and antithetical. This merely serves to illustrate the inability of men to come to the truth solely by the use of general revelation.

It is for this reason that certain of the arguments formerly used by theologians to demonstrate, for example, God's existence—the cosmological argument, the

[10] Bernard Ramm, *Special Revelation and the Word of God* (Grand Rapids: Eerdmans, 1961), p. 21.

teleological argument, the ontological argument, etc.—are little used any more. There appear to be two reasons for this. In the first place, they fall short of absolute proof. In the second place, even if they did prove God's existence, their failure to provide information concerning his nature and requirements renders them virtually useless.

The arguments from the nature of the universe are of little more value. Such attributes as omnipotence and righteousness are not necessary conclusions from an observation of the universe. To the believer all these factors may contribute to a genuine feeling of thankfulness and awe in the presence of his God, but to the unbeliever their value is either nonexistent or very limited.

Nature of Special Revelation

If then special revelation is of supreme importance, the next question becomes, What is the nature of that revelation? This question is particularly relevant as it relates to modern dialectical theology, whose advocates, unlike so many others in the modern period, take special revelation seriously, even though from the perspective of the conservative theologian they take it wrongly. If this movement has one distinguishing characteristic, it is its tendency to separate its conception of special revelation from the Bible. It does so by erecting a series of antitheses which I regard as false. In the first place, these theologians insist that revelation must be personal. It can never be propositional. Neo-liberal and neo-orthodox theologians set up a false antithesis between revelation as communication and revelation as encounter. An inspired experience is substituted for an inspired Scripture.

This spirit appears to be founded more on a theological revolt than on careful theological thought. It is a reaction primarily against doctrinal theology. It takes one part of the solution to the problem and makes it the whole solution. To be sure, God is given to us as a person in revelation. But if we are to carry anything away from the encounter of lasting value, we will also carry some truths and concepts from that encounter.

That the possibility of revelation coming in propositional form must be left open is seen from at least two points of view. In the first place, when one says that propositional revelation is impossible he gives the appearance of stating categorically what is and what is not possible for God. Would anyone seriously question the right and ability of God to reveal himself via the means he chooses?

A second reason for insistence that revelation may come in propositional form is that this is the only way in which its truth may be asserted and shared by all. If revelation is purely a personal matter, we find a situation developing in which the individual personality becomes the final judge of the truth of revelation. This is mysticism. To be sure, Christianity has elements of mysticism in it, but it is always a mysticism that is checked against an objective standard—the Bible. If that standard be removed, there is no telling where this mystic tendency may lead—or has led, for that matter.

A second modern antithesis, related to the first, insists that all revelation must be from subject to subject, not from object to subject. This would appear to be one of the contributions that existentialist philosophy has made to this theological camp. The objections to this antithesis are in general the same as they were to the one discussed above, but there is a further important fallacy in this position. It fails to take seriously the sovereignty of God. We are not dealing here with a man-to-man relationship, but rather with a man-to-God relationship, and that relationship has been disrupted by sin. This being so, man's approach to God must be made in submission. He must wait for the divine self-disclosure, and he must accept it in humility however it comes.

A final antithesis that is sometimes drawn sets up the Word of God against the text of Scripture. This antithesis states that in view of textual criticism any attempt to identify the revelation of God with the text of Scripture is untenable. We shall discuss briefly, subsequently, the question of the text of the New Testament. It is sufficient here to note that for all practical purposes we have the original text of the New Testament, so that particular antithesis dissolves.

It may appear that we are spending an undue amount of time in examining dialectical theology and its revelational position. We feel that this attention is necessary, however, for two reasons. While the dialectical theologians have spent most of their efforts in the field of theology rather than in that of history, their studies are based at least in part on the results of the critical historical school. In the second place, any apologetic for a particular approach to the problems under discussion in this book must seek to define and clarify its position in relation to the other possible alternatives.

Let us, therefore, summarize the position at which we have arrived. Conservative theology, as we have sketched it, based as it is on a recognition of man's depravity and the inadequacy of general revelation to tell man what he needs to know about God, insists on the necessity of special revelation. That revelation he finds in the Scriptures. The only test that can be used to evaluate that revelation, therefore, is the test of logical consistency. If the Scriptures pass this test they may be accepted as God's special revelation. What we contend here is that the Scriptures pass this test and are, therefore, a meaningful revelation for rational man.

As against this, dialectical theology finds itself in real difficulty. It attempts to hold a loftier concept of God than liberalism did, along with the old liberal idea of Scripture. These two elements do not mix well, and as a result it lapses into irrationalism.

We have to this point developed a conservative concept of special revelation from the point of view of logic. It also can and should be developed briefly from the point of view of history. The conservative theologian begins here with the belief that God desired to reveal himself to man. The process by which he chose to do so is what we have revealed for us in the Bible. That revelation begins with the creation of man but later, because of his rebellion, involves a smaller fragment of mankind. Thus with Adam and Noah the circle of revelation involves all mankind. With Abraham, however, the process of selection begins. Israel is now the body to whom he reveals himself. But even Israel rebels, and as a consequence God's revelation is narrowed to only a remnant of Israel. Finally, he sends his Son to this lost and wayward world. By the time of the Son's coming man is fully aware of his need for God's help, and of his inability to please God apart from such help.

In the person and work of Christ man's need is fully met. It is met in two complementary ways: (1) Something is accomplished for man in the life, death, and resurrection of Christ which man is powerless to accomplish apart from those events; and (2) the personalities surrounding those events are given an authoritative interpretation that does not leaves their significance in doubt. This is, no doubt, part of the reason for the high regard for the apostles by the New Testament Church. They were there when the events happened, and they were given understanding as to the meaning of those events.

These events and their interpretation were, of course, immediately available to the members of the primitive Church, but as that Church moved away from those events historically, and as the witnesses to those events became aware of their decrease in numbers, it became apparent to them that because of their importance they must be preserved for posterity. It became apparent to them, that is, because it had always been apparent to God.

If, therefore, this revelation was not to be repeated in successive generations, it became obvious that it must be adequately preserved for them. As Bruce observes, "The historical 'once-for-allness' of Christianity, which distinguishes it from those religious and philosophical systems which are not specially related to any particular time, makes the reliability of the writings which purport to record this revelation a question of first-rate importance."[11]

The process of revelation, therefore, did not end with the events, but when those events had been written into

[11] F. F. Bruce, *The New Testament Documents: Are They Reliable?* (Grand Rapids: Eerdmans, 1960), p. 8.

an accurate and reliable account on the basis of which all subsequent generations could act. Thus the New Testament came into being.

Nature of Inspiration

We have concluded so far that special revelation is absolutely necessary if man is to know God in a meaningful way. We have further concluded that while that revelation consisted in a series of actions on the part of God that were revelatory to man, it was finally put in a fixed form so that it would be available to all future generations. The next question that arises is, What assurance do we have that the Bible is an accurate and valuable account of that revelation? This is what is referred to in the doctrine of inspiration. As Ramm insists, "If 'special revelation' is one side of the coin, the 'inspiration of the Holy Spirit' is the other."[12] We may put this in a slightly different way: If by revelation we mean that God has desired to make something known to man, by inspiration we mean the medium by which God chose to communicate that knowledge.

If on the basis of the previous section we have concluded that God's revelation is in at least some sense to be linked to the Bible, we may begin our investigation of inspiration with an examination of some of the biblical materials on the subject. This will be particularly profitable if we attempt to see how the New Testament views the Old. The words of our Lord here must be considered especially important. Here, as elsewhere in this chapter, our treatment must be illustrative rather than comprehensive. We note here, in particular, two passages of supreme importance. In the early part of the Sermon on the Mount in Matthew, Jesus makes what sounds to modern man like a very shocking statement: "Think not that I have come to abolish the law and the prophets; I have come not to abolish them but to fulfil them. For truly, I say to you, till heaven and earth pass away, not an iota, not a dot, will pass from the law until all is accom-

12 Ramm, p. 61.

plished" (Mt. 5:17-18). The importance of this lies in Jesus' insistence on the value of the most minute element in the law. The *iota* was the smallest of the Greek letters and corresponded to the smallest Hebrew letter, the *yodh*. By "dot" he probably refers not to any given letter but rather to the minutest portion of any letter.

The other passage we shall notice is Jn. 10:35, which contains the parenthetical expression, "and scripture cannot be broken." This verse apparently gives Jesus' estimate of the extent to which the writings of the Old Testament are inspired. It would then seem fair to conclude that Jesus felt God's guidance was present in the formation of the Old Testament in two complementary ways: (1) It extended even to the minutiae of the documents; and (2) it made every part of the revelation of supreme importance so that one is not at liberty to pick and choose what he will accept and what he will reject.

Coupled with this one must notice how consummate was Jesus' desire that the Scripture should be fulfilled in his life. He constantly puts the necessity of obedience, suffering, death, and resurrection in terms of the necessity to fulfil Scripture.

The rest of the New Testament is equally pervaded by a strong doctrine of inspiration. The doctrine of inspiration itself takes its rise from the statement of Paul in II Tim. 3:16: "All scripture is inspired by God and profitable for teaching, for reproof, for correction, and for training in righteousness." The words "inspired by God" are a translation of the Greek *theopneustos*, which means literally "God-breathed." This is a very strong statement, to say the least, and is intended at minimum to indicate that what we have in Scripture is an authentic message from God. It is not a product of human thought even at its best, but a message from God to man. In the opening of his letter to the Romans, Paul refers to "the holy scriptures," a phrase that purportedly would attribute to them the same vital connection with God.

The second epistle of Peter contains a similarly strong statement on the inspiration of the Scriptures: "First of all you must understand this, that no prophecy of scripture is a matter of one's own interpretation, because no prophecy came by the impulse of man, but men, moved by the Holy Spirit, spoke from God" (II Pet. 1:20-21). This statement, while indicating that the source of the communication is God, is most explicit as to the precise role men played in the transmission of that communication.

The remainder of the New Testament is equally emphatic, either by way of implication or by direct statement, as to the inspiration of the Old Testament. The writer of Hebrews, for example, quotes the Old Testament profusely, and simply identifies the speaker as God or the Holy Spirit.

Finally, the divine origin of the Old Testament was not something ascribed to it either by our Lord or by the authors of the New Testament. That authority was acknowledged prior to the time of our Lord.

This then, briefly, covers the Old Testament. What can we say about the New? It need hardly be emphasized that the life of our Lord stands at the center of the biblical story. The narration of that life and the actions and words that made up a part of that life are thus of paramount importance to us. How can we be certain that what we have in the Gospels in this regard is accurate? We have the best clue to this in Jesus' farewell discourse with his disciples recorded in Jn. 14-16. Here he states, "These things I have spoken to you, while I am with you. But the Counselor, the Holy Spirit, whom the Father will send in my name, he will teach you all things, and bring to your remembrance all that I have said to you" (14:25-26). We have stated here the same high doctrine of the Spirit's guidance with respect to the future as we saw claimed for the writings of the past—the Old Testament. This, then, should be sufficient to account for the inspiration of the New Testament.

There are, in addition, some indications in the New Testament books themselves that show that their writers laid claim to this promise. Most specific in this regard are the promises (1:1-3) and warnings (22:18-19) in the book of Revelation. Paul also gives evidence that he is conscious of an authority from God himself. A few of the many passages that may be mentioned are I Thess. 5:27; II Thess. 3:14; I Cor. 14:37; and Col. 4:16.

If it seems that there are few biblical claims to its inspiration, a moment's reflection should clarify the issue. Apparently there are two primary reasons for this: (1) As we have said previously in reference to the Old Testament, we say now in reference to the Bible as a whole: its authority is intrinsic, not extrinsic. Its authority is found in the character of the message it portrays. This was the way the Old Testament reached its acknowledged position of authority, and this is precisely what we should expect in the case of the New Testament. A book of the character of the Bible need not go to lengths to claim inspiration. Books that do this usually bear witness to the falsity of their claim.

(2) But there is a second reason for the paucity of biblical claims to its own inspiration. It will be recalled that at the beginning of this section we noted the interrelationship of revelation and inspiration. There they were shown to be two sides of a coin. But considered from another perspective they must be regarded as sequential. Revelation is first in order of time, and first in order of importance. It is the function of revelation to tell man what he needs to know about God. It is the function of inspiration to preserve that revelation.

The process by which the words and actions of God in his special revelation to mankind have been taken under the guidance of the Holy Spirit and put via the instrumentality of men into the books of our Old and New Testaments has been referred to by some conservative commentators as "inscripturation."

It doubtless will appear odd to some that in a section entitled the "Nature of Inspiration" we have come so far without attempting to define inspiration itself. This has been deliberate, for we thought it well first to survey the material before us before we committed ourselves to any definition. Even now we must exclude some mistaken notions of inspiration. There are two conceptions of the doctrine that must be ruled out because they do not say enough, and one that must be ruled out because it claims too much. The first of these deficient theories is known as the naturalistic or intuition theory. As Strong defines it, "This holds that inspiration is but a higher development of that natural insight into truth which all men possess to some degree."[13] The books of our Bible are primarily the works of men of particular religious genius. Just as there are people who have particular ability in science, in literature, etc., so we have in the Bible the productions of men who were particularly adept in the area of religion. This theory is based on a modified form of belief in general revelation to the exclusion of special revelation, and thus the same arguments that make general revelation to the exclusion of special revelation unacceptable, equally make this theory unacceptable.

The second inadequate conception is the illumination theory. "This regards inspiration as merely an intensifying and elevating of the religious perceptions of the Christian, the same in kind, though greater in degree, with the illumination of every believer by the Holy Spirit."[14] This theory, which puts the inspiration in the writers rather than in their writings, has gained much currency in our century. It states that the Bible is not the Word of God, but that it contains the Word of God. This theory is first of all based upon a confusion of biblical terms; that is, it takes a term that should be used to describe the means by which the contemporary believer *understands* the revelation of God and changes it into a term that indicates the device by which God *communicated* that revelation. But it is beset also by a further difficulty. If the Bible merely contains the Word of God, it is ultimately left up to the individual to determine what is the Word of God and what is not, and thus we are thrown back into a situation little different from the preceding one in which "man is the measure of all things" and only general revelation is necessary.

If there is danger in making a doctrine of inspiration too weak so that we cannot be certain we have an authentic revelation from God, there also is danger in

13 Augustus Hopkins Strong, *Systematic Theology* (New York: Armstrong, 1902), p. 97.

14 *Ibid.*, p. 99.

making the doctrine too rigid so that the end product is completely divorced from the efforts of the writers of the books. This second danger is seen in the dictation theory: "This theory holds that inspiration consisted in such a possession of the minds and bodies of the Scripture writers by the Holy Spirit, that they became passive instruments or amanuenses—pens, not penmen, of God."[15] The dictation theory does not give adequate attention to the individual vocabularies and stylistic peculiarities of the individual writers. This, as other elements in our study, could be developed at great length by statistical studies of various words used in the Bible and by other studies of stylistic tendencies. We give here just two examples, which should be sufficient to illustrate the issue. The Synoptic Gospels are the best suited to illustrate our case. The New Testament uses primarily one Greek word for our word "sea." All three of the Synoptic writers use it, but the Gospel of Luke uses it most sparingly. On five occasions Luke employs a different word for the Sea of Galilee, which may be properly translated "lake." This is of interest because he uses his peculiar term in exactly the same place in which the parallel passages in Matthew and Mark use the more conventional term for "sea."

There are in the Gospels primarily two Greek terms for our adverb "immediately," or "at once." Mark uses one of these words so frequently that it has almost emerged as a characteristic of his literary style. The other term, with the exception of its use in two adjacent verses of Matthew's Gospel, occurs only in Luke, where it is found ten times.

It is very difficult to explain such phenomena on the basis of a theory of dictation. If the Holy Spirit dictated the Scriptures word-for-word to the biblical writers, why should he characteristically use one vocabulary when dictating to one author and another vocabulary when dictating to another?

The essential elements of an adequate definition of inspiration are these: (1) Inspiration is verbal. The Scrip-

15 *Ibid.*, p. 100.

ture passages we cited would seem to insist on this. This means that the influence of the Holy Spirit on the Scripture writers was so pervasive that it extended to the actual words they chose. This allowed Mark to use the word "sea" for the Sea of Galilee while Luke used "lake," but it prevented either of them from using the word "mountain."

(2) Inspiration is plenary. What is true of the words of Scripture is also true of Scripture as a whole. The influence of the Holy Spirit extended to all parts of Scripture. This element is necessary to keep man from setting himself up as an authority over and above the Bible and determining what in it is and what is not an authentic word from God.

(3) Inspiration has both a divine and a human element. The writers of the biblical books were not merely pens, but penmen. Their vocabularies, backgrounds, and thoughts shine through. Yet the work of the Holy Spirit is equally evident. Thus the end product is one of dual authorship.

These three elements, it would seem, are a bare minimum, and the only means whereby we may be certain that God has revealed himself to mankind in a special way and that that special revelation has been preserved for us in a lasting and accurate form that is worthy of our confidence.

Before we press on to the question of the canon, we will deal with two other areas of concern. There are in the first place some mistaken notions of the view of inspiration here presented. Of these, we will notice briefly three. The name "verbal inspiration" or "dynamic inspiration" has given rise to one of these mistaken impressions. These terms are adequate if the investigator is aware of what is included in them. In some circles, however, dynamic inspiration carries with it a far less objective significance than here presented, and in others verbal inspiration has come to be equated with dictation. While verbal inspiration may indeed mean dictation to some, it certainly need not mean that. Therefore the charge made by many critics, that verbal inspiration is equal to dictation, is not justified. Our own discussion of the dictation theory should have made that clear. It is perfectly possible to maintain that the superintendence of the Holy Spirit extended to the words used by the various authors, and yet maintain that the words used come from the vocabularies of the individual writers involved.

A second mistaken impression by critics of this position is that verbal inspiration is equal to bibliolatry. Such a charge is founded on ignorance of the conservative regard for Scripture and the reason for that regard. If any sort of bibliolatry ever existed it was that of the Jews in Jesus' day, and of this he himself was most critical. His comments to the Jews in Jn. 5:39-40 are relevant here: "You search the Scriptures, because you think that in them you have eternal life; and it is they that bear witness to me; yet you refuse to come to me that you may have life." The Jews had made too much of the object of Scripture and had failed to apply it to their lives. Jesus' criticism was not leveled at them for using the Scriptures. Their fault lay in that they failed to go where the Scriptures should have logically led them.

Some people act as if the Bible were some sort of magical potion that could heal all sorts of ills simply by its possession, but this is contrary to what orthodox Christianity has always said. The Scriptures are an instrument. They are important because they record events in the history of God's relationship with man, and because when conjoined with the work of the Holy Spirit they bring about deep and basic changes in men's lives. The conservative thus insists on the Bible *and* the work of the Holy Spirit. The Bible without the Holy Spirit would be mere history; the Holy Spirit without the Bible would be sheer mysticism.

The third objection to this view of inspiration is not so much a mistaken impression as a failure to see how integrally this view of inspiration is tied to the idea of special revelation. We have already noticed that some contemporary critics feel that to accept any concept of special revelation would involve a "sacrifice of the intellect" (p. 15 above). This doctrine is most particularly related to the Roman Catholic idea of biblical authority, where the authority of the Scriptures reposes in that the

Church says they have authority, and the interpretation of a given passage is determined by the Church if it so pleases to give an authoritative interpretation. Alluding to this notion, the critical school accuses conservatives of setting up a "paper pope."

There are two kinds of replies that can be made to this objection. The acceptance of any authority is entirely dependent on the worth of that authority. If, for example, I go to a doctor with a certain set of symptoms which he on the basis of further tests, his medical training, consultation with his medical books, etc., comes to feel is tuberculosis, and as a consequence he treats me for it, it would be ridiculous for me to accuse him of "sacrifice of the intellect" for using such devices external to himself for arriving at his decision. This is what the conservative Protestant feels makes his position differ from that of Romanism. He sees no reason to submit either to a Church or a representative of the Church for procuring an authoritative revelation from God. That revelation, he feels, came first in history, and it has now been preserved in an accurate way in the Christian Scriptures, which bear their own recommendation and authority.

The second kind of reply that can be made to this objection concerns the kind of inference it makes on the nature of the human intellect. Those who make this charge are at least by inference raising the human intellect to the level of deity. Is man's intellect the pure and sinless constituent of his personality? If such be the case, we maintain that neither the facts of human experience nor the biblical doctrine of sin has been evaluated properly. Paul's charge of the futile thinking of natural man comes up for consideration here again: "Claiming to be wise, they became fools, and exchanged the glory of the immortal God for images resembling mortal man or birds or animals or reptiles" (Rom. 1:22-23). Modern man may not set up the same crude idols as did ancient man, but in his implicit attempt to make the human intellect the judge of all things he is guilty of a far more heinous form of idolatry, besides virtually putting himself in the place of God.

The other issue with which we must deal before we

pass on to a brief discussion of the canon is that of alternative possibilities to the view of inspiration here presented. The liberal view of Jesus that has passed out of favor had at least one thing to commend it. While it felt that Scripture was fallible, it at any rate had confidence in man's ability to arrive at an adequate religious understanding, because it had supreme confidence in man's ability. But as Ogletree has stated, "Once the fallibility of Scripture has been acknowledged, there are no means remaining to check the historical reliability of the biblical testimony to Jesus other than those provided by critico-historical study."[16]

But while the view of biblical fallibility and human ability fit nicely together in liberal theology, the resulting loss of confidence in human ability in modern dialectical theology and its allies would apparently lead to a position of absolute skepticism. For in effect it tells us that now we can trust neither ourselves nor the Bible.

But modern theology attempts to ride the fence between skepticism on the one hand, and confidence in the reliability of the Scriptures on the other, which is manifestly impossible. The new questers appear to be most painfully aware of this precarious position. Käsemann says: "But at precisely the same moment, the very people who have hitherto been the opponents of the liberal quest of the historical Jesus are obviously going in fear and trembling lest the doors should for the first time be really opened to radical scepticism and lest, with the abandoning of any direct attack on the historical question, the historical reality of revelation itself should be endangered."[17]

Bornkamm assures us that "The Gospels justify neither resignation nor scepticism."[18] However, after he has assured us that historical data are available to us, he con-

[16] Thomas W. Ogletree, *Christian Faith and History* (Nashville: Abingdon, 1965), p. 212.

[17] Ernst Käsemann, *Essays on New Testament Themes*, trans. W. J. Montague (Naperville: Allenson, 1964), p. 17.

[18] Günther Bornkamm, *Jesus of Nazareth*, trans. Irene and Fraser McLuskey and James M. Robinson (New York: Harper, 1960), p. 24.

cludes, "This opinion may be boldly stated, despite the fact that on historical grounds so many of the stories and sayings could be contested in detail, despite tendencies evidently active in the tradition, despite the impossibility of finally extracting from more or less authentic particulars a more or less assured whole which we could call a life of Jesus."[19]

This kind of approach to the subject is completely inadequate. We deny the possibility of setting up adequate historical criteria in the twentieth century to arrive at anything approximating historical truth relative to the life of Jesus based on the Gospels, if we once throw out the view of inspiration we have presented here. It would be interesting to compile a list of those items which criticism at its various stages has at one time or another decided are either (1) historical or (2) unhistorical. I am convinced that one could without very diligent search find every single item of any significance at all in both lists, with critics on both sides affirming and denying its historicity.

Furthermore, how do we go about determining what is essential and what is not? There is danger in asserting that what is important and what therefore is historical is nothing other than what the particular contemporary critic regards as being important. In that respect there is no guarantee that the contemporary critic is any better equipped than was the one who gave us a liberal life of Jesus.

Even beyond this, if it were possible for us to determine what in the Scripture is "detail," which possibility we deny, what assurance have we that the "important" element is any better preserved than are the matters of "detail"? If the Scriptures were not divinely produced via the means of their self-witness through the instrumentality of the Holy Spirit, as the dynamic or verbal theory of inspiration asserts, then there is no warrant for basing anything other than a vague humanistic faith on them, or perhaps even more properly, arriving at a position of absolute skepticism in regard to what we should then have to designate as "Christianity."

19 *Ibid.*, p. 25.

Content of the Canon

If then we are correct in assuming that the Scriptures are inspired in the sense in which we have defined inspiration in the preceding section, how are we to determine what is the extent of those Scriptures? This is basically the question of the canon. Here, once again, we shall trace our position briefly. As with inspiration, the view of the Old Testament in the New must be our starting point. In the first place, almost all the Scriptures we cited in connection with the doctrine of inspiration apply with equal force here. The statement of Jesus with respect to the law in Mt. 5:17-18, his comment that the "scripture cannot be broken" in Jn. 10:35, and the statement of Paul in II Tim. 3:16 are of chief importance. To this we add only one verse to indicate the attitude of Jesus. When Jesus is commissioning the disciples for their work he makes this remark: "These are my words which I spoke to you, while I was still with you, that everything written about me in the law of Moses and the prophets and the psalms must be fulfilled" (Lk. 24:44). This is very significant because Jesus appears deliberately to be mentioning the three major divisions of the Hebrew Old Testament. The third is designated by its first and largest component—the Psalms.

To this direct New Testament evidence certain indirect evidence may be added. There is not the slightest indication anywhere in the New Testament that there was any dispute among either Christians or Jews that the Hebrew canon was a universally accepted minimum. Such disputes as we do find are primarily of two sorts: (1) The dispute of the Pharisees with the Sadducees as to whether the oral tradition bore authority. The Pharisees said it did; the Sadducees said it did not. (2) The occasional dispute of Jesus with the Jews regarding their tradition that went beyond the Old Testament itself, for example, in Mt. 15.

Furthermore, there is no mention whatever of the Jews ever challenging Jesus on the issue of the canon. To be sure, this is an argument from silence; but in view of the claims made by Jesus and of the position of the Jewish authorities regarding their Scripture, such a silence is explicable only if there was no basis for disagreement between Jesus and the Jews on that subject.

Moreover, Jesus often bases his most minute arguments on a passage from the Old Testament. The passage regarding David's Lord in Mt. 22:41-46 is a case in point.

With regard to the remainder of the New Testament we merely cite two passages which, interestingly enough, are found in the same class of literature in which we have previously found warrant for inspiration. In II Timothy, it will be recalled, we found the passage that asserted that the Scripture, i.e., the Old Testament, was "God-breathed" (3:16). In I Timothy we find a very interesting verse: "For the scripture says, 'you shall not muzzle an ox when it is treading out the grain,' and, 'The laborer deserves his wages' " (5:18). This is very interesting because the first of the quotations in this passage is taken from Deut. 25:4, and the second from Lk. 10:7, and yet they are both lumped together as "scripture."

We have already noted the role of the Holy Spirit in the works of the prophets, according to II Pet. 1:21. In the same book at least some of the writings of Paul appear to be classed with other books as "scriptures": "So also our beloved brother Paul wrote to you according to the wisdom given him, speaking of this as he does in all his letters. There are some things in them hard to understand, which the ignorant and unstable twist to their own destruction, as they do the other scriptures" (3:15-16).

The critic may, of course, counter with the objection that the Pastoral Epistles and II Peter are not authentic works and, as a consequence, their value in setting the boundaries of the canon is limited. The conservative scholar, however, feels that he is in a strong position in pleading for their authenticity.

There are, however, some additional factors here too which should be brought to our attention. Anyone who claims the name "Christian" at all thereby acknowledges that the person and work of Christ in the first century transcends in significance anything that preceded it in the Old Testament. Is it therefore logical to assume that the Church should be left with a canon of the preparatory revelation and with no equivalent canon of the climax of that revelation?

The only problem is therefore to determine whether or not the books contained in our New Testament are authentic productions. When they are exhibited to be such, the question of their canonicity is settled. With the exception of the works by Luke and Mark, all claim to be the work of apostles either by direct statement or by implication. Both Mark and Luke were very close to apostles and presumably received the majority of their materials from them. This puts their works in the same general category.

Here again the conservative theologian feels that there was more than chance on the side of the Church. As Bruce puts it, ". . . the historic Christian belief is that the Holy Spirit, who controlled the writing of the individual books, also controlled their selection and collection, thus continuing to fulfil our Lord's promise that He would guide His disciples into all the truth."[20]

The one question remaining for us is, How was the canon itself actually decided upon or brought into its concrete form? Here there are chiefly two positions in contemporary biblical scholarship. The critical school has tended to say more or less definitely that the canon is a result of human decision. Certain people at certain times in the Church made decisions on what should be included and what should not. If, however, the Holy Spirit was operative in the determination of the canon, as he was in the inspiration of the Scriptures, human decision could not have been the determining factor. Rather, the selection of the canon was more of a recognition by the Church of what did and what did not belong in the sacred Scriptures. This is not to say that it did not take a considerable period of time for certain parts of the Church to realize the worth of the entire canon. But it is to say that the writings themselves bore the impression of a special divine revelation from God, and that the ultimate inclusion of them all in the canon was a foregone conclusion.

[20] Bruce, p. 21.

While we may put the ultimate determination of the books to be included in the New Testament canon at the end of the fourth and the beginning of the fifth century, we must not look upon this period as one in which a radical break was made with all that preceded it. It was rather a time when the largest part of the Church gave expression to what had for practical purposes occurred much earlier. This is to say neither that there had been no variation before this time, nor that there was to be no variation with regard to certain persons' perception of the canon thereafter, but that by this time most Christians had become satisfied as to the extent of the New Testament.

Accuracy of the Text

The next question of importance is the accuracy of the text. If God did inspire the writers of our Bible so that they were enabled to give us an authentic revelation from him, and if the Holy Spirit did give guidance in the selection of the canon, what assurance have we that the text which we have of that Scripture is an accurate text?

In the first place, it must be stated that the message is primary and the text secondary. This is not to deny importance to the text, but it is to put it in proper perspective. If the text were of primary importance, then the biblical devotee could be accused of bibliolatry. This is not the case with the conservative exegete. But this is not to say that the text is not of real importance. For we are dependent on the text to give us the message. Considered therefore from this perspective, the message and the text are integrally woven together, and the question of the text is a question of first-rate importance.

If this is so, why did God not inspire all of the copyists of the text in order that we might have a perfectly accurate record of that revelation? On the contrary, there are thousands of textual variants in the extant manuscripts. To answer this question fully we would have to be God, but we can make some intelligent guesses. Why the original manuscripts were lost is not a difficult problem to solve. The history of humanity has been a history of idolatry. The idolatrous use that would have been made of such original manuscripts is not difficult to see.

But there is a further very likely reason why the transmission of the manuscripts has not been devoid of error. The history of the Judaeo-Christian faith itself testifies that even though God gives man a revelation of himself, man constantly neglects, abuses, and corrupts that revelation. While the transmission of the text of the Bible is not a conspicuous example of this tendency on the part of man, it nevertheless apparently shares in this tendency. Here as elsewhere, however, man is not allowed the complete freedom to obliterate that revelation.

How important an issue are we raising when we talk of the corruption of the text? To begin, we must notice briefly the Hebrew characteristics of transmission when we speak of the Old Testament. If God had arbitrarily decided to reveal himself to a racial group that would have preserved and revered that revelation more zealously and more accurately than any other people, he could not have done better in giving it to any other people than he did in giving it to the Hebrews. The Hebrew scribe stands as a paragon of accuracy in the entire history of mankind. The minuteness of the regulations for copying manuscripts seems almost ludicrous to us today.[21]

When we come to the New Testament, we are no longer dependent on a period of lengthy transmission on which we cannot check. The preface to the Revised Standard Version states this very well:

> We now possess many more ancient manuscripts of the New Testament, and are far better equipped to seek to recover the original wording of the Greek text. The evidence for the text of the books of the New Testament is better than for any other ancient book, both in number of extant manuscripts and in the nearness of the date of some of these manuscripts to the date when the book was originally written.[22]

[21] Frederic Kenyon, *Our Bible and the Ancient Manuscripts*, rev. A. W. Adams (New York: Harper, 1962), pp. 78-79.

[22] Preface to the Revised Standard Version of the New Testament, p. xii.

When we come down to an actual consideration of the textual variants, we must view them from both a quantitative and qualitative perspective. There are some 150,000 variants in the extant manuscripts of the New Testament. Of these only about four hundred affect the meaning of a given passage, and of these fewer than fifty are of any real importance.[23]

On the level of Christian doctrine, however, the significance of even these variants is of no importance. The scholars who worked on the Revised Standard Version of the New Testament tell us, "It will be obvious to the careful reader that still in 1946, as in 1881 and 1901, no doctrine of the Christian faith has been affected by the revisions, for the simple reason that, out of the thousands of variant readings in the manuscripts, none has turned up thus far that requires a revision of Christian doctrine."[24]

From what has been said here two things should be obvious: (1) The original biblical texts and the texts we possess today are substantially identical; and (2) the problem of the text is no real obstacle to the view of revelation and inspiration presented in this chapter.

Interpretation of the Text

We come, finally, to the issue of how we are to get the proper sense out of the text. We shall deal with the subject of interpretation at much greater length in the chapter on mythology. All we shall do here is define a basic approach to interpretation. To begin, we affirm that the only method of interpretation that has proved its worth historically is the literal method. We must, however, explain what we mean and what we do not mean by literal interpretation. By interpreting literally, we mean

23 Ira Maurice Price, *The Ancestry of Our English Bible*, rev. William Irwin and Allen P. Wikgren (New York: Harper, 1956), p. 222.

24 American Revision Committee, *An Introduction to the Revised Standard Version of the New Testament* (New York: Nelson, 1946), p. 42.

we must seek to discover what was the literal significance of a given biblical passage to its author. This means a great deal more than picking up an English translation of the Bible and interpreting the passage in the sense of the current English meaning of the words. It means, among other things, that we must know the language of the biblical writer, the culture that formed the background of his writing, and the history of the period in which he wrote as well as of the period preceding his writing. The better we come to know these factors, the better our interpretation will be.

But what we do not mean by literal interpretation is equally important. By our plea for literal interpretation we do not seek to rule out such things as metaphor and symbolism. But metaphor and symbolism gain their meaning by comparison with literal statements. Unless along with metaphor and symbolism there are literal statements, we are unable to understand a book.

Furthermore, we do not make a plea for literal interpretation in such a way as to set it in opposition to application. The biblical passage had an application for the contemporaries of its author. But it also has an application for us, and we must press on to find it. For example, in our contemporary Christian society we are not in danger of making a Christian brother stumble by eating meat that has been offered to idols as were the Corinthian Christians to whom Paul wrote. On the other hand, if we seek to discover the truth involved in this passage, it may alter our conduct radically in relation to our Christian brother in ways that were beyond the conception of first-century Corinthian Christians.

To some readers the basis of interpretation sketched here might seem too self-evident to require statement. The history of biblical interpretation, however, does not bear this out. Throughout its history the Church has been afflicted by a perverse form of biblical exegesis commonly called allegorical interpretation. This form of interpretation refuses to see in the literal rendering of the text the real significance of the passage. It insists rather on finding hidden meanings. Early Jewish and Christian Alexandrian writers perfected the technique and passed it on to the Middle Ages, during which period it was the predominant method. It continually recurs in biblical interpretation and figures prominently in one large segment of the contemporary critical school.

What we maintain here is that unless the biblical passage professes to be allegory or gives some obvious indication that it is such, this is a completely illegitimate means of interpretation. It results in the interpreter finding in the passage what he wishes, rather than what its author intended.

There is one other matter in the interpretation of the text to which we will briefly direct our attention. Given the view of revelation and inspiration here traced, we need to insist not only on literal interpretation, but on total interpretation. That is, we must interpret all of Scripture. This is not to say that every verse of Scripture will be as important to us as every other verse, but that the Bible as a whole is the revelation of God to us, and we must therefore strive to understand all of it. We may not accept what we like and reject what we dislike. We will rather seek God's total message for us and try to apply it to our lives.

Alternative Positions

Our consideration to this point has of necessity involved itself with matters that are integrally connected with the Bible itself. Our conception of special revelation and inspiration has made that a necessity. Are there any other approaches to the subject that are equally valid? Although any alternative approach of necessity denies the proper biblical concept of special revelation, let us nevertheless examine their source and validity. To begin, approaches different from the one developed here cannot claim that they have the advantage of a presupposition-less point of departure. Ernst Kinder makes this clear:

> We cannot approach the Bible without presuppositions, nor seek in any kind of immediacy to understand its claim in a way which might oppose the Church's claim. If we do not approach the Bible from the standpoint of the Church, we do

so from the standpoint of some world view. There is no third
possibility such as neutrality without presuppositions.[25]

The result of all this and its effect on one's approach
to the Bible are forcefully stated by Kinder:

> If "biased" witnesses are rejected, then preference must be
> given to the "unbiased" person and to the postulates and
> criteria of the person who is not inwardly a participant.
> Preference is given to the categories and norms of the natural
> man who is not inwardly grasped by the substance of the Bible
> over those of the "biased," participating, and believing
> man . . . . He [the "unbiased" witness] makes a definite deci-
> sion regarding the Bible, however, a decision providing him
> with his formal and neutral criteria and norms which he
> postulates as a priori and absolute . . . . When historical and
> literary methods are posited as primary and absolute norms
> they are no longer merely methods; they have become "isms,"
> and they possess the content of a definite philosophy, though
> such be unintentional.[26]

Thus the relationship of philosophy to biblical study is
of great importance. In this regard two preliminary points
must be made clear: (1) We have no desire here to set up
philosophy against the Bible in an either/or antithesis. No
philosophy that has ever been held by any large number
of men is devoid of the truth. The point is not whether
philosophy contains truth, but whether *specific* philosophical systems are absolutely true. (2) However, there
is a legitimate and an illegitimate use of philosophy. The
necessity of the use of philosophy is pointed out by
Cairns. It has value as illustration in theological thinking,
and yet the Christian must ever be wary of the danger of
falling prey to a nonbiblical philosophical system.[27]

Ramm points out the danger in this necessary use of
philosophy:

[25] Ernst Kinder, "Historical Criticism and Demythologizing,"
Kerygma and History, ed. and trans. Carl E. Braaten and Roy A.
Harrisville (Nashville: Abingdon, 1962), pp. 66-67.

[26] *Ibid.*, pp. 67-68.

[27] David Cairns, *A Gospel Without Myth?* (London: S.C.M.,
1960), p. 27.

The theologian uses philosophy but he does not produce *another* philosophy. The knowledge of God is not another metaphysical system or ideology. It is theology, not religious anthropology. It is *logia* (carefully controlled discourse) of God, and not *theoria* (speculation) of God. The knowledge of God is not a projection of human ideas into the spiritual order, for this is but religious anthropology and not *logia tou theou*. [28]

We have stated earlier that one of the saddest features of the history of biblical interpretation has been the use of allegorical interpretation. One of the features that has contributed to this sad state of affairs has been the place from which this kind of interpretation has gotten its content. All too often it has come from an anti-Christian philosophical system. It thus becomes a matter of what is primary. Has God revealed himself in a special and meaningful way? If so, that revelation must be our point of departure. If, as we have maintained here, we have that revelation in the Bible, then it will be our starting point. We may use philosophical categories and terminology to help us understand it, but our movement will always be from the Bible to philosophy, not vice versa. If, however, the knowledge we need is only a product of human insight, we may travel in the opposite direction. It thus becomes a matter of which of these two standards we allow to control our thought. Our distrust for depraved human thought pushes us either in the direction of the Bible or in the direction of skepticism.

Therefore, while the Bible is not a philosophical system on the one hand, and yet philosophy is of value to us in the interpretation of theological concepts on the other, we need to ask the question, At what point must the primacy of the Bible be exhibited? Its main contribution appears to be in the area of showing what may not be allowed in a philosophy from a Christian perspective. The Scriptures have something to say on almost every branch into which philosophical study has been divided. We give here a few illustrations; however, a long list could be compiled. In the area of cosmology, the approach of the

[28] Ramm, pp. 141-42.

Bible is theocentric. As a result, any cosmological system that is dualistic, pantheistic, or materialistic must of necessity be ruled out.

Similarly, in the field of epistemology, there are certain kinds of systems that need to be ruled out. Any system that is by nature atheistic, materialistic, or agnostic is not suited to being incorporated into a Christian system of thought.

Perhaps of greatest interest to us here is the branch, philosophy of history. Here large elements in the Christian Church in the twentieth century have fared very poorly. From the philosophical point of view there have been two major theological schools that have dominated a great deal of the theological thought of this century—idealism and existentialism. Idealism has at its base an optimistic view of history which sees mankind as being redeemed in the historical process. Existentialism has a tendency to ignore the history of mankind and rather center on the experience of the individual. Neither of these philosophies of history is acceptable from a biblical point of view.

None of these philosophies which have found wide acceptance among non-Christians is completely acceptable from a biblical point of view. They contain rather greater or lesser degrees of truth. For this reason, whenever Christian theology becomes dominated by *a philosophical system*, it is a Christianity that has in some sense departed from its biblical foundations. This has occurred repeatedly in the history of the Christian Church. Let us look first at two examples of this prior to the twentieth century. In the early centuries of Christianity there developed a school of exegesis that sought to combine Christianity with Greek philosophy. This school in many respects followed the pattern that had been set by Philo as he developed and perfected the method whereby he could accept the Old Testament, as he felt he must as a Jew, and yet maintain those elements of Greek philosophy which attracted him so much. Clement and Origen, the two most distinguished members of this Christian exegetical school, brought the New Testament and Greek philosophy together via the same route.

The pervasive influence of the philosophy of Aristotle on the theology of Thomas Aquinas in the Middle Ages is well known. This influence and its continuing effects have resulted in the transformation of Catholic theology into a system that is at many points more Aristotelian than biblical.

The twentieth century likewise has been marked theologically by the dominance of two types of philosophy over theological studies. The pervasive influence of idealism on liberal theology is well known. Throughout the nineteenth century and into the early decades of the twentieth, the influence of Hegel, Schleiermacher, and Kant was dominant in biblical studies in the critical school. This now is universally admitted and disdained even by the largest portion of that school itself.

Consequently, it is difficult to understand why it is that contemporary theological and historical study has so thoroughly embraced the newest philosophy—existentialism. This is particularly true of those engaged in the critical quest of Jesus, as one can see by even a casual glance at its representatives. Thus Bultmann, speaking almost precisely in terms of the early Heidegger, desires existential encounter with the kerygma; Robinson tells us we may have an existential encounter with Jesus' selfhood; Fuchs and Ebeling are interested in an existential encounter with the New Testament; and while Jaspers and Ogden are less specific, they still advocate existential encounter with the kerygma or with something else.

The question then arises, How valid is the approach of philosophical existentialism when one compares it to the witness of the Bible? Here our concern is not to assert that this philosophy contains no truth but to show that it is not *the* truth. One of the best analyses of this problem is by J. Rodman Williams.[29] He gives credit to this philosophical approach where credit is due, but he also points out many areas where it is in direct and clear opposition to biblical Christianity. He notes that existen-

[29] J. Rodman Williams, *Contemporary Existentialism and Christian Faith* (Englewood Cliffs, N.J.: Prentice-Hall, 1965).

tialism is foreign to the Christian faith in its relativism, excessive individualism, and subjectivism. He criticizes Bultmann when he comments that with him "the subject [man] is always involved, theology and biblical interpretation must begin there and make the best of it through existential analysis."[30]   Against this Williams sets the true Christian perspective: "On the contrary the expositor of scripture renders the cause of Christian faith the best service if he earnestly seeks to subordinate his own subjectivity to the word that may then break through."[31]

Williams notices in the second place that existentialism has a tendency to rate man too high or too low. As a result the theologian who begins with existentialist presuppositions becomes completely wrapped up in man and can never get beyond him even when Christian revelation demands that he does.[32]

As a corollary to its previous problem, existentialism, because of its emphasis on the centrality of man, "has difficulty finding God anywhere."[33] It is a system that consequently emphasizes anthropology and de-emphasizes theology in the traditional sense. This is once again contrary to the biblical approach, which begins with God rather than finishing with him or ignoring him.

In its attitude toward death, existentialism allegorizes the biblical message and talks of the future only in terms of the present. Williams points out the source as well as the inadequacy of Bultmann's position in this regard when he writes:

Since death as final and resurrection as existence (or rise) of faith stem ultimately from Bultmann's Heideggerian limitations, it becomes a secondary matter to challenge him on New Testament grounds. In any event the theology of Bultmann shows itself to be a "theology without hope," based on an inadequate approach to Christian faith.[34]

30 *Ibid.*, p. 22.
31 *Ibid.*
32 *Ibid.*, p. 38.
33 *Ibid.*, p. 64.
34 *Ibid.*, p. 99.

The attitude of existentialism toward anxiety is another of its antibiblical features. As Williams puts it, "Anxiety is due to man's sin, not his being human; it is the result of his faithlessness, not of his finitude."[35]

Finally, with respect to its goal of authentic existence, existentialism once again comes up short: "Christian faith holds that authentic reality does not, and cannot, include elements of death, anxiety, guilt, meaninglessness, and despair; rather does it radically exclude them all."[36] Against this Williams sets the true Christian perspective: "Christian faith on the contrary holds that God has *already* made known authentic reality in Jesus Christ—He is 'the way, and the truth, and the life' (John 14:16)—and this reality has been made available to every man through His incarnate life, death, and resurrection."[37]

Williams' summary is excellent and makes the opposition of existentialism to biblical Christianity most clear:

> Truth does *not* begin with man but with God in His own self-revelation, existence does *not* center in man but in God who has made man "to glorify Him and enjoy Him forever," God is *not* the inner power and ground of man but stands over against him as the Creator who is totally other, eternity is *not* just some dimension of present human existence but is the reality of God's presence that knows no end at death, anxiety is *not* a natural condition that must be assumed and endured but by the grace of God can be overcome in faith, and authentic existence is *not* the goal of living but only the kingdom of God. Existentialism is ultimately wrong because it fails to understand man in the light of God.[38]

We have offered this critique of existentialism at considerable length because it happens to be the currently popular philosophy in theological circles. It is no longer necessary to refute previous philosophical tendencies in previous theological systems. This says something to the conservative. Any philosophical system that is developed

35 *Ibid.*, p. 128.
36 *Ibid.*, p. 164.
37 *Ibid.*, p. 172.
38 *Ibid.*, p. 176.

apart from a biblical perspective is doomed to be short-lived. Contemporary existentialist theologians do not by and large say that Stoicism was the correct Christian philosophy for the first century, Aristotelianism for the Middle Ages, and Idealism for the nineteenth century. They say that these philosophies to some important extent were in error. Do we dare have the audacity to deny that some day existentialism will be looked upon in the same way?

The consequences of this for the study of the Jesus of history are profound for two reasons: (1) Due to its preoccupation with existentialism, contemporary historical study of the life of Jesus has found basically what it has wanted to find in the life of Jesus. Hugh Anderson points this out in writing of the new quest: "The suspicion is created that the exponent of the 'new quest,' in which historical research is bound up with a particular brand of philosophical understanding, is selecting from and finding in the traditional materials relating to Jesus only what he is looking for, only what accords with 'existence philosophy.' "[39]

The end product of such an investigation is described by Fuller in commenting on the work of Robinson: "All he does is come up with a Jesus who talks suspiciously like a modern existentialist of the early Heidegger stripe."[40]

(2) If this be the product of our investigation, there is little likelihood that the picture it paints of Jesus will last any longer than have its predecessors. Robinson, surprisingly, points this out in a footnote quotation from Pierre Prigent: "We smile today at the humanistic portrait of Jesus which the nineteenth century painted. But do you think that the same smile will not rise on the lips of those who detect tomorrow, in certain recent works, Jesus the existentialist?"[41]

[39] Hugh Anderson, *Jesus and Christian Origins* (New York: Oxford, 1964), p. 261.

[40] Daniel P. Fuller, *Easter Faith and History* (Grand Rapids: Eerdmans, 1965), p. 135.

[41] James M. Robinson, *A New Quest of the Historical Jesus* (London: S.C.M., 1959), p. 76.

The study of the Jesus of history has undergone the same turmoil and instability that all theology has since the period of the Enlightenment in the middle of the eighteenth century. In that movement man became the measure of all things, and human reason was lifted to a place of supremacy. We have no desire to offer a wholesale condemnation of that movement, but when this spirit is taken into theology it results in a virtual deification of man. Man is now competent to solve his religious problems and to sit in judgment on the Bible. Special revelation now ceases to have any real function. Furthermore, our theological systems tend to be based on the currently popular human philosophy rather than on the Word of God. Along with this, our picture of Jesus tends to be drawn in accordance with that philosophy. In the past he was a humanist. In the present he is an existentialist. In the future . . . ?

And this brings up a further feature about the critical movement which we may not ignore. The school of thought that has historically been the hardest on the results of higher criticism has been the critical school itself. In time all of its theories suffer eclipse. It has become almost axiomatic of the movement that "today's assured results are tomorrow's discarded hypotheses." As a consequence the movement is self-defeating and tends to move in cycles rather than on a straight road to the truth.

What, then, is the net result of it all? Apparently there are only two alternatives. Either one decides to cast his lot with this movement in full awareness of the variety of contradictory positions it has held and may hold in the future, or he decides on the basis of the kind of investigation we have been following here to cast his lot with a meaningfully inspired Bible that conveys to us a special revelation from God. If he chooses the first of these alternatives, he should realize that on the grounds of the lack of historical certainty for any of its successively stated constructions, he may—even must—arrive at a position of ultimate skepticism regarding the life and significance of Jesus.

Necessity of Criticism

If the position we have reached in this chapter is sound, the question will logically arise, Why should the orthodox theologian ever attempt to defend the historical accuracy of the New Testament? Why should a conservative theologian even enter the arena of biblical criticism? Is it not true that such a theologian adopts a position that guarantees the accuracy of the documents before he ever looks at them?

It could be that some theologians adopt this approach, but to say that this is the only possible attitude of orthodoxy is unwarranted. These questions may also be looked at from another point of view. This other approach begins with the claims of the New Testament itself. What we have done in this chapter has been to systematize these claims. Then the real question becomes, Will a critical examination of the New Testament support the claims of its self-witness?

Now when one has critically examined the literature itself, there are two chief types of reply that can be made to this question, outside that of a few who would feel that a final answer to this question is impossible: (1) The New Testament supports the claims of its self-witness; and (2) the New Testament does not support the claims of its self-witness. The presumptions one brings to these books may dispose him to be more favorably inclined to one of these answers than the other, but these presumptions must not determine his conclusion.

There are basically three kinds of presumptions regarding the accuracy of the New Testament: (1) the presumptions of those who are inclined to have confidence in it; (2) the presumptions of those who are inclined to distrust it; and (3) the presumptions of those who confront it with neither positive nor negative inclinations. Because the New Testament is conceptually an essentially adult book with which most of us have had contact long before adulthood, the number of us who respond to it as adults in the third way is relatively small.

We must then ask, Which of the first two sets of presumptions is most acceptable? It would seem that the first set is highly preferable. There is nothing unique about our approach to the New Testament in this respect. When we pick up any piece of literature, be it sacred or secular, our basic impulse should be to accept its statements as true unless for some strong reason, either in the document itself or external to the document, we are compelled to reject its truth.

Large segments of the critical school have felt it necessary to reject the revelational position we have traced in this chapter. Our contention is that this rejection has not been based primarily on an analysis of the documents themselves, but rather on factors external to the documents. Primary among these external factors has been the adherence of this type of criticism to some currently popular philosophical position as its basis of authority.

Orthodoxy, on the other hand, feels that a careful examination of the New Testament leads one to a rationally defensible position with respect to its reliability. If on the basis of his critical study the conservative theologian finds that the New Testament abounds in absurd and unhistorical statements, e.g., "the moon is made out of green cheese," he will be forced to abandon his revelational position. If, on the other hand, he finds it to be of a generally reliable character historically, to say nothing of its religious and moral insights, he will investigate it carefully to see if the claims of its self-witness must not be accepted.

It is our position that a critical examination of the New Testament will support, rather than deny, the claims that it makes for itself. All too often conservative biblical scholarship has waited around to pick up the pieces after a theological explosion and has gloated over the demise of a former enemy. Too infrequently it has been on the battle front with the proper kind of equipment. Rather than applying serious thought to its source book and seeking on the basis of its revelation to construct an intellectually respectable apologetic position, it has dealt in trivia.

We believe that Christianity is a faith supported by the facts. This factual basis of the Christian faith can be demonstrated by the entry of the conservative into the field of biblical criticism. The conservative does not claim to enter the field without presuppositions, and he denies that anyone else enters without them either. He believes that by careful investigation he can demonstrate that no one can write off his theological position on the grounds that it is in conflict with facts or that these facts lack importance. Furthermore, he feels that these facts have importance and tangency to present experience. When he brings forth a faith that is thus factually true and experientially reliable, he feels he has arrived at a sound position.

The words of Ramm express very well the feeling of the writer:

> Unless we engage in literary criticism we are too credulous. Literary criticism alone can tell us if the documents we revere so highly are authentic and genuine. We want a faith grounded in a Bible with a respectable pedigree. The author has no sympathy with Fundamentalists of the narrow pietistic school who consider all Biblical introduction as unnecessary, and who think that the certainty of religious experience gives them a hand to be dogmatic in literary criticism . . . . His quarrel is with the radical critic who rules out any considerations of inspiration or providence or the supernatural. He also objects to the identification of scholarship or science with radical views of the Bible. He believes firmly that the highest scholarship and soundest learning may go with a reverent and devout approach to literary criticism. He also resists the disjunctive type of reasoning which states that we either believe in inspiration and some magical theory of the origin of the Bible, or in radical criticism and no theory of inspiration. We believe in the conjunctive relationship of *inspiration and criticism.* [42]

It is, consequently, in this spirit that we shall pursue our investigation in the chapters that follow.

[42] Ramm, *Protestant Christian Evidences* (Chicago: Moody, 1957), p. 79.

CHAPTER TWO

The Jesus of History

Background

The writing of a biography or history of Jesus' life ought to be undertaken with the realization that such an enterprise, due to the Gospel records, no matter how one may evaluate them, must work within certain limitations. In the first place, a biography as it is usually conceived of deals with the entire period of a person's life. To be certain, some periods of that life may be emphasized more than others, but modern biography, as we normally think of it, treats the individual from birth to death. We have great problems in attempting to do this in the case of the life of Jesus, for while the Gospels contain narratives of his infancy, there is only one other event recorded for us concerning the life of Jesus until we reach the final two or three years of his ministry. Out of those final years a great deal of attention is given to the final week of his life.

Because this is true, it would perhaps be well to confine ourselves to the possibility of writing a history of Jesus' life, or even a history of that portion of his life contained for us in the Gospels. Even here, however, we must be wary of a temptation to make of the Gospels more than they profess to be. They make no pretension of being chronicles or diaries of the life of Jesus—even for that period which they record. We should make both a positive and a negative observation in this regard. It must be definitely stated in the first place that the Evangelists set out to write history. There are indications that they used great care in arranging the materials at their disposal in sequence. Luke is the most explicit in this regard. In the prologue to his Gospel he professes to write "an orderly account" (1:3). While this phrase is not to be interpreted as exclusively chronological, neither must the idea of chronology be divorced from it. Furthermore, that Luke to a great extent appropriates the Markan framework indicates the satisfactory nature of that framework from Luke's point of view.

On the other hand, it should not be asserted that because the Gospel writers had a basic historical purpose in mind, that sequence was their only concern. The consideration the authors had for sequence extended to the broad chronological outline rather than to the exact sequence of events. There is nothing unique about this. Whenever one narrates a series of events in which a personality plays a particularly large part, he may at times be writing primarily from the standpoint of the personality and at other times from the perspective of the events. This would lead one to expect two things:

(1) The order of the events should be expected to be approximately in the order in which they occurred; and

(2) in certain cases, the concern of the writer for the personality may cause him to modify the chronological sequence slightly.

It may, of course, be objected that the sequence of events in the Gospels is a creation of Mark and that it passed over from him to the other Synoptic writers. We shall deal with the idea of the messianic secret that gave rise to this theory in a later section of this chapter. We make here just two general observations that would tend to destroy that thesis. Many of the events recorded in the Gospels are of such a character that they indicate in themselves where they belong in the historical narrative. Secondly, it is unthinkable that the early Church should have devoted its time exclusively to the collection of detailed incidents in connection with the life of Jesus and

at the same time should have ignored the broad chronological outline of that life.[1]

Matthew illustrates a further point in connection with
the order of events. In writing narrative, one may proceed
either chronologically or topically. Matthew apparently
gives to his work a topical arrangement. It would then be
unfair to criticize him on the basis that his book is not
arranged in precise chronological order. His purpose is
rather to deal with the main features of the life of Jesus,
and he brings in incidents as they illustrate those various
features. Nonetheless, his general framework is comparable to that of the other Synoptics, and in narrating the
events of passion week Matthew agrees very closely with
both the content and sequence of Mark and Luke.

We should be wary of any attempt to trace Jesus'
psychological development. This was one of the serious
limitations of the old quest. Most contemporary critics
tend to see the fault of such a procedure in the nature of
the sources. The real limitation here would appear rather
to be in the nature of the personality. If Jesus was the
person that the New Testament uniformly represents him
to have been, then the use of analogy to trace his psychological development is out of the question. Here many
modern critics would do well to listen to Martin Kähler,
who at many points shows more insight into the issues
than those who have appropriated a part of his methodology: "Will anyone who has had the impression of being
encountered by that unique sinless person, that unique
Son of Adam endowed with a vigorous consciousness of
God, still venture to use the principle of analogy here
once he has thoroughly assessed the situation? . . . The
distinction between Jesus Christ and ourselves is not one
of degree but of kind."[2]

On the basis of these considerations, then, the real
question before us is not whether we are able to write a
biography in the modern sense, or whether we can trace

[1] E. F. Scott, *The Validity of the Gospel Record* (New York:
Scribner, 1938), pp. 184, 186.

[2] Martin Kähler, *The So-Called Historical Jesus and the Historic
Biblical Christ,* trans. Carl E. Braaten (Philadelphia: Fortress,
1964), p. 53.

the psychological development of Jesus. The real question is, Are the Gospels trustworthy historically? This in
turn divides itself into two further questions: (1) Is it
important to find history in them? (2) Can we place
confidence in that history?

Importance of History

Christianity and history

It cannot be stated too strongly that Christianity is an
historical religion, and that it is so intimately tied to
history that if the historical credibility of its sources were
to be proven false, it would at once collapse as a possible
claimant for our loyalty.

Of the other world religions that seriously claim an
historical base in the sense that the unfolding of history
itself was an unfolding of the religion, only Judaism and
Islam can convincingly make that claim. Christianity
shares with Judaism its historical tradition and adds to it
its own. Islam takes from both Judaism and Christianity
and supplements this with novel elements of its own.

The idea of God acting in history and of a religion
being born in history is, of course, central to the biblical
idea of special revelation. There is no way in which, from
a Christian point of view, man could either know what he
needs to know about God, or develop the content of such
a religion, apart from the direct intervention of God in
history. This in itself sets Christianity off by itself and
differentiates it from the vast majority of the world's
religions and from all speculative philosophy. History
itself, therefore, from a Christian point of view, has been
revelatory.

If, therefore, God has acted in history, it is extremely
important to the Christian to know the truth about those
eras in which God has revealed himself in a special way.
Inasmuch as the events surrounding the life of Jesus are
of chief importance to the Christian in the history of
divine revelation, it is more important than ever for the
Christian to know about them.

But we must go even further than this. In no other religion is there a central personality whose life itself is as important to the faith as is the case with Jesus and Christianity. If then this is so, an accurate knowledge of the life and teachings of Jesus is indispensable to an adequate understanding of that faith.

Danger of Docetism

It is a remarkable fact that most of the troubles that have besieged the Christian Church from the point of view of doctrine in its long history are not new. So it is that the de-emphasis on history in the Gospels as developed in the thought of Rudolf Bultmann is in fact the recurrence of one of the earliest heretical tendencies in the Church—Docetism. This doctrine, which as far as we know was first held by Cerinthus, stated that Jesus had really not come in the flesh, but merely seemed to be human. Now, of course, it is not true that Bultmann denies that Jesus lived, but in his denial of nearly all the history of that life as contained in the Gospels, he has run the risk of doing so in effect.

Once again, the earthly life of Jesus is so intimately tied up to the Christian faith that if one denies the life, he has no faith left. As Scott says, "There is a world of difference between something imagined and something that has been realized."[3] For this reason the early Church fought the Docetists with all its resources, for it realized that apart from the earthly life of Jesus its faith was drained of all its substance.

As this was the case in the first century, so it remains in the twentieth. Scott puts it in terms of our century: "If Christianity is to quicken and direct the lives of men, it must rest on the assurance that the story of Jesus is real. If it could be proved to be nothing more than a glorious legend, woven out of the dreams and longings of the early believers, our religion would fall to the ground."[4]

3 Scott, p. 194.
4 *Ibid.*, p. 195.

While neither Scott nor Cairns would affirm what we have said in our previous chapter, they are at one in their insistence on the historical foundation of Christianity. The latter writes, "Christian faith is indeed vitally interested in the actual occurrence of 'certain events at a certain period in world-history'. Those who deny this are in the 'unenviable position' of declaring Christian faith to be independent of the historical fact of Christ."[5]

This concern for history as opposed to the docetic tendency in Bultmann has apparently given rise to two of the movements that have followed him. Both the critics to the right of Bultmann and the members of the new quest school are fearful lest, as a result of the work of Bultmann, Christianity may be proven to be nothing other than a religious idea.

This gives rise to another question: Why is it that Bultmann insists on the "event of Christ"? It will be recalled that the critics to his left are critical of him for retaining even this. To answer this question for him may be dangerous, but we could perhaps make two suggestions: (1) In all likelihood Bultmann is aware of the charge of Docetism and the consequences that go with it. The retention of the "event" is in part an attempt to guard against that, even though it may not be a very successful one. (2) Consequently, while he designates that event as the "event of Christ," it may rightly be asked whether he is talking about a Christ-event or the event of the primitive Christian faith. However, by using this term he is able to hold on to "the faith of the early Church" in the name of Jesus. Ellwein is critical of Bultmann here, for he feels that the net result has been the severance of the connection between Jesus and the primitive Church.[6]

Seemingly, the critics to the left of Bultmann have seen the issue more clearly than he has. The "authentic existence" which he seeks and which he claims is possible

5 Cairns, *A Gospel Without Myth?*, p. 151.

6 Edward Ellwein, "Rudolf Bultmann's Interpretation of the Kerygma," *Kerygma and History*, ed. and trans. Carl E. Braaten and Roy A. Harrisville (Nashville: Abingdon, 1962), p. 44.

only because of the event of Christ, is not to be limited, according to these critics, to that event. It need be limited, according to them, only to *some* event. Doubtless, from the evangelical perspective, both Bultmann and the critics to his left set their sights too low, but if "authentic existence" is all they seek, there is no need to tie it either to Christ or to the Christian faith.

Nature of history

If then the maintenance of an accurate historical record is essential to the nature of Christianity as revealed religion, and if the loss or the denial of the accuracy of that record results in the evaporation of Christianity into a religious idea rather than an historical faith, the next question we must ask is, What is the nature of history? If one reflects for a moment he will come to realize that the way various critics answer this question has a great deal to do both with the way they approach the Jesus of history and with the conclusions they reach concerning him.

The simplest way to put this is as follows: *History is composed of fact and interpretation.* We may apply it more directly to the Gospels, and consequently to the subject at hand, in this way: *The Gospels are a combination of history (in the sense of fact) and kerygma (interpretation).* In the preceding sentence we used the word "history" in the more restricted sense of fact, because it is often set up in this way as opposed to the kerygma by contemporary kerygmatists. Furthermore, any historical writing of necessity must contain both fact and interpretation. They vary in quantity in relation to one another. If the particular writer emphasizes the facts, we have a chronicle. If he emphasizes the interpretation, we have a romance.

For the most part the critical study of the life of Jesus has fallen prey to several erroneous conceptions with respect to the quantity and relationship of these two elements to one another as we have them in the Gospels. The nineteenth-century quest put most of its interest on the fact. To be sure, Bultmann and the members of the new quest emphasize this in a way that is extreme, but nevertheless there was a tendency among these critics to get at the "bare facts" about Jesus. In so doing they attempted to cut away the theological interpretations of his life, and thus to present us with the historical Jesus as he was in the first century. There were two main faults with this kind of procedure. In the first place, it failed to realize that any proper historical writing involves both elements of fact and elements of interpretation. Consequently, all historical writing is in some sense the interpretation of facts. When one comes to an historical work with a desire to put fact and interpretation in two neatly divided compartments, he is as a consequence attempting an impossibility. Even if he could come up with these facts they would be of no significance.

The real question is, Did the Gospel writers interpret the facts correctly? Do we have in the Gospels an accurate accounting of what happened in the first century *and* an accurate interpretation of those happenings?

But there was a greater problem that besieged the original quest. It was found not so much in its desire to find the "bare facts" as in its general orientation, which dictated what it would allow in the category of fact. Thus, the miraculous or prophetic was rejected or rationalized, while elements of the Gospel story that were commodious for humanism were at once seized upon as "historical." As a result, the Jesus of the nineteenth-century quest approximated a refined humanist gentleman of the nineteenth century.

Although Ethelbert Stauffer is aware of the "new sources" available since the time of the old quest, he shares to a considerable degree the burdens of that quest. He is, in the first place, to an extent that even goes beyond most of the writers in the school of the original quest, confident that he can arrive at the "bare facts" of Jesus' life minus their interpretation by the early Church. But beyond this, he will not even interpret Jesus for himself.[7] This is a sheer impossibility, for not only did

7 Ethelbert Stauffer, *Jesus and His Story*, trans. Richard and Clara Winston (New York: Knopf, 1960), pp. xiii-xiv.

the writers of our Gospels interpret, but we too must interpret when we are presented with their works.

If the fault of the original quest was its overemphasis on the factual element in attempting to construct a history of Jesus, the fault of Bultmann and his successors has been their overemphasis on the element of interpretation as we have it in the Gospels. Here everything has been poured into the kerygma. The faith of the early Church is central. To be sure, the exponents of the new quest have in a measure reopened the historical question, but even with them the greatest emphasis remains with the kerygma.

In light of this it is worth our while to notice the words of Scott. He feels that one of the reasons why the Gospels were produced was to restrain erroneous interpretations. The Church was beginning to struggle with such groups as the Docetists, and it felt that it must have an accurate record of the facts in order to restrain the Docetists from their excesses. Doubtless the following quotation is extreme on the side of fact, but it points up a truth which must never be forgotten:

> Most probably we owe our Gospels to nothing else than to this consciousness on the part of the church that fact and interpretation must be kept separate. There was a place for doctrine and mystical vision, but these could have no meaning unless the historical facts were put on record. However the revelation might be understood, it was contained in the life of Jesus as it had once been lived on earth, and the knowledge of this life was the one thing necessary.[8]

However, our problem is much greater here than a decision as to which is more important—fact or interpretation. For members of the kerygmatic school of thought go on to assert that the kerygma produced the history, or the interpretation produced the facts. In other words, what we have in the Gospels is not so much an authentic life of Jesus as it is a stylized life of Jesus produced by the early Christian Church on the basis of its faith. How such a process could come about is beyond conception. It

[8] Scott, p. 196.

would almost be as if the Church developed its message from some unknown source and then at a later time wrote up a record of the life of Jesus to justify that message. Besides the logical impossibility of such a procedure, it has in it the presumption that the life of Jesus and the preaching of the early Church were for a time kept completely separate; or perhaps we may say more properly, it has in it the presumption that for a time the life of Jesus was almost completely ignored in the Church.

But beyond this logical impossibility, such thinking has presented critical New Testament scholarship with a paradox. As Davies observes, "The Kerygma, it has been claimed, rests on historical events; but the substance of these in history is declared to be either unimportant or unknowable."[9]

Before we seek a solution to this paradox, let us review the historical ground we have covered: (1) The original quest was guilty of emphasizing facts at the expense of interpretation. (2) The kerygmatists have been guilty of emphasizing interpretation at the expense of facts. (3) This in turn has led them to assert that the interpretation produced the facts. What we maintain here is rather that the facts produced the interpretation. There are several reasons for believing that this was the case: (1) It is more likely that facts produced the faith than that faith produced the facts. How may one account for the rise of such a faith as we see portrayed in the New Testament? Did it arise in a vacuum? Was it a product of someone's ingenious thought? If this is so, why has it attained such a place of prominence in the history of our world? Why has not another system of equal worth and commanding equal loyalty arisen since it? These questions cannot be answered apart from the assertion that something happened in the first century of our era that gave rise to this tremendously dynamic and incomparable faith.

(2) Moreover, the interpretation or kerygma points to

9 W. D. Davies, *Christian Origins and Judaism* (Philadelphia: Westminster, 1962), pp. 9-10.

facts. We are told about a personality who lived and acted and spoke to a particular people at a particular time. If one were to remove the historical element from the kerygma nothing would remain. If the kerygma were composed of a series of general truths that could be explicated independent of the person Jesus, then perhaps one could make the kerygmatists' claim stick. But in fact the life of Jesus is at the very core of the kerygma.

(3) Any doubts that the movement was from history to kerygma should be erased when we consider the writings of Luke. Because Luke first composed his Gospel and followed this with the book of Acts, it is obvious to us what his thinking was. The teaching and preaching of the early Church finds its anchor in the Jesus of history. What we have therefore in the New Testament is the climax of God's special revelation to mankind in the person of Jesus, and the inspired interpretation of that life.

Let us summarize all that we have been saying here relative to the nature of history and its relationship to the life of Jesus and the Gospels: It is not a case of history (in the sense of fact) at the expense of kerygma (interpretation). It is not a case of kerygma (interpretation) at the expense of history (in the sense of fact). It is a question of kerygma (interpretation) on the *basis* of history (in the sense of fact).

Birger Gerhardsson makes an observation of which all contemporary kerygmatists must be reminded:

> It seems to be an extremely tenaciously-held misapprehension among exegetes that an early Christian author must *either* be a purposeful theologian and writer *or* a fairly reliable historian. This misapprehension is applied to the author of Acts, to the Evangelists, and to those who preceded the Evangelists in forming the various elements of the gospel tradition. The pioneer form-critics Dibelius and Bultmann have contributed materially to the perpetuation of this error. They work on the basis of an over-simplified alternative, maintaining that the men who shaped the gospel tradition had no wish to preserve memories for posterity, but *instead* wished by their proclamation to arouse faith in Christ. This is a false alternative. To present the problem in this way fails to do justice to the

deep-rooted respect for divine revelation which was felt in Antiquity (and elsewhere): to that profound reverence associated with the words which were "heard" and the things which were "seen," i.e. those events which were understood and interpreted in religious categories. Nor does it do justice even to the reverence commanded by the authoritative teacher or a received authoritative tradition. The fact of the early Christian Apostles, teachers and Evangelists having presented their material with a religious end in view does not necessarily mean *per se* that their memories ceased to function, or that their respect for historical facts vanished.[10]

Quantity of history

If a knowledge of history is absolutely essential to the Christian faith with regard to its origin, if the neglect of such history will open it to the charge of Docetism, and if the kerygma of the Church rose on the basis of history, the next question we should logically ask is, How much of the history of Jesus must we know? Here Bultmann asks for less than any except the critics to his left. We are not expected to know or be able to find the events of Christ's life, but only "the event of Christ," the mere "thatness" of his existence. The adherents of the new quest expect to find slightly more, but even they do not expect to find a great deal. Robinson states it in two ways: "We can know very little about the historical Jesus,"[11] and "Christian faith is not interested in the historical Jesus."[12] By these statements he means that we can learn and must learn very little about Jesus via the study of the scientific historian.

Bultmann goes on to assert that it is not only impossible to know more about Jesus than the mere "that," but it is illegitimate from a Christian perspective. The attempt to discover the Jesus of history by means of historical research and as a result to find a basis for faith is to ground faith in a "work."

[10] Birger Gerhardsson, *Memory and Manuscript*, trans. Eric J. Sharpe (Uppsala: Gleerup, 1961), p. 209.

[11] Robinson, *A New Quest of the Historical Jesus*, p. 31.

[12] *Ibid.*, p. 32.

Our radical attempt to demythologize the New Testament is in fact a perfect parallel to St. Paul's and Luther's doctrine of justification by faith alone apart from the works of the Law. Or rather, it carries this doctrine to its logical conclusion in the field of epistemology. Like the doctrine of justification it destroys every false security and every false demand for it on the part of man, whether he seeks it in his good works or in his ascertainable knowledge. The man who wishes to believe in God as his God must realize that he has nothing in his hand on which to base his faith. He is suspended in mid-air, and cannot demand a proof of the Word which addresses him. For the ground and object of faith are identical. Security can be found only by abandoning all security, by being ready, as Luther put it, to plunge into the inner darkness.[13]

How are we to evaluate this lack of concern for history on the part of these critics? In the first place, we should frankly ask the question, Does the New Testament speak of an event or a life? The only reason one would put the "event of Christ" above the life of Christ is that that is all he needs to satisfy his philosophical-theological desires. Here, once again, the theologians who seek the event have been victimized by the presuppositions that they have brought with them to the New Testament.

But we can go beyond this. Apart from any considerations of what we today may regard as important or unimportant, what is important from the perspective of the Gospel writers as they present the narrative to us? Those who talk in terms of "the event of Christ," limit their concern almost exclusively to the death of Christ and the events immediately surrounding it. Is this enough? The Christian Church as a whole throughout most of its history has said that it is not. The death of Christ has meaning only in terms of the life that preceded it. This is the assertion of Jesus at the very beginning when he is baptized by John over the latter's objection: "Let it be so now; for thus it is fitting for us to fulfil all righteousness" (Mt. 3:15). Paul comments more fully in terms of Jesus' entire life: "God sent forth his Son, born

[13] Rudolf Bultmann, "Bultmann Replies to His Critics," *Kerygma and Myth*, I, ed. Hans Werner Bartsch, trans. Reginald H. Fuller (London: S. P. C. K., 1964), pp. 210-11.

of woman, born under the law, to redeem those who were under the law" (Gal. 4:4-5). It thus is the case that every part of his life is the unfolding of the divine plan for human redemption. Jesus met in his person the requirements of the law perfectly, and thus he was able to take man's place and redeem him. The life, then, is as important as the death. It is not a case of either/or, but one of both/and. Furthermore, we dare not terminate our interest with his death, for as his death without his life would have been meaningless, his death without his resurrection would have been futile.

Scott writes in terms of his prepassion life, "The record of the death contained the essential message, but it could not stand alone. It had always been felt that the later part of the history could not be understood without the earlier."[14]

There are no logical critical grounds for accepting the death of Jesus and rejecting the largest portion of the life that preceded it and the resurrection that succeeded it. The sources all stand on the same level. The only reason for accepting the one and rejecting the other is to be found once again in the particular set of presuppositions which the individual critic brings with him.

It appears that Kähler saw very clearly the problem involved in any kind of attempt to get at a critically constructed life of Jesus:

> Where do we come to know this Jesus? Only a few are sufficiently trained to evaluate such work. To be sure, such work would relieve us of the authority of the Bible, but it would in turn subject us to the authority, not of an empirical science, but of the alleged results produced by this science. Meanwhile there is no one who can answer our question, Where is that fifth evangelist capable of providing us with the picture of the exalted Christ, the picture of God revealed?[15]

If, therefore, we are placed at the mercy of the historical sciences in order to know anything certain about the Jesus of history, we find ourselves in the position of

14 Scott, p. 47.
15 Kähler, pp. 61-62.

having to recognize that only a few people are capable of such endeavor, and that most of these have been found in comparatively recent years. Moreover, what would a Jesus presented to us by this means prove to us? He could certainly do something for our minds, but that this would destroy faith or make faith unnecessary is far from the truth. As Ladd observes, "Historical proofs have to do with the mind and critical reason; faith has to do with the whole man."[16]

At this point we see one of two great errors on Bultmann's part with respect to the historical question. That historical research may demonstrate an event as historical in the Gospels has no basic effect on faith. Cairns points this out: "These events have a verifiable aspect, as events, but the fact that here God acted in miracle, or that God acted in revelation is not verifiable in any sense which could remotely endanger the nature of faith itself." [17] There were those in the world of Jesus' day to whom the events of the life of the Jesus of history were much more available than they are to any contemporary critical biblical historian, and yet they did not believe. This should be enough to refute the idea that knowledge of the life of Christ either by historical research or by any other means is enough to destroy faith.

We agree that if historical research is necessary to faith, this would make faith basically a "work." On the other hand, if we accept the historical record as it has come down to us as a special revelation from God, then we may act on the basis of that record and come to experience faith. But even if we accept it as a special revelation, this does not obliterate the necessity of acting on it, and so faith still remains a necessity. Is this not what we have in the concluding verses of Jn. 20: "Now Jesus did many other signs in the presence of the disciples, which are not written in this book; but these are written that you may believe that Jesus is the Christ, the Son of God, and that believing you may have life in his name" (20:30-31)?

16 George E. Ladd, "The Resurrection of Christ," *Christian Faith and Modern Theology*, ed. Carl F. H. Henry (New York: Channel, 1964), p. 280.

17 Cairns, p. 144.

The second great error of Bultmann has to do with his understanding of how a man comes to faith after the evidence, by whatever means, has been presented to him. This is not a case of human decision made possible by "the event of Christ." It is a divine work brought about by the Holy Spirit. This is the point that Jesus in New Testament times had such difficulty getting across to Nicodemus, and it is a point that modern man has equal difficulty understanding. Paul says this as explicitly as does anyone: "He saved us, not because of deeds done by us in righteousness, but in virtue of his own mercy, by the washing of regeneration and renewal in the Holy Spirit, which he poured out upon us richly through Jesus Christ our Savior" (Tit. 3:5-6).

What purpose, then, has historical research at all? It would appear that in relation to faith its force would be that of verification rather than awakening of faith. It keeps the contemporary Christian from being deluded or naïve in his faith. It is of great help to him to know that what he takes as the special revelation of God is in accordance with the facts of historical research.

There are, in addition, two other reasons or purposes for pursuing historical research. To some people the demonstration of the evidence may be the means the Holy Spirit uses to bring them to faith. As Austin Farrer observes, "What turned the scales might be the historical persuasion that the seeds of the Church's faith were not only in the Gospels but in the historical fact behind the Gospels."[18]

In the second place, historical research may make the Christian even more thankful for the grace of God that has been revealed to him. Cairns states it this way: "To those who received faith, however, both his contemporaries and later generations, the story of Jesus' life and manner of his death have been immensely important, for in the light of faith these historical facts are seen to be the disclosure of the heart of God."[19]

[18] Austin Farrer, "An English Appreciation," *Kerygma and Myth*, I, ed. Hans Werner Bartsch, trans. Reginald H. Fuller (London: S. P. C. K., 1964), pp. 219-20.

[19] Cairns, p. 218.

Selection impossible

We have noticed that from the point of view of the sources, there is no logical reason for accepting some of the life of Jesus and rejecting the rest. This is not to say that some contemporary critics have not attempted to establish criteria for doing this. We shall consider some of these criteria shortly. Here we shall deal briefly with the result of any attempt to work out such a process of selection.

The major feature of attempts at selection from the Gospels is the subjectivity which of necessity must dominate them. Davies points this out: "Roman and Protestant scholarship in the Synoptics has been made difficult and frustrating because of the extreme subjectivity of its approach. Each student has felt free, not only to make his own assumptions, but to create his own criteria." [20] While Davies feels that the establishment of such criteria is possible, the current writer doubts this in light of the nature of the sources, if one does not take the biblical witness to its origin seriously.

If, then, subjectivity is characteristic of the critics, what are some of the pitfalls of such an approach? It is interesting here to note the remarks of Mackinnon. We do so not because his statement is superior to others that could be given, but because of the date of his book. He wrote before the full effect of criticism had been felt in life-of-Jesus research, and in consideration of the situation that currently prevails his words sound almost prophetic:

Whilst the historian is greatly indebted to the labors of higher criticism, it would be unwise to regard all their opinions as fully ascertained verities. One is often mystified rather than edified by the jangle of conflicting views that grates on the ear of the seeker of historic truth. The assumptions made and the conclusions reached seem, at times, lacking in sound judgment and real historic insight. Some of them certainly suggest the

[20] Davies, p. 11.

mere hunt for novelty, the desire to make a reputation on the strength of the ingenuity of the critic.[21]

While we are certain that the quest for novelty is never completely absent from the critical school, there are even greater dangers that confront it in its attempt at selection. One of the greatest is that the historical critic may come to the Gospels with a notion of what he thinks is true and may use the Gospels primarily by way of illustration, while at the same time creating the impression that the life of Jesus with which he presents us is the authentic one. Johannes Munck has stated it this way: "Historical research which is in principle not free will never achieve results contrary to its own assumptions. It can begin to run idle without realizing that it is finding only what it looks for and is establishing only what it already knows."[22] This tendency is, of course, most pronounced when a theological movement is captivated by some nonbiblical philosophical movement, as is the case with Bultmann and the new questers. We shall return to this issue later in this chapter. Here we limit ourselves to the methical validity of any selective procedure. Later we shall speak of where such a procedure gets its content.

The great trap that awaits anyone who attempts to go about a process of selection is that he will judge a statement to be early or late, historical or kerygmatic, genuine or spurious purely on the basis of his point of departure. We have all come to see that this was true of the nineteenth-century lives. We had presented to us Jesus the humanist. The most honest of all these critical lives was doubtless the one of Schweitzer, for he developed his most fully on the basis of all the Gospel materials. But due to his naturalistic point of departure, he presented us with a picture of Jesus that was more to be pitied than reverenced.

[21] James Mackinnon, *The Historic Jesus* (New York: Longmans, Green, 1931), p. xiii.
[22] Johannes Munck, "The New Testament and Gnosticism," *Current Issues in New Testament Interpretation*, ed. William Klassen and Graydon F. Snyder (New York: Harper, 1962), p. 232.

Following Kähler, Bultmann threw out the possibility of selection and professed to take the whole record. But the only way he could accept the whole record in accordance with his pre-understanding was to interpret it mythologically, or as we would state it more properly, allegorically. We shall evaluate such interpretation in a later chapter. We note here, however, that when he comes up against historical evidences that are objectionable to him, he enters into the same process of selection as those whom he criticizes. A most blatant example of this occurs in the very article in which he sets forth his new approach. In dealing with the subject of the resurrection this comes out. He writes, "The resurrection cannot be a miraculous proof capable of demonstration and sufficient to convince the skeptic that the cross really has the cosmic and eschatological significance ascribed to it." [23] This, of course, does not fit the evidence of the New Testament very well, as he himself admits: "It cannot be denied that the resurrection of Jesus is often used in the New Testament as a miraculous proof."[24] He cites two passages (Acts 17:31; Lk. 24:39-43) and then concludes, "These are most certainly later embellishments of the primitive tradition."[25]

In dealing with the cross, however, he professes to be dealing with an historical event: "In its redemptive aspect the cross of Christ is no mere mythical event, but a historic (*geschichtlich*) fact originating in the historical (*historisch*) event which is the crucifixion of Jesus." [26] Thus the crucifixion is historical, but the resurrection is mythical. Here it appears that the basic difference between Bultmann and his predecessors is not in the selection and rejection of parts of the Gospel records, but rather in the quantity of selection. We shall consider the reasons for this in due course.

[23] Rudolf Bultmann, "New Testament and Mythology," *Kerygma and Myth*, I, ed. Hans Werner Bartsch, trans. Reginald H. Fuller (London: S. P. C. K., 1964), p. 39.

[24] *Ibid.*

[25] *Ibid.*

[26] *Ibid.*, p. 37.

Harald Riesenfeld points to the fault in such a methodology:

> Scholars have set out from a conception of Jesus which has been constructed *a priori* and have then asked what portions of the Gospel material accord with this conception. They have more or less unconsciously used as the measure of their inquiry what Jesus can or cannot have done, without taking account of the fact that from the very first the tradition understood the deeds no less than the words of Jesus as something wholly unique which can be understood only in an eschatological setting. But an imperative requirement in the matter of method is that the nature of the investigation, and the criteria by which the material is judged, should be appropriate to the subject of inquiry. And this is something that we can now see more clearly than was possible a few decades ago.[27]

Assumptions of Historical Mistrust

Aftermath of form criticism

Markan framework (chronological accuracy of the Gospels). One of the most widely accepted presumptions of higher criticism today is that the framework of the Gospel of Mark, and therefore the chronology of Jesus' life, is that Gospel writer's own invention. If, then, Mark was the first of the Gospel writers, and Matthew and Luke used his Gospel along with other sources in the writing of their Gospels, the chronology of the life of Jesus in all three of the Synoptics partakes of this artificial Markan scheme.

The source of this belief is to be found in the theory of the messianic secret developed by Wrede. Briefly, this theory claims that Jesus never regarded himself as the Messiah. The messianic faith came as a result of the resurrection. Mark, however, wrote his Gospel in such a way as to demonstrate that Jesus had claimed to be the

[27] Harald Riesenfeld, *The Gospel Tradition and Its Beginning* (London: Mowbray, 1961), pp. 9-10. More recently this essay has appeared in a collection of Riesenfeld's essays published by Fortress Press.

Messiah, but had kept it a secret from the public, revealing it only to his disciples. Bultmann, fifty years after the work of Wrede, holds virtually the same position.[28]

The effect of this theory was to undermine confidence in the chronological sequence of the life of Jesus presented in the Synoptics. While the theory has undergone some revision at the hands of Bultmann's successors, [29] the net effect of that revision has not materially affected the historical problem. It is still felt by the successors of Bultmann that each pericope must be evaluated in and of itself with no connection to any other. The chronological sequence is merely a fictitious, although pious, invention.

In considering the value of this assumption, we must consider first the validity of its predecessor and causative agent—the messianic secret. One need not deny that the idea, as Wrede developed it, is possible. The real question is, Is it the only possible interpretation of the narrative in Mark, or even, is it the most logical interpretation? If we take the Markan narrative as we have it, can we discern any reason for Jesus' secrecy as it is presented in that book? We contend that such a reason is obvious in the book itself, and as a consequence we need not resort to the inventive fancy of the device of the messianic secret.

The confession of Peter in Mk. 8:29 was not made, as is that of contemporary Christians, in the context of belief in Jesus' deity. His confession was made in the context of the Jewish idea of the Messiah—a political Messiah. Jesus' commendation of Peter at that time cannot be taken to mean that the full and final realization of Jesus' messiahship had dawned on Peter. One need merely read the rest of the Gospel to see that. Peter is filled with militaristic ideas and actions, and when Jesus finally fails to come forward as Peter would like him to, Peter denies him.

[28] Rudolf Bultmann, *Theology of the New Testament*, I, trans. Kendrick Groebel (New York: Scribner, 1955), p. 32.

[29] Reginald H. Fuller, *The New Testament in Current Study* (London: S.C.M., 1963), p. 95.

In the light of the subsequent history we can see good reasons for Jesus' admonition to silence: (1) He felt compelled to give his disciples a good deal of instruction concerning the nature of his messiahship. It was not political, but spiritual. The abstruseness of the disciples at this point is difficult for us to understand; however, we can understand the disciples' actions more clearly if we attempt to put ourselves in their shoes. Their messianic concept had been developed over centuries of Jewish history. A well-fixed idea like that was difficult to change. (2) If Jesus had allowed his disciples to proclaim him as Messiah, the people would have been aroused to a political and perhaps a military campaign that would have concluded his ministry before it began. We must be reminded that in spite of Jesus' frequent injunctions to secrecy, from the point of view of the Romans he was eventually crucified for his claim to be the Messiah (Mk. 15:26, etc.).

The only logical reason for denying this construction is to be found in an a priori assumption that Jesus could not have been in any way the metaphysical Son of God, could not have regarded himself as the Messiah in the spiritual sense, and could thus not have known the future. We are thus thrown back to the old antithesis—general revelation versus special revelation.

There is, however, additional evidence which must be brought in to support the chronology of Mark. The earliest external evidence we have of the authorship of the Gospel is contained in a quotation preserved by the fourth-century church historian Eusebius of the remarks of Papias, Bishop of Hierapolis, in the third decade of the second century:

Mark became the interpreter of Peter and he wrote down accurately, but not in order, as much as he [Peter] related of the sayings and doings of Christ. For he was not a hearer or a follower of the Lord, but afterwards, as I said, of Peter, who adapted his teachings to the needs of the moment and did not make an ordered exposition of the sayings of the Lord. And so Mark made no mistake when he thus wrote down some things as he [Peter] related them; for he made it his especial care to omit nothing of what he heard, and to make no false statement therein.[30]

Modern critical scholarship has tended to center on the phrase "not in order." This may be taken in two ways. It may mean either that Mark was not a chronicler or that chronological sequence is completely absent from his treatment. While the form critics have taken it in the latter sense, there is good reason to take it in the former sense. Before we turn our attention to that, however, let us see whether there is reason to accept the remarks of Papias that behind the Gospel we have the testimony of Peter and that in its construction we have the work of Mark.

Donald Guthrie has pointed to the work of two men who have done much to establish the genuineness of the Petrine reminiscences in the book as we now have it. C. H. Turner, for example, has shown that in a number of passages in the Gospel in which Mark used the third person plural, one could with little difficulty use the first person plural; and this to him is evidence that at these points we have eyewitness reminiscences of Peter.[31]

T. W. Manson picked up Turner's work, and showed how a number of passages adjacent to the ones Turner identified could be explained only in connection with those passages. As a result, a large portion of the material must be attributed to Peter.[32] Furthermore, much of the remaining material gives evidence of having been arranged into blocks prior to Mark's using it, which would indicate its use prior to the time of the writing of Mark.[33]

In connection with Mark we also notice a few additional things without going into all the matters of introduction. I Pet. 5:13 associates Peter and Mark and Rome (Babylon). We know from the early narratives in Acts

[30] Eusebius, *Ecclesiastical History* iii.39.15. Translation here is from Henry Bettenson (ed.), *Documents of the Christian Church* (London: Oxford, 1967), p. 27.

[31] Donald Guthrie, *New Testament Introduction: The Gospels and Acts* (Chicago: Inter-Varsity, 1965), p. 135.

[32] *Ibid.*, pp. 135-36.

[33] *Ibid.*, p. 136.

that Mark at that time was in Palestine. It is very likely that during these days he could have picked up much information from eyewitnesses to the events. It would appear that the only way this presumption could be denied is to assert that his decision to write was a spur-of-the-moment impulse. This is highly unlikely. It is also a reasonable guess that the young man who fled naked in Mk. 14:51-52 at the time of the trial of Jesus was Mark himself. Why such an event should be included in the Gospel if it were not Mark himself would be difficult to explain. If this individual was Mark, it would be logical to assume that he was a witness of at least this part of Jesus' life.

We return now to the question of chronological sequence. C. H. Dodd based his contention as to the chronological dependability of the Markan order on two things: (1) The summaries, which are supposedly the editorial work of Mark, when put together form a consecutive historical outline; and (2) the speeches in Acts, particularly that of Peter in Acts 10:37-41, bear the same general chronological pattern as does the Gospel of Mark.[34]

James Robinson has criticized Dodd primarily on two counts: (1) The attempt of Dodd to find such history was based on the positivistic historicism of the nineteenth century; and (2) the kerygma, from Robinson's point of view, shows no interest in the public ministry of Jesus. [35]

In light of what we have said earlier in this chapter regarding the necessity of both fact and interpretation in history, it is obvious that Robinson has gone too far with interpretation, as some of his predecessors went too far with fact; thus his first criticism must not be weighted as heavily as he would like us to think. We shall deal more fully with the second criticism later in this chapter.

There are, however, a number of additional observations which we may make that would appear to weight the case in the direction of Markan accuracy rather than

[34] C. H. Dodd, *The Apostolic Preaching and Its Developments* (New York: Harper, 1936).

[35] Robinson, pp. 56-57.

against it: (1) The passion narrative in the Gospel is in chronological order. This form critics and their successors have been forced to admit. That the events of the final week of Jesus' life must in general follow the sequence of Mark, they will not and cannot dispute. The reason for this they find in the importance of those events for the early Church. But are we to assume that while the Church was interested in passion week because of its tremendous significance from the beginning, it showed no interest in the chronology of the life of Jesus that preceded it? Or are we to assume that while in one part of his narrative Mark showed great concern for chronology, in the other part he totally neglected it? It would take a great deal of imagination to believe this.

(2) The quantity of narrative material in the Gospel outweighs that of any other character. Robert Bartels has for the sake of analysis divided the materials in the Gospels into six categories: "(1) John the Baptist narratives . . . (2) Narratives which are biographical in nature . . . (3) Miracles or wonders . . . (4) References to Jesus' preaching . . . (5) Jesus' teachings . . . (6) Parables of Jesus."[36] Of these six categories, Mark includes 288 of his 677 verses in the category of narratives that are biographical in nature. This far exceeds the number in any other category.[37]

From this evidence Bartels concludes that we must admit the possibility of at least two things:

> First, that in the early Church the brunt of the proclamation of the Gospel of Jesus' Messiahship may be expected to have rested upon a recitation of episodes or of a series of episodes (including especially the Passion) which showed Jesus in messianic action . . . . Second, the analysis indicates that Mark himself, perhaps of necessity and in keeping with the nature of the tradition as he had already heard and knew it, placed immense value upon the actual shape and progress of Jesus' life and ministry.[38]

[36] Robert A. Bartels, *Kerygma or Gospel Tradition . . . Which Came First?* (Minneapolis: Augsburg, 1961), pp. 41-42.

[37] *Ibid.*, p. 42.

[38] *Ibid.*, pp. 44-45.

(3) If the reminiscences of Peter lie behind the Gospel, and if in addition Mark had access to the testimony of other eyewitnesses in writing his Gospel, perhaps including in part his own, there is no warrant for believing that these witnesses would have from the beginning omitted any concern for matters either of geography or of chronology. The amount of time between the happenings and the writing of the Gospels shall occupy our attention shortly. Here, however, we must anticipate that subject by saying that chronology of necessity had to interest the eyewitnesses.

(4) As a consequence of our last observation, the occurrence in the Gospel of numerous notations of time and place is inexplicable apart from their accuracy. This is a necessary observation in light of the frequent claim that Mark generalizes. While this is in part true, in many instances he is very specific in reference to time and place. To do something like this inaccurately, in the presence of eyewitnesses to the events who regarded them as important, is impossible.

(5) The way Mark uses Old Testament materials to bolster belief in Jesus as the fulfilment of prophecy is added evidence on the side of his historical accuracy. Sometimes authors give the impression that Old Testament prophecy is responsible for the picture of Jesus developed in the Gospels. The Gospel writers, they say, of whom Mark was the first, fabricated a life of Jesus in accordance with what was expected of the promised Messiah. Hunter points out the error in this assumption; and while he comments in terms of all of the Gospels, his remarks have special relevance for the Gospel of Mark:

> All the Evangelists claim that in Jesus the Old Testament finds its fulfilment. Yet ... precisely because their telling of the story is controlled by the authentic memory of the original facts about Jesus, they do not dare to represent the Old Testament prophecies as having been literally, or conventionally, fulfilled in Jesus. The Messiah (to take only one example) was to be a King .... The Evangelists do affirm that He was a King, but they no less affirm that His Kingdom was "not of this world," and that His royalty was to be construed in terms of service. We may conclude that the Christ of the earliest

Christian tradition was no dream figure conjured up from Old Testament prophecy.[39]

(6) Finally, the work of Mark should not be considered a break with the past in respect to the life of Jesus. It should rather be considered as drawing upon the oral tradition that preceded it. We shall consider soon the nature of that oral tradition. It is sufficient here to note that the assertion that Mark's Gospel represents either a deliberate or accidental departure from that tradition is in no way warranted.

The sum of these considerations would appear to be a severe challenge to the theory of the messianic secret as developed by Wrede and Bultmann, and to favor the chronological accuracy of Mark's Gospel. In saying this, however, we again do not intend to assert that his work is to be regarded as a chronicle.

There are some additional factors that also must occupy our attention in our attempt to evaluate the contention of lack of chronological accuracy in the Gospels. One of these has to do with what has been designated "the formative period," i.e., the period between the crucifixion of Jesus and the writing of the Gospels. We begin by acknowledging the existence of such a period. It must not, however, be thought that a great length of time passed between the events of Christ's life and the first recording of those events. Most Synoptic critics now feel that the Gospel of Mark was written about A.D. 65, and that Q, whatever its nature, was in existence by A.D. 50. We are thus talking about a period of no more than twenty years between the events and the first organized account of them, and a period of no more than thirty-five years between the events and the publication of the First Gospel.

There is, in addition, scriptural confirmation of what we should expect to have been the case—that is, of the handing down of the tradition from eyewitnesses. Luke's preface makes this clear, and there is a most explicit

[39] Archibald Hunter, *Interpreting the New Testament 1900-1950* (Philadelphia: Westminster, 1951), p. 48.

statement to this effect in Paul: "I delivered to you as of first importance what I also received" (I Cor. 15:3).

Gerhardsson has called our attention to the Jewish expectation of this requirement: "Against the background of the Jewish milieu, it is evident that the early Christian Apostles were *compelled* to present their message as an eyewitness account, as 'that which we have seen and heard.' . . . "[40]

How, then, are we to evaluate this "formative period"? Form criticism and the successors of that movement give the impression that in this period there was a tremendous shift from the Jesus of history to the Christ of faith. But it may be objected that there was not nearly enough time for what is claimed by the form critics to have happened. The Gospels came from the second and third generation after Jesus, and as we have already seen, they were based on documents that dated back to even earlier days. Thus both the record and the message were from primitive Christian days. We have in the Gospels not the work of later critical historians; we have the works of men who were in real contact with the events.

The impossibility of any serious alteration from the standpoint of time is obvious if we look at the two principal Gospel sources and make an intelligent guess about what happened before that time. Mark, as we said, stands no more than thirty-five years from the events, Q no more than twenty years. Furthermore, if something as extensive and well defined as Q was in existence twenty years after the events, it would appear that there would have been other, briefer, written accounts much earlier. The possibility must not be ruled out that on occasion notes were made in conjunction with an actual event in the life of Jesus. We shall consider later in this chapter the possibility that Jesus required his disciples to memorize his teaching.

Riesenfeld has pointed out that the words and the deeds of Jesus were perhaps first recited in the early Christian community, as recounted in Acts 2:42.[41] The

[40] Gerhardsson, p. 330.
[41] Riesenfeld, p. 22.

association of these words and deeds with the Old Testament in such assemblies would emphasize both the importance and the accuracy of their transmission. Gerhardsson notices a development that perhaps followed very soon: "It is probable that relatively comprehensive 'tractates' of Jesus-traditions had to be compiled at a fairly early stage for use of missionaries and teachers who went out from Jerusalem."[42]

Moreover, as Albright has pointed out, there are benefits to be found in a period of oral transmission, brief though that might be. Once a record has been written down it attains fixity, and if it is in error the error is made permanent. In a relatively short period of transmission, such errors may be corrected.[43] Gerhardsson has drawn attention to the locus and the methodology that resulted in the solidification of the tradition and its parallelism to what occurred elsewhere in contemporary Judaism: "In the course of this present investigation we have come to the conclusion that the leading *collegium* in the Jerusalem church carried out a direct work on *ho logos tou kyriou* (i.e. the Holy Scriptures and the tradition from, and about, Christ). From certain points of view this work resembled the labours of Rabbinic Judaism . . . and the work carried out in the Qumran congregation . . . ."[44]

We would agree with the critics that some transformation such as they claim could have come over the material if the formative period had been two hundred rather than twenty years, but such a transformation in the length of time available was simply impossible. Bruce has well summarized the matter:

> We have then in the Synoptic Gospels, the latest of which was complete not much more than forty years after the death of Christ, material which took shape at a still earlier time, some of it even before his death, and which, besides being for the most part first-hand evidence, was transmitted along indepen-

[42] Gerhardsson, p. 333.

[43] William Foxwell Albright, *From the Stone Age to Christianity* (Baltimore: Johns Hopkins, 1957), p. 387.

[44] Gerhardsson, p. 331.

dent and trustworthy lines. The Gospels in which this material is embodied agree in their presentation of the basic facts of the Christian faith—a threefold cord not quickly broken.[45]

We may, however, go further than the notice of time in our attempt to establish the reliability of the Gospel records. Due to the length of the formative period, the source of the materials that we have in the Gospels must be attributed to eyewitnesses of the events. The apostles, of course, are the first to come to our mind, but they were only representative of a much larger group of witnesses. If they regarded what Jesus had said and done as important, as they most certainly did, they would be most zealous in guarding the accuracy of the tradition. The high esteem in which they held him would cause them to guard his words and the accuracy of their transmission with utmost zeal.[46]

If exponents of the form-critical school are correct regarding what happened in the formative period, we would be forced to deny the integrity of the apostles. It would mean that during the lifetime of the apostles, and with their full knowledge, they allowed a distorted and false life of Jesus to replace the account of his life as it was really lived.[47] The consequences of such a creation make it even less attractive to us, but we shall consider this shortly.

The purity of the record, we can further affirm, was guarded not only by friendly witnesses, but by those who were basically hostile to the new faith as well. Any elaboration or alteration of the events of Jesus' life would have at once been challenged. Peter in his Pentecost sermon refers to this general knowledge of the events of Christ's life by those who were not believers (Acts 2:22).

Although Jesus and his disciples did not come from official rabbinic circles, it is likely that he used mnemonic devices to help his disciples remember those parts of his teaching which he regarded as being particularly impor-

[45] Bruce, *The New Testament Documents: Are They Reliable?*, p. 46.

[46] Gerhardsson, pp. 258, 329.

[47] Ramm, *Protestant Christian Evidences*, p. 154.

tant. Gerhardsson has observed that if Jesus used a methodology similar to his contemporary Jewish and Hellenistic teachers we may conclude, "He must have made his disciples learn certain sayings off by heart; if he taught, he must have required his disciples to memorize."[48]

Riesenfeld agrees with this judgment. He notices, for example, that Jesus taught his disciples the Lord's Prayer. He also notices that behind many of the words of Jesus we can hear echoes of an Aramaic original that offers evidence that the sayings were formulated in such a way as to make them suitable for transmission.[49] While such a technique was later developed much more highly by the rabbis, memorization always played a most important role in Jewish religious life.[50]

The words of Vincent Taylor have become almost classic in emphasizing the guard of eyewitnesses over the tradition: "If the form critics are right, the disciples must have been translated to heaven immediately after the Resurrection. As Bultmann sees it, the primitive community exists *in vacuo*, cut off from its founders by the walls of an inexplicable ignorance."[51]

There has been no greater factor in the destruction of the theory of the formative period as it has been developed by form critics and their successors than the most recent realization of the date of authorship of the Gospels. About a century ago it was believed in many quarters of biblical criticism that the Synoptic Gospels did not exist until the first decades of the second century. The German scholars of the Tübingen school were the most pronounced in this regard, but many others shared their views in a less extreme form. If such were the case, a transformation in at least some degree would be possible. It is today recognized, however, that the Gospels are first-century documents. As a matter of fact, the twenti-

48 Gerhardsson, p. 328.

49 Riesenfeld, p. 24.

50 Guthrie, p. 199.

51 Vincent Taylor, *The Formation of the Gospel Tradition* (New York: Macmillan, 1933), p. 41.

eth century has been characterized by the progressively earlier dating of the Gospels. Due to the discovery of the Greek papyri of the Gospels, this is no longer a question. Furthermore, archaeological investigations have served to demonstrate that the setting for the Gospels is most certainly to be found in first-century Palestine. The Gospels simply will not fit a second-century setting. In addition, at a number of places the historical accuracy of incidents in the Gospels has been vindicated, even against what was formerly thought to have been error.

In connection with this earlier dating of the Gospels and their reliability, Bruce makes an interesting observation: "If the New Testament were a collection of secular writings, their authenticity would generally be regarded as beyond all doubt. It is a curious fact that historians have often been much readier to trust the New Testament records than have many theologians."[52]

One of the main devices used since the rise of form criticism to cast doubt on the chronological accuracy of the Gospels has been the comparison of accounts given in the Synoptics. For that reason we will address ourselves briefly to this subject. In the first place, it must not be assumed that when two accounts of apparently identical historical origin appear in two of the Gospels and vary to some degree, this is an indication that one author is taking liberties with his source. There are a number of possibilities involved in such a circumstance. In the first place, the two Gospel writers may be using independent sources. The only way one may deny such a possibility is to assert that only one written account of any incident in the life of Christ was in existence at the time of the Evangelists' writing.

With respect to the teaching of Jesus there is an even simpler explanation. If Jesus gave teaching that he regarded as particularly important, is it not likely that he would repeat that teaching on a number of occasions? It would seem logical to assume that this would be the case. If so, then it is remarkable that we do not have more repetition and variation in that repetition than we have in

52 Bruce, p. 15.

the Gospels. If Jesus repeated the teaching it would not be necessary for him to repeat it all and repeat it in precisely the same form on any given occasion. To take a conspicuous example, it is not necessary to assume that the Sermon on the Mount in Mt. 5-7 and the Sermon on the Plain in Lk. 6 are either from the same source or represent Jesus' teaching on the same occasion.

Gerhardsson wrestles with the dual problem of the early standardization of the tradition and the variation of sayings in parallel accounts in the Gospels. While he entertains the possibility that some of the variation could be due to such things as translation on different occasions, faulty memorization, or redaction by the Evangelists, he does not feel that this should be our first approach to variation:

> First and foremost, we must make a very careful attempt to decide when we are actually dealing with variations of one and the same basic saying, and when with sayings of Jesus, delivered by Jesus himself in more than one version. The ease with which many scholars explain all differences between related traditions as being secondary versions of one basic saying, seems most remarkable to anyone who has noted the role played by the category of "theme and variations" in Jewish teaching.[53]

In regard to narrative portions the same thing may be said. The feeding of the four thousand and the feeding of the five thousand are represented by many critical scholars as doublets, because both narratives occur in the same Gospel. But on closer inspection it will be seen that one of these accounts has to do with Jesus' contact with the Jews and the other with his contact with the Gentiles. Because this is the case, it is likely that they are really two independent and distinct incidents. In the one, Jesus presents himself as the bread of life to the Jews; in the other, he presents himself as the bread of life to the Gentiles.

It is often stated that in the Gospels themselves we see indications of development of the tradition. This is

[53] Gerhardsson, pp. 334-35.

usually illustrated by pointing out ways in which the
other two Synoptics expand on Mark. When this is done,
however, critics fail to realize that just as often the
movement is in the opposite direction. In many cases the
accounts in Matthew and Luke are briefer. Such is the
case, for example, in the narratives concerning the demoniac boy (Mt. 17:14-20; Lk. 9:37-43a; cf. Mk.
9:14-29); the Gerasene demoniac (Mt. 8:28-34; Lk.
8:26-39; cf. Mk. 5:1-20); and the death of John the
Baptist (Mt. 14:1-12; Lk. 9:7-9; cf. Mk. 6:14-29). The
possibilities of different sources in these instances must
also be entertained.

One of the most constantly noticed differences, yet
one of the least significance, is that on occasion Matthew
introduces two individuals in instances where the other
Synoptic writers have only one. Such is the case in the
instance of the Gerasene demoniac (Mt. 8:28) and the
blind man at Jericho (Mt. 20:30). In the story of the
resurrection Luke similarly mentions two angels at the
tomb (Lk. 24:4). This cannot be treated as a serious
difficulty. The authors who mention only one in these
cases tell the story from the perspective of the one
mentioned. As E. F. Harrison has insisted, "One could
properly speak of error here if the texts which specify a
single participant made it definite that there was one and
only one."[54]

In comparing the Synoptic narratives with one
another, one should bear in mind also the purpose of
each of the authors in writing. For example, Matthew
seeks to illustrate various facets of the life of Jesus,
whereas Luke tells us that his purpose is to set forth "an
orderly account." Although we are justified in asserting a
general chronological pattern for the writers of the
Synoptic Gospels, each of them had particular themes
that caused them to vary it slightly. This leads us to say
two things: (1) Chronological sequence is both expected

54 Everett F. Harrison, "The Phenomena of Scripture," *Revelation and the Bible*, ed. Carl F. H. Henry (Grand Rapids: Baker,
1958), p. 246.

and stated; and (2) chronological sequence in each precise detail is not demanded.

We will consider one other topic here that affects the subject of the chronological accuracy of the Gospels. It is that of source criticism. While source criticism should not be set up in opposition to form criticism, it must be admitted that most of those who have come out of the form-critical school of thought do not show any intense interest in the area of source criticism. We feel that there are good reasons for this, which we shall point out shortly. The vast majority of scholars today accept the Gospel of Mark as the first of the Synoptic Gospels written. There is even a noticeable trend in this direction by Roman Catholic scholars who long have held out for the primacy of Matthew.

There is also a large amount of agreement among biblical scholars as to the existence of the second source, Q. This source is identified by the great amount of common material in Matthew and Luke which is not found in Mark. While a great number of scholars hold to the existence of Q, there is less agreement today as to its nature than was the case a few decades ago. Because we do not have the source itself, a great many questions have arisen about it. We do not know, for example, whether it was one source or a series of sources that the Evangelists held in common. We do not know whether it was a written source or an oral source. We do not know whether the source was more extensive than the common materials in Matthew and Luke. For that reason we do not know whether the special material in either Matthew or Luke came from that source or not.

In spite of these questions, there is general agreement that such a source(s) existed and that it was pre-Markan in date. Fuller mentions some of the reasons for attributing to it an early date: (1) There is indication from the passages that we have in Q that Palestinian Jewish life was still centered around the Temple. (2) There is indication that the followers of John the Baptist and the Pharisees may still have been a problem for the Christians. (3) The Christian mission is apparently pretty well limited as of this time to the Jews.[55]   Taking all this evidence into consideration, it is a good guess that Q must be dated about A.D. 50.

Some have attempted to identify Q with a source mentioned by Papias. A statement by him preserved by Eusebius reads, "So then Matthew recorded the oracles in the Hebrew tongue, and each interpreted them to the best of his ability."[56]   Most contemporary scholars do not feel that the Gospel of Matthew is a translation of that document, but some feel that what may be referred to here is Q.[57]   Others, however, doubt the validity of this conjecture.[58]

If the Gospels of Matthew and Luke, then, are based in part on Q, whatever its nature, coming from about A.D. 50, and the Gospel of Mark, coming from about A.D. 65, and if on the basis of recent textual and archaeological information all three Gospels must be recognized as first century, then here as elsewhere in this section of study we have good evidence for trusting the chronological accuracy of the Gospels.

Community sayings. We mention here one other item of carry-over from the form-critical school in current critical scholarship. Ever since the origin of form criticism, it has been asserted by its adherents that many of the sayings in the Gospels attributed to Jesus find their origin rather in the primitive Christian community. The theory behind this assertion was developed briefly as follows. In the early Christian community problems developed which Jesus did not and could not have foreseen. In order to meet these problems in its *Sitz im Leben* (situation in life), the early Church put words into Jesus' mouth which they thought would represent the way he would have dealt with the problem. We have many of these sayings preserved for us in the Gospels. If this should be the case, then we can have little assurance that

[55] Reginald Fuller, pp. 88-89.

[56] Eusebius, *Ecclesiastical History* iii.39.16. Translation here is from Bettenson, p. 27.

[57] Bruce, p. 40; Hunter, p. 46.

[58] Guthrie, p. 34.

the accounts in the Gospels are accurate representations of the words and deeds of the historical Jesus.

Against this background we must notice two responses to the work of the form critics with respect to the *Sitz im Leben* of the Gospels. The first is a movement that is basically sympathetic with the approach of the form critics. It, like form criticism, is German in origin and goes by the name *Redaktionsgeschichte*, or, as it is known to English readers, "redaction criticism." The name was given to the discipline by W. Marxsen in 1954 and developed more fully in a work of 1956 on the Gospel of Mark.[59] His work in the area was preceded, however, by that of Bornkamm on the Gospel of Matthew in 1948,[60] and by that of Conzelmann on the Gospel of Luke in 1954.[61] Since that time a number of redaction-critical studies have appeared. A number of the German studies were analyzed in a doctoral dissertation by Joachim Rohde which has subsequently been translated into English.[62]

While the redaction critics in general accept the work of the form critics, their work goes beyond that of the form critics in several respects which we may illustrate by way of some comparisons: (1) Form criticism was concerned with the forms or small units that made up the Gospels. Redaction criticism is concerned with the Gospels as a whole in their redaction. (2) Form criticism considered the Evangelists as collectors and transmitters. Redaction criticism considers them as redactors and therefore to some extent authors. (3) Form criticism considered the oral tradition behind the Gospels. Redaction criticism looks more closely at the existing written

59 Eng. trans.: W. Marxsen, *Mark the Evangelist*, trans. Roy A. Harrisville (Nashville: Abingdon, 1969).

60 Eng. trans.: G. Bornkamm, G. Barth, and H. J. Held, *Tradition and Interpretation in Matthew*, trans. Percy Scott (Philadelphia: Westminster, 1963).

61 Eng. trans.: H. Conzelmann, *The Theology of St. Luke*, trans. G. Buswell (New York: Harper, 1960).

62 Joachim Rohde, *Rediscovering the Teaching of the Evangelists*, trans. Dorothea M. Barton (Philadelphia: Westminster, 1968).

Gospels. (4) Form criticism adopted an anti-individual-istic point of view regarding the work of the Evangelists. Redaction criticism regards the framework of the Gospels as the achievement of the Evangelists.

The approach of the redaction critics is usually based on the two-source theory (Mark and Q), and they pro-ceed to demonstrate the theology of the individual Evan-gelists by comparing the Synoptic Gospels. Such theology they feel is revealed in the individual Evangelist's choice of material, order of material, arrangement of material, and alterations of the material he received.

More important for our study here is their point of view with respect to the *Sitz im Leben*. Marxsen in particular has emphasized that we must now think in terms of a threefold *Sitz im Leben* with respect to the Gospel data: (1) Some of the material has a setting in the life of Jesus. (2) Some of the material has a setting in the life of the early Church. (3) Some of the material has a setting in the purpose and theology of the Evangelists. [63] Form criticism concerned itself primarily with the second of these settings. It was its contention in varying degrees that the bulk of the materials in the Gospels must be considered the product of the early Church. Redaction criticism has concerned itself primarily with the third of these settings. For that reason it has not pretended to give us much information about the Jesus of history. The net result of the work of the redaction critics, however, would be to give us even less confidence in the Gospels as sources for the life of Jesus. If what they say is true, we are removed not just one important step from the setting in the life of Jesus to the setting in the early Church, but a second important step to a setting in the purpose and theology of the Evangelists.

There are some desirable tendencies in the redaction-critical approach which have been absent in previous criticism. The willingness to consider the Gospels as products of an individual and not those of a community, and the return to a sounder analysis of the Gospels on the basis of literary sources are two of these. But there are

[63] Marxsen, p. 23.

also serious problems connected with it. Some of these problems it holds in common with form criticism. For example, we must believe that the Christian community would act as a check on the supposed theological tendencies of the Evangelists. This would be particularly the case if our Gospels were written as early as we must now suppose so that eyewitnesses to the events were a part of that community. Also, as with form criticism, vast assumptions are made about the transformation of the material from the time of the occurrence of the event to the time of its inclusion in the Gospels. How certain can we be about what elements the Evangelists passed on as they received them and what elements they edited?

Other problems are more particularly those of redaction criticism itself. Perhaps the principal one is its tendency toward overinterpretation. Critics build grandiose theological assumptions on the basis of tiny bits of evidence. Rohde calls attention to this repeatedly in his study,[64] and one is left with the impression when he finishes reading Rohde's book that if the Evangelists had known how much significance would be attached to minute details in their accounts by future critics, they would never have mustered the courage to sit down and write.

But let us return to the issue of the *Sitz im Leben* of the Gospels in terms of a second response to the form critics. This is found in the work of the Swedish theologians Riesenfeld and Gerhardsson. They take up the issue of the *Sitz im Leben* claimed for the Gospels by the form critics. Riesenfeld in particular deals with a couple of the assumptions of form critics with respect to the *Sitz im Leben* of the Gospels. He notes that one group of critics assumes that the *Sitz* is to be found in the mission preaching in the early years of Christianity. Riesenfeld raises the question as to what the missionary preaching might have been. He feels that he can get a general idea of its content by studying the book of Acts and certain echoes in the New Testament epistles. On the basis of these materials he discerns that the kerygma concerned

64 Rohde, p. 258.

itself with "formulae about the saving work of Christ." [65] He then concludes, "But of anything which recalls the materials from which our Gospels were constructed we have, alas! not the least trace."[66]

Riesenfeld then deals with the assumption of another group of form critics: that the *Sitz im Leben* of the Gospel tradition is to be found in the communal instruction of the early Church; that is, the *Sitz* is not found to be external to the Church but within the Church. He also finds this difficult to accept:

> If we suppose the existence of such an interrelation between early Christian community preaching and Gospel tradition, then it remains inexplicable that while in the Christological and theological parts of the New Testament Epistles we have countless allusions to the sayings of Jesus (though not to the narrative material of the Gospels), we have no express citations of his words. There can be only one explanation of this strange fact, namely, that the primitive Christian letter-writers, and among them Paul, took express pains to avoid citing the sayings of Jesus in the context of their original utterance. Their method, that is, was directly the opposite of that of preachers of our own day. The sayings of Jesus, and hence the tradition about Jesus, were presumed to be already known, but this tradition was not cited in its verbal form.[67]

Riesenfeld goes on to illustrate his contention in reference to the epistles of the New Testament and then concludes, "The *Sitz im Leben* and the original source of the Gospel tradition was neither mission preaching nor the communal instruction of the primitive Church."[68]

What, then, was the *Sitz im Leben* of the Gospel tradition? Riesenfeld feels we can find the answer to this in the writing of Luke. On the basis of Lk. 1:2 he concludes that the sayings and deeds of Jesus were regarded as a holy Word comparable to the Old Testament. Because they were so regarded, the handing down of this record was entrusted to special persons. That is why, for

[65] Riesenfeld, p. 12.
[66] *Ibid.*
[67] *Ibid.*, pp. 14-15.
[68] *Ibid.*, p. 16.

example, it was so important that the successor to Judas
Iscariot among the apostles should be someone who was
acquainted not only with the resurrection of Jesus, but
with the entire course of his public ministry (Acts
1:21ff.).

This brings Riesenfeld to the question before us:

> Now can we find in the most primitive Christianity any *Sitz im
> Leben* of such a special "holy" tradition about Jesus? We are
> helped in answering this question if we consider the literary
> genus of this tradition which precedes the Gospels in their
> definitive written form. Comparison with the style of the
> Prophetic discourses of the Old Testament on the one hand
> and with the Rabbinic material on the other, suggests that the
> tradition was recited; and, since the tradition was not esoteric
> in the narrower sense, that it was recited not exclusively to
> hearers who were destined to become future transmitters of
> the tradition. But as soon as ever one reflects on the character
> of this Christian tradition as holy word, as the Word of God
> and as something parallel to the holy writings of the Old
> Testament, the very smallest knowledge of the Palestinian
> milieu forces the conclusion that the words and deeds of Jesus
> were not just improvised, that there was no question of freely
> narrating or of inventing, even when the speaker was possessed
> by the Spirit. On the contrary, the strict laws relating to holy
> tradition will have prevailed from the outset and determined
> both what was uttered and what was transmitted, in spite of
> the fact that in points of detail variations could not but appear
> and, indeed, did appear.[69]

As a result of his investigation Riesenfeld concludes
that the words and deeds of Jesus were first recited in the
assemblies of the Christian community, that their association with the sacred words of the Old Testament
imparted to them the same sacred authority, and that this
process occurred at a very early date in the Christian
community.[70]

It would appear that Riesenfeld has put his finger on
the fundamental error in the form-critical analysis of the
Sitz im Leben of the Gospel tradition. It has failed to pay

[69] *Ibid.*, pp. 21-22.
[70] *Ibid.*, p. 22.

proper attention to the fact that the Gospels arose in the Jewish milieu of Palestine in the first century, and not in a Hellenistic milieu.

These, then, are some of the features of contemporary criticism in relation to form criticism. Let us now look at some other features of contemporary criticism that have contributed to mistrust of Gospel history.

Further developments

Lukan accuracy. One of the contributing factors to the rise of the form-critical movement was that three of the Gospels, the Synoptics, are very similar in nature, yet contain significant differences. It was only natural that the critical scholars in this movement should concentrate their attention on Mark's Gospel inasmuch as it was the earliest written. More recently, however, it appears that the scholars of this lineage have been devoting increased attention to Luke's Gospel. There appear to be two main reasons for this. In the first place, the Lukan prologue, no matter how one may take it, apparently announces the intent of the author to launch into a more systematic and technical study of the life of Jesus than his predecessors had. It makes little difference whether we take the words "orderly account" to mean chronological or logical. One cannot escape the conclusion that the author intends to write history. This has led critics to evaluate his work as an historian.

In the second place, more emphasis has been placed on the study of Luke in conjunction with Acts. If it may be demonstrated that Luke was a poor historian in the book of Acts, this would reflect on the historical validity of his Gospel. If, conversely, it can be shown that Luke did a fine job from an historical perspective on the book of Acts, the historical value of his Gospel would be enhanced. Our task here, then, shall be to compare Luke with two sets of literature; first to the other Synoptics—principally Mark—and then to Acts.

When Luke is compared to Mark, certain features of his work immediately impress one. The chronological pattern for Jesus' life is repeated by Luke in essentially the same form it is given by Mark. There are neither any major transpositions of that chronology, nor any omissions that would set Luke over against Mark and force one to choose the chronology of one against the other. The importance of this general similarity is emphasized when one realizes that of the additions made to Mark by Luke, more are narrative in nature than there are of any other kind. If we use for convenience' sake the six-category breakdown of Bartels once again, we find that 269 of the additional 626 verses in Luke are narratives of a biographical nature.[71] The main feature of Luke's Gospel is thus expansion, not alteration or omission, though we shall examine the omissions that do occur shortly.

The care of Luke with respect to his sources extends even to his editing of the language of his sources. Gerhardsson has noticed this in a couple of respects: (1) In his use of Markan material "Even the language is subjected to comparatively little correction,"[72] and (2) "The writer of the prologue to Luke's Gospel had a different personal style from that which he uses when reproducing the gospel traditions."[73]

The major expansion is the so-called Perean section comprising Lk. 9:51-18:14. Although Mark gives to this only one verse (10:1), it will fit nicely into his chronological setting. It has been further observed that in some of Luke's special passages, the linguistic style of the source itself is discernible. This in itself is a demonstration of his faithfulness to his source.

The question of the omissions of Mark in Luke is somewhat more difficult to answer, but here several probabilities either singly or in groups may be suggested. Inasmuch as he added materials not found in Mark, space limitation would be a factor. Limitations to the scroll length and the comparative unavailability and expense of writing materials may have caused him to shorten parts of Mark as well as to add to it. It is also possible that he

71 Bartels, p. 49.
72 Gerhardsson, p. 209.
73 *Ibid.*, pp. 209-10.

chose other passages in his selection of sources over the ones available to him in Mark. A third possibility is no longer as popular among critics as it once was, but it remains a possibility. The so-called Ur-Markus theory states that there was a primitive edition of Mark's Gospel different from ours from which Luke drew his material. There would appear, however, to be no need to look for any other explanation for the Lukan omissions than the deliberate choice of the author.

Luke's preface would indicate that he got his materials from a variety of places. It should be supposed, for example, that during the Caesarean imprisonment of Paul, Luke had a great deal of time in which to procure materials. Since he used the written source Mark, and whatever materials comprised Q, it would be likely that he also used other written sources. Any written sources he procured during the time Paul was in Caesarea would probably have been at least as old as Q. Further, from our analysis of the careful way in which he used Mark and Q, the presumption as to his faithful use of any other sources must be in his favor.

Although the book of Acts is somewhat out of the chronological scope of our study, at least as far as the events it contains are concerned, it is necessary that we look at some features of recent criticism concerning it which reflect on its accuracy. If this book is accurate, it would tend to raise our estimate of Luke in his writing of the Gospel. If, on the other hand, Luke's lack of accuracy in Acts could be demonstrated, it would reflect badly on his Gospel.

As early as 1923 Martin Dibelius began to publish a series of essays in which he attempted to apply form-critical techniques to the book of Acts.[74] The general effect of these articles was to undermine the historical reliability of that book, but more particularly they attributed the speeches in the book of Acts to the creativity of Luke himself. Since that time this theory has been widely held among critical scholars.

[74] Martin Dibelius, *Studies in the Acts of the Apostles*, trans. Mary Ling (New York: Scribner, 1956).

Such was the method of Greek historians. They composed speeches that fit the character of the men they portrayed and put them in their histories. The first Greek historian of substance was Thucydides (c. 454-400 B.C.). He drew up a set of rules for himself as an historian. He admitted that on occasion he would not give a word-for-word reproduction of the speeches he recorded, but was always careful to make them conform to the general sense of the utterance. Although Thucydides exercised great caution in doing this, his successors became increasingly more careless and freely invented speeches for the characters they portrayed. Is this the procedure Luke followed?

Inasmuch as all the speeches are relatively brief, this may appear to be the case; however, their brevity can be accounted for on other bases. Since Acts is a second volume by the author, and since the first volume deals so extensively with the life of Jesus, it is to be supposed that in writing the speech of any given occasion, Luke would omit from his account the materials in the speech that dealt with the life of Jesus. This in many cases might have been the greater portion of the speech. Another likely omission in the speeches would be the possibly lengthy references to Old Testament Scriptures as they would be applied to the life of Christ. Bartels has observed that Luke's readers were probably well informed on the Old Testament.[75] Luke could not possibly have covered the scope of history he did in the book of Acts if he had written out in full each of the speeches, and the value of his having done so for the purpose of his book would have been relatively small.

Certain further considerations appear also to weigh in favor of the authenticity of the speeches recorded in Acts. There is first of all the question whether Luke in his writing followed the Greek tradition of historical writing or the Jewish tradition. Although Luke himself was a Gentile, he was associated more with the Jewish tradition than with the Greek. He had at his hands such writings as the Old Testament and such intertestamental writings as

75 Bartels, p. 93.

the books of I and II Maccabees. If this be the case, then our analysis of the speeches themselves must guide us in determining which historical tradition he followed, and as a consequence, how much we may rely on them.

Perhaps the greatest single factor that weighs in favor of the authenticity of the speeches is the pronounced Semitic flavor that we find in them. Bartels has noticed this: "A strong Semitic element still lingers in the early speeches in Acts, which indicates that even in translating Luke must have been careful not to destroy the original flavor of the speeches which his sources supplied him." [76] Others have concluded on the basis of this evidence that the speeches we have in Acts were once in Aramaic. [77]

Also, that a speech fits the situation may be an indication of one of two things. Either it was made in that situation, or it was composed by the historian to fit the situation in the manner of Greek history writers. All admit that Luke's speeches fit the situations ideally. In choosing between these alternatives, therefore, the Aramaic flavor would tip the balance in favor of their authenticity. The likelihood of a Greek author composing a speech with a Semitic flavor to it would be slight.

Finally, our observation of Luke's use of sources in his Gospel should raise our estimate of his ability to reproduce faithfully the sources he had at hand. It would appear, then, that aside from the necessary abbreviations of the speeches, Luke has given us a very accurate account of what was said by the speakers on the various occasions.

A second area in which the reliability of Luke has been questioned is that of his political knowledge. Luke's use of political titles is remarkably accurate, as the findings of archaeology have demonstrated. Further, in instances in which Luke has been thought to have been in error, added information has demonstrated his accuracy. The most dramatic evidence of this had to do with the verification of Lysanias as tetrarch of Abilene at the time of

[76] *Ibid.*, p. 86.

[77] Hunter, p. 35.

Jesus' public ministry.[78] Perhaps the greatest problem that remains is that Luke identifies Quirinius as governor of Syria at the time of Jesus' birth. It is known from other sources that Quirinius was governor of Syria in A.D. 6, and that he supervised a census in that year. Further evidence, however, has indicated that Quirinius may well have been in Syria at the earlier date as well. [79] It would appear here that modern critical biblical scholarship has not learned its lesson. It overreached itself in the case of Lysanias, and it has done the very same thing in the case of Quirinius, although in this case it is not even necessary to hypothesize a second individual by the same name as was the case with Lysanias.

A third area in which the accuracy of Luke has been challenged has to do with the relationship of Acts to Paul and his writings. It is observed, for example, that according to Acts, Paul visits Jerusalem three times in his early ministry (9:20ff.; 11:30; 15:2), while in Galatians only two such visits are mentioned. This alleged discrepancy is claimed on the assumption that Galatians gives a complete report of all of Paul's visits to Jerusalem. Others have maintained that the two sets of writings represent Paul in a contradictory way in reference to the Jewish law, but it is apparent that Paul looked on the law differently from the perspectives of Jews and Gentiles. In other areas also, which range from specifics to Luke's general portrait of Paul, differences have been claimed, but none of these appears to be of any substance, and the net result of it all is that such examinations tend to strengthen our confidence in Luke as an historian.[80]

The conclusions that we may justifiably reach on the basis of our examination of Acts are two: (1) Inasmuch as Luke has proven reliable in areas where we may test him, the presumption should be in his favor in areas where we as yet cannot; and (2) the fact of Luke's

[78] J. M. Creed, *The Gospel According to St. Luke* (London: Macmillan, 1930), pp. 307-09.

[79] Everett F. Harrison, *Introduction to the New Testament* (Grand Rapids: Eerdmans, 1964), p. 193.

[80] Guthrie, pp. 322-26.

reliability in Acts lends weight to the idea of his general reliability, i.e., the reliability of his Gospel.

Early Church and history. Since Bultmann, it has been characteristic of his followers to assert that there is no primarily historical purpose behind the writing of the Gospels. The following sample citations are merely illustrative:

> The significance of this Jesus for faith was so profound, that even in the very earliest days it almost entirely swallowed up his earthly history.[81]

> Nothing could be more mistaken than to trace the origin of the Gospels and the traditions collected therein to a historical interest apart from faith.[82]

> The aim was not to communicate who Jesus had been, and how he had once been regarded, but who Jesus is and [how he] may now be understood in faith.[83]

> It can never be certainly decided whether any indisputably genuine saying of Jesus has been handed on to us . . . . What have been handed on to us . . . are stylized formulations of the early community or of the evangelists.[84]

> Neither St. Paul nor St. John mediate an historic encounter with the historic Jesus. Even if the synoptic gospels appear to do so, that is only when they are read in the light of the historical problems which have arisen since their day, not when they are read in their original sense.[85]

It is sometimes stated that one of the reasons for the lack of historically reliable materials in the Gospels is that

[81] Käsemann, *Essays on New Testament Themes*, p. 23.

[82] Bornkamm, *Jesus of Nazareth*, p. 23.

[83] Gerhard Ebeling, *The Nature of Faith*, trans. Ronald Gregor Smith (Philadelphia: Fortress, 1961), p. 51.

[84] Ernst Fuchs, *Studies of the Historical Jesus*, trans. Andrew Scobie (Naperville: Allenson, 1964), p. 179.

[85] Rudolf Bultmann, "A Reply to the Theses of J. Schniewind," *Kerygma and Myth*, I, ed. Hans Werner Bartsch, trans. Reginald H. Fuller (London: S. P. C. K., 1964), p. 117.

the Gospel writers lacked the insight of modern critical historians. To this objection two things may be said. In the first place, we are in danger of underestimating the Gospel writers as historians. Scott has pointed out that the first century became a century in which history writing came to the fore in view of the decline in the arts and literature.[86] Furthermore, as we have noticed previously, the Gospel writers had at hand such things as the Old Testament, the Apocrypha, and Josephus. Scott goes on to notice that the Gospel writers used methods that historians of worth in any age have used. They went to sources for their information. They compared and evaluated sources, and when their sources on a subject were silent, they too were silent. "That brief preface in which Luke tells us what he has sought to do describes almost to the letter the aims and methods of any serious historian in our own time."[87]

In the second place, when the Evangelists are accused of lack of critical insight, there is danger of our putting them in a category in which they do not belong. An example may help clarify this. If I were to sit down today and attempt to write a history of the Peloponnesian war, it would require a great deal of research and critical analysis on my part. If, on the other hand, I were to write an account of a series of incidents that occurred in my home town twenty years ago in which I was personally involved and which had a profound effect on me, such research would not be necessary. I could draw on my own experience and that of those associated with me. And we contend that the Gospels are in the latter category, not the former. The whole point is that the Gospels were written in the era of the happenings; the availability of eyewitnesses to the events prevented their distortion; and the writers themselves used great caution to protect their accounts from error.

The real question, then, becomes this: Did the religious experience of the Evangelists or of the early Christian community cause them to submerge history? This is the

86 Scott, p. 17.
87 *Ibid.*, p. 18.

assertion that is being made. What we intend to demonstrate here is that a positive answer to such an assertion is unwarranted.

First of all, such an assertion makes several assumptions about the era of the New Testament which are completely untenable. To separate the community's concern for its own existence from its interest in the one who had given meaning to the life of that community is absurd. Jesus was of tremendous importance to that community. It can only be maintained with the most bizarre imagination that this same community evidenced no interest in the events of the life of that one who had come to mean so much to it. Jesus was the focal point of the interest of the community. As Gerhardsson has written, "All historical probability is in favor of Jesus' disciples, and the whole of early Christianity, having accorded the sayings of the one whom they believed to be the Messiah at least the same degree of respect as the pupils of a Rabbi accorded the words of *their* master!"[88] Or, once again, "Remembering the attitude of Jewish disciples to their master, it is unrealistic to suppose that forgetfulness and the exercise of a pious imagination had too much hand in transforming authentic memories beyond all recognition in the course of a few short decades."[89]

In addition, the early Church had to face the unbelieving world. The least effective way it could have done so would have been to confront it with a story full of exaggerations, distortions, and untruths. Both from the perspective of the centrality of Jesus to their faith and from that of antagonistic witnesses that confronted it, the Church would be forced to develop accurate accounts of the events.

A further assumption of this predominance of faith over history on the part of the early Church is one that pictures the Church as existing for a period of time really not knowing who Jesus was or what he meant to it. Finally, from some place there developed a vibrant and

[88] Gerhardsson, p. 258.
[89] *Ibid.*, p. 329.

vital faith on the part of the community, and then it somehow became interested in Jesus and proceeded to draw up an account of his life. How a series of events like this could have occurred is beyond the ability of this writer to imagine.

But we must go beyond this to the actual books of the New Testament themselves. It should be stated at the beginning that with the possible exception of the Gospel of John, none of the books of the New Testament were written primarily for evangelistic purposes. They were all written to people who were already believers. They were thus written either to establish people in the faith, to impart some additional information to them, or to deal with some problem. Almost without exception the churches, communities, or individuals being addressed had a previous knowledge of the life of Jesus. The people to whom the Gospels were addressed knew the least. That is the reason why they contain so much material on the life of Jesus.

If this be the case, the surprising thing is that the New Testament books make such frequent reference to the life of Jesus, not that they mention that life so little. Take, for example, the book of Acts. Modern kerygmatists have made a great deal out of the fact that so little mention is made of the life of Jesus in the kerygma in Acts. When this is done, it is apparent that modern critics have overlooked the fact that Acts is the second volume of a two-volume work. The Gospel of Luke deals extensively with the life of Jesus. We have already seen that one of the places at which Luke perhaps abbreviated the speeches of Acts was where they referred to the life of Jesus. Theophilus, to whom the book is addressed, knew all about this from the first volume. It would be very unsafe, therefore, to conclude on the basis of the book of Acts that the early Christian kerygma was not vitally interested in the Jesus of history.

We are fortunate to have this two-volume work by Luke, for it gives us a basis for what was the likely procedure of the Church in its missionary endeavor. Paul and the other missionaries as they traversed the Roman world likely presented to the new communities materials very similar to those we have in the Gospels. It is interesting to note in this regard that in all the correspondence by Paul that we have in our New Testament, there is never the slightest intimation that any of the Churches or people to whom Paul wrote ever asked a question concerning the course of Jesus' life. There can only be one explanation for this—they knew.[90] Even if they could have regarded that life as theologically irrelevant, which is inconceivable, plain curiosity would have prompted them to ask some questions about it. What is true for Paul is equally true for the other New Testament authors and the recipients of their letters.

It is amazing, then, that writers writing to people who already knew should place such a great emphasis on history. In the Gospels the most emphatic statements in this regard are found in the prologue to Luke and in Jn. 20:30-31. That Acts contains as many historical references as it does in light of Luke's Gospel is surprising. Paul, too, refers to the principal events of Jesus' life, although here, too, previous knowledge must be assumed. The early verses of I Cor. 15 are a summary of what the Corinthians already knew and are used by Paul to introduce the subject of the resurrection. There are numerous other references to incidents in the life of Jesus that were already known by the recipients of Paul's other letters.

Hebrews gives a sustained argument for the superiority of Christianity over Judaism, and in so doing it refers repeatedly to the life of Jesus. The Petrine letters refer also to the life, transfiguration, death, and resurrection of Jesus—once again to people who already knew about it. The Johannine epistles are directed against people who deny that Jesus has come in the flesh. The problem of Docetism was a problem for the Church of the first century as it is for the Church of the twentieth. The accumulative evidence is impressive. The life of Jesus gave rise to the early Church. The events of that life were the revelation of God. Apart from that life the faith of Christians of any era is vain.

There are two other matters which we will discuss

90 Riesenfeld, pp. 14-15.

briefly in our consideration of the importance of the life of Jesus to the early Church. The first has to do with a misinterpretation of a verse in Paul by contemporary kerygmatists. In II Cor. 5:16 Paul writes, "From now on, therefore, we regard no one from a human point of view: even though we once regarded Christ from a human point of view, we regard him thus no longer." The verb "regard" or "know" here has been seized upon by dialectical and existentialist theologians as the great proof text for their position. It is claimed that Paul is here stating that the earthly, objective life of Jesus now has little significance, and in its place one must put the heavenly Christ.

This cannot be the case. Paul is not saying here that he had known or seen Jesus in the time of his earthly life. For this we have no evidence, and the possibility of Paul's knowing him in any meaningful sense is remote. Further, he is not talking about a body of earthly knowledge he may have acquired about Jesus in contrast to his knowledge of him as risen Lord. Finally, he is not talking about knowledge he has received from the disciples versus his own mystical experience of Christ. That these last two interpretations of the passage are false is demonstrated by the rest of Paul's work. He lays constant emphasis on the life of Christ even to people who already knew about it. In this very passage in 5:15 and in 5:18-21 he refers to it. For Paul the knowledge of the facts, the objective, was basic, and one could not proceed until he had that in hand.

Furthermore, if one looks at the passage carefully, it will become obvious that Paul is not setting the earthly Jesus against the heavenly Christ. It is not only Christ that is not regarded from a human point of view—no one is to be regarded any longer from a human point of view. But we may go even further than this. From the way the Greek sentence is constructed, "from a human point of view" qualifies "regard" and not "Christ."

What, then, is Paul saying? He is talking in terms of his conversion experience. Before he had come to believe in Christ there was nothing in his life that attracted Paul. His obscure birth, his unsensational life, his shameful death, all ran contrary to everything he had expected of the Messiah. But from the time of his conversion he had come to regard him not after the flesh, but after the spirit. The meaningfulness of that life had now dawned upon him. It may be, too, that Paul is here confronting the "Christ party" that he mentions in I Cor. 1:12. They may well have used against Paul the fact that they had traveled with Christ and seen him in the flesh while Paul had not. Paul counters by saying that he had knowledge of that life also, but that knowledge was not sufficient. Acting on the basis of that knowledge was essential.

The chief point here, then, would appear to be that neither is faith to the exclusion of facts possible, nor are facts to the exclusion of faith consequential, but one must have faith on the basis of the facts, and those facts entail the whole life of Christ from birth to ascension.

The second matter with which we will deal here in our consideration of the importance of the life of Jesus to the early Church is the New Testament idea of tradition. Since the earliest days of form criticism the idea of tradition has been referred to in the Gospels in a way that gives them the connotation of unreliability. There are a number of places in the New Testament itself where the word "tradition" is used in reference to that which has been handed down; and in other places, while the specific word is not used, the idea of passing along what has been received is prominent. Paul uses the word in I Cor. 11:2 and II Thess. 2:15; 3:6, and refers to the same idea repeatedly without the use of the word. Perhaps the best-known passage in the latter category is I Cor. 15:1-3.

The difficulty we have here, it would appear, is our failure to distinguish our Western idea of tradition from the Jewish concept. The idea of tradition to us has a very indefinite character. It is passed along not by individuals but by the community. For that reason the source from which it comes and its trustworthiness are difficult to ascertain.

Behind the Jewish idea of tradition, however, there stands rather the idea of authority. This is the sense in which we must think of it in the New Testament. There is behind it the authority of the apostles. It is not of importance primarily because of its age. It is not of importance primarily because it is the possession of some church body. It is of importance because it comes from the witnesses of the events—the apostles. The work of Riesenfeld on the *Sitz im Leben* of the Gospels, which we discussed earlier in this chapter, should reinforce our confidence in the reliability of the Gospel tradition.

In addition to the different connotation of the words, there is the further difficulty that on occasion the word is used in the Gospels by Jesus in a derogatory sense, e.g., Mk. 7:8. In these cases, however, it is not the quality of the transmission that is being disparaged, but rather the absolute value of that tradition. These instances, therefore, would not reflect on the Gospels in any way.

The question naturally lingers, however, as to the degree of certainty we can have with regard to the accuracy of that transmission. We have already largely dealt with these matters, but we shall merely list some of those factors by way of review which give us confidence regarding the accuracy of the transmitted record: (1) The period of oral transmission was a relatively short one—certainly not over twenty years and in case of part of the material much shorter. (2) The brief period of oral transmission served to guarantee the accuracy of the written record rather than to militate against it. (3) The presence of eyewitnesses to the events in the formative period prevented any radical departure from the facts. (4) Unfriendly witnesses as well as friendly ones were a guarantee against any process of free invention by the early Church. (5) The record was transmitted mainly in the area in which the events had occurred. For this reason such things as culture, geography, politics, etc. served as a background and helped keep the record pure. (6) The message of Jesus was so inextricably involved with his life that, apart from an accurate transmission of the record of that life, the message would have collapsed. (7) The early Church's need of materials for teaching and worship was a further motivation for accurate transmission. (8) The Gospels themselves give evidence of the conscientiousness with which that tradition was transmitted. They can somewhat accurately be described as compilations. Their authors used the materials handed down to them with all care. Invention and falsification could not be permitted.

The net effect of all this evidence should be enough to demonstrate that the early Church was vitally interested in the history of Jesus' life, and took all precautions to see that the record of that life was faithfully transmitted, first of all among its own members, and then via the Gospels to all those who should come after.

New negative criteria. In his major work on form criticism, when dealing with the class of sayings that he calls similitudes, Bultmann writes, "We can only count on possessing a genuine similitude of Jesus where, on the one hand, expression is given to the contrast between Jewish morality and piety and the distinctive eschatological temper which characterized the preaching of Jesus; and where on the other hand we find no specifically Christian features."[91]

The followers of Bultmann in the new quest school have seized on this judgment, expanded it to all the sayings attributed to Jesus, and even applied it to the Gospel materials in general. We see this exactly stated by Käsemann,[92] Robinson,[93] and Ebeling.[94] Let us notice it as stated by Käsemann: "In only one case do we have more or less safe ground under our feet; [1] when there are no grounds either for deriving a tradition from Judaism or [2] for ascribing it to primitive Christianity."[95]

With respect to the first of these criteria, it is amazing how criticism of the Gospels can swing from one extreme to the other. A few decades ago it was popular to say that only that part of Jesus' life which could be accounted for on the basis of his Jewish upbringing was historical. One almost got the impression in reading some works that Jesus must have been the most totally uncreative figure in the history of the human race. Thus in the History of Religions School, Paul became the real founder of Chris-

[91] Rudolf Bultmann, *The History of the Synoptic Tradition*, trans. John Marsh (New York: Harper, 1963), p. 205.

[92] Käsemann, p. 37.

[93] Robinson, p. 99.

[94] Ebeling, p. 52.

[95] Käsemann, p. 37.

tianity. Paul was farther from Jesus than was Jesus from Judaism. So, too, with many of the liberal historians. Anything in the sayings of Jesus attributed to the character of prophecy or insight into the future must be eliminated. Anything that set him up as more than an extraordinary man could not be accepted.

Why, we may ask, need we insist on this radical kind of disjunction before we will accept anything as historical? Was Jesus completely divorced from the past? Could he have had any vital effect on anyone if he threw out completely what had gone before? If one studies the Gospels even superficially he will see that Jesus was in fundamental agreement with Judaism—or is this part of the inventive fancy of the Synoptists too? Jesus had no fundamental disagreement with Judaism as it was meant to be. It was only with perverted and base Judaism that he had his differences. If this be true, why could he not have said and done many things that were in perfect conformity with the Judaism of his day? His own statement concerning his coming to fulfil the law, not destroy it, would indicate that in intention he looked upon himself as one who had come to live the life of a perfect Jew in order that in his death he might provide the perfect sacrifice.

Behind the second of these criteria lies the great presumption of so much of modern theology. Dialectical theology in reaction to the liberal lives-of-Jesus movement came around to saying that the Jesus of history had little significance. It was the Christ of faith that had the real significance. Thus there was driven the wedge between these two personalities: the Jesus of history, a Galilean teacher of varying degrees of uniqueness depending upon who the individual interpreter was; the Christ of faith, the great transforming figure of the Church's post-Easter faith. It has been stated in various ways ever since: historical (*historisch*) Jesus and historic (*geschichtlich*) Christ; history and kerygma, etc. It is surprising how resistant this formulation has been. We assert here that the separation of these two entities is impossible and completely unwarranted from a biblical perspective.

We repeat here what we said early in this chapter.

History *always* involves fact plus interpretation. It becomes distorted when the attempt is made to separate them. The necessity of a factual basis is emphasized by Hepburn:

> Questions of objective history . . . cannot be smuggled out of the way by extolling the "significance for life" of the doctrines concerned. The appeal to significance cannot properly displace the anxiety and risks attending historical research into New Testament origins . . . . Events of history have to be realized existentially, if they are to be more to us than brute facts about the past. But to be realized existentially, they must first be facts. Prayer to a living Jesus today is a possibility only if Jesus did rise in the first century A.D.[96]

On the other hand, history cannot be written without interpretation as well. We have dealt with this, too, earlier. This is necessary in all history and above all in anything that attempts to be biographical. The Gospels cannot be criticized on the basis that they contain interpretation. Scott asks a very pertinent question in this regard, "One cannot but wonder sometimes what kind of Gospels some writers are wanting when they reject the present ones as unsatisfactory. Would they have preferred something by a scribe or a Sadducee, who saw nothing in Jesus but a Galilaean carpenter?"[97]

It has been this desire to hold together fact and interpretation that has in part motivated the new quest, but it bears with it the legacy of its predecessors in that it is certain that the facts as we have them in our New Testament have been altered by the interpretation. Rather, the sequence as it has been drawn up by Thompson would appear to be more appropriate:

> Thus the order would be: *divine redemptive activity—seen in the ministry of Jesus as Messiah—apprehended by those who witnessed His life, death, resurrection—confessed as Lord (Kyrios) having supernatural authority—embodied in the cor-*

[96] R. W. Hepburn, *Christianity and Paradox* (London: Watts, 1958), pp. 102, 104.

[97] Scott, p. 30.

porate life of the ecclesia—and recorded in the Holy Scrip-tures.[98]

The tenacity with which the Jesus of history and the Christ of faith must thus be held together is in the estimate of this writer nowhere stated better than by Gerhard Kittel:

> The Jesus of History is valueless and unintelligible unless He be experienced and confessed by faith as the living Christ. But, if we would be true to the New Testament, we must at once reverse this judgment. The Christ of faith has no existence, is mere noise and smoke, apart from the reality of the Jesus of History. These two are utterly inseparable in the New Testament. They cannot even be thought apart. There is no word about Christ which is not referred to Him who suffered under Pontius Pilate, and which is not at the same time intended as the Gospel applicable to all men of every time and place. Anyone who attempts first to separate the two and then to describe only one of them has nothing in common with the New Testament.[99]

It is our firm belief that this second negative criterion of Bultmann and his successors implies the possibility of such a separation, and for that reason is completely meaningless.

Reasons for Historical Mistrust

History and contemporary philosophy

It may appear to the reader that we have already sufficiently covered the subject of the reasons for histori-cal mistrust on the part of contemporary critics. Our investigation, however, has been based mostly on the way in which those critics look upon the texts. It becomes obvious when one studies the modern critical movement

[98] Claude H. Thompson, *Theology of the Kerygma* (Englewood Cliffs, N.J.: Prentice-Hall, 1962), p. 21.

[99] Gerhard Kittel, "The Jesus of History," *Mysterium Christi,* ed. G. K. A. Bell and G. A. Deissmann (London: Longmans, Green, 1930), p. 49.

in biblical scholarship, however, that there is a much more deep-seated reason for its historical mistrust than what it finds in the documents. There is basic to much of this critical movement a contempt for history as the vehicle of God's revelation. Of all contemporary authors, the one who has done the best in pointing this out is Oscar Cullmann. After writing of the biblical concept of history and the centrality of Jesus in that history, he concludes, "Here the close connection between Christian revelation and history comes to light, and here in the final analysis lies the 'offense' of the Primitive Christian view of time and history, not only for the historian, but for all 'modern' thinking, including theological thinking; the offense is that God reveals himself in a special way and effects 'salvation' in a final way within a narrowly limited but continuing process." [100]

While this contempt for history as the vehicle of God's revelation has come in various forms, the way in which it is currently most often stated is in the primacy of the subject over the object in historical study. Bultmann states this very directly: "Faith needs to be emancipated from its association with every world view expressed in objective terms, whether it be a mythical or a scientific one." [101]

The importance of the object, however, cannot be overstated. It is not enough to proceed solely on the basis of one's inner impulses. If one does not find his "object" in history, he will find it somewhere else. If history is rejected, then some philosophical and speculative system will become the "object." One does not develop a system out of nothing. If the factual character of past history is not given its place, then present meaning is likely to take its place. The result of all this could well mean that one could be devoted to a fiction or to self-delusion.

On the other hand, one must not stop with the objective. If the fault of much contemporary existentialist

100 Oscar Cullmann, *Christ and Time*, trans. Floyd V. Filson (Philadelphia: Westminster, 1951), p. 23.

101 Bultmann, "Bultmann Replies to His Critics," *Kerygma and Myth*, I, 210.

historiography is found in its rejection of the objective, the fault of much of the positivistic historiography that was at the basis of the original quest was its inattention to the subjective. The mere collection and arrangement of facts is not enough either. The proper way to proceed would appear to be from object to subject. This is basic to the biblical view of revelation, and this is basic to the biblical view of history as the vehicle of that revelation.

Critics like Bultmann give the impression that the reason for their mistrust of biblical history is that it comes from a nonscientific era of the world's history. Yet they must acknowledge that much contemporary knowledge is gained by the use of the objective. It then becomes necessary for such critics to talk about two kinds of knowledge, and when they do this they reveal the real reason for their rejection of history—their existentialist presuppositions.

In applying existential philosophy to the New Testament, however, Bultmann and his successors have not solved anything from an historical perspective, they have merely avoided the question of history and at the same time pretended to present us with a better kind of history. Hugh Anderson is particularly critical of the efforts of the new quest in this regard: "We do not believe that the attempts of the 'new seekers' to disengage the historical from the kerygmatic in the Gospel tradition are foolproof or infallible. Rather is it their philosophical standpoint of 'existential openness' toward Jesus that has produced the impression that the goal of Jesus-research has at last been reached." [102]

If the New Testament record is not taken as basic, then we bring something to it from the outside that is basic. Which of these two courses one chooses is up to the individual, but it is not honest to bring in some foreign system and proclaim gleefully to all the world that this is really what the New Testament has been saying all the time anyway.

Of course no such alien system will completely fit the New Testament, so it then becomes necessary for its

[102] Anderson, *Jesus and Christian Origins*, p. 261.

advocates to seize on statements in the New Testament that support their position to some degree and to ignore others. In so doing the advocates for the new quest are little better off than were their predecessors of the old quest of whom they are so critical. The difference is not that the old quest selected some and rejected other parts of the New Testament, while the new quest does not. The difference is in what is selected and rejected and why it is selected and rejected. If history, in the sense of fact, has no particular relevance for faith as in Bultmann, why worry about it? If history is necessary only to protect one from the charge of Docetism as in the new quest, just establish a few things and then let your existentialist philosophical system take care of the important matters.

How complete is the dominance of existentialism over the Bultmannian and post-Bultmannian critical school can be illustrated by a few pointed observations. It will always remain a question with the conservative whether existentialism or form criticism was the real determinative element in the construction of Bultmann's system. There will always be the suspicion that he, although his complete thought in this area had not developed yet, approached the New Testament as an existentialist, and therefore had to dispose of it as an objective basis for faith.

Similarly, with Robinson we see the dominance of existentialism. Why is the new quest possible? A new concept of selfhood and a new concept of history make it possible. But what basically has my selfhood to do with determining what happened in the past? I may respond to it or not. I may like it or not. I may do any of a thousand things regarding it, but what I am in the present does not in any way alter the occurrence. Similarly, the new concept of history is not to be found in new historical techniques of investigation. It is found in the self. This may be desirable from a philosophical perspective, but the net effect of it all might be that we run from history.

It would appear that men like Jaspers and Ogden have reached a far more logical conclusion. If the source of truth ultimately comes from the depths of man, why insist on any event? Why insist on any particular history?

Why not just respond to some event of the past in which we may find meaning and let that be our basis for the discovery of authentic existence?

Bultmann, his critics to the left, and his successors of the new quest are concerned that we do not tie the Christian faith to the thought forms of the New Testament world. The concern of the present writer is that we do not tie Christianity and the Christ of the New Testament world to the categories of modern philosophy.

Validity of nonhistorical approach

The biblical, historical approach, like that of most of the historical approaches of man in his history, deals with man in reference to three kinds of time—the past, the present, and the future. Furthermore, speaking from a biblical perspective, all of these three kinds of time are regarded as very important, and man at any era must seek to relate himself meaningfully to them. It is therefore wrong both from the perspective of biblical interpretation and from the perspective of biblical truth when this is ignored. Yet this is precisely what Bultmann has done. Ellwein notes that "the past, the present, the future, the resurrection, the last day, and eternal life are all collapsed into one and merged into one single simultaneous occurrence."[103]

It is because the present is of all-consuming importance to the existentialist mode of interpretation that this is done. Yet if we grant to God the possibility of revealing himself as he will, we must also grant the possibility that at some point in the history of our world he has revealed himself in a unique, verifiable, and unrepeatable way. If this be the case—and it is difficult to avoid this view from a simple and natural reading of the Bible—then it is important for us to know something about those events in order that we may order our lives in accordance with that revelation.

The same is true with respect to the future. If in that revelation of God in the past he gave to man some

103 Ellwein, p. 52.

information which would help him order his life properly with respect to the future, it is important for man to know and use that information. Fuller is critical of Bultmann at this point as he writes, "The whole New Testament conception of cosmic redemption refuses to pass through the sieve of existential interpretation, and must therefore in practice be eliminated. The same applies to the 'myths' of Christ's pre-existence, the virgin birth and the second coming. These too have a significance which transcends the existence of the individual." [104]

It is thus the case in Bultmann that only when one comes into an existential confrontation in the present by the joining of preaching and faith does anything really significant happen. Whether or not an item in the past is historical is not of importance. This has led Cairns to say, "If Bultmann's view . . . be right, then it is extremely difficult to see how the personal encounter with God can ever be more than a blank immediacy." [105] To put this in other terms, one's encounter with God from Bultmann's perspective becomes a pure and absolute mysticism that occurs and can be checked only by its happening.

Let us see, then, how all this reflects on the biblical concept of history from Bultmann's point of view. In the first place, biblical history prior to the "event of Christ" is largely neglected. In the second place, everything in the New Testament which has about it a futuristic sense is ignored in that sense. Biblical eschatology is thought of only in terms of the present, and thus, from any traditional way of thinking, is eliminated. Faith is rather "eschatological existence" or a radical "openness to the future."

The reason for this kind of interpretation of the future is not to be found in the biblical texts themselves, but rather in the presuppositions of the interpreter. As Anderson has pointed out, "The tendency to rid Jesus' message of the expectation of a concrete eschatological future, whether it be by exegetical reinterpretation of the texts or by spiritualizing or demythologizing the eschato-

[104] Reginald Fuller, p. 30.
[105] Cairns, p. 143.

logical prediction, has arisen from the zeal to make the
message applicable for modern man and his moral problems." [106]

The violence done to the biblical record via this kind
of interpretation should be self-evident. Old Testament
expressions like "in the last days," "the day of the
Lord," etc., and New Testament expressions like "the
kingdom of God" (in part), "the Son of Man," "coming"
(*parousia*), as well as many other express statements,
point to future happenings in time in connection with the
end of history. Even apart from special terminology used
in conjunction with that end, the use of the future tense
itself, if naturally interpreted, points to a future consummation. The only way to get around passages like these—
and there are many of them—is to allegorize them.

The ways the references to the future in the Gospels
have been interpreted in the twentieth century are indica-
tive of modern man's reluctance to take the New Testament at face value. Most of the critics in the school of the
original quest regarded the eschatology of the Gospels as
a creation of the early Church in its contact with Jewish
apocalyptic. Nothing like this was to be found in the
teaching of Jesus.

Schweitzer, it will be recalled, accepted New Testament eschatology as being original with Jesus. Jesus expected to return as the Son of Man on the clouds of
heaven, but in this he was mistaken.

C. H. Dodd, the popularizer of "realized eschatology,"
seizing on the statements in the New Testament in which
Jesus professes that the kingdom has come, held that
eschatology had been realized in the present.

Bultmann looked upon eschatology as being fulfilled
for each individual in his existential situation. It thus has
or will have no significance for the history of the world.
The advocates of the new quest largely follow Bultmann
with some minor variation.

As against all these views, orthodoxy has maintained
that Jesus looked forward to a consummation in time
which is still future to us. Jesus brought in the kingdom

[106] Anderson, p. 126.

in part at his first coming, but that kingdom still awaits its eschatological fulfilment. In a sense the kingdom has come, and yet the kingdom is coming. All other views represent in some way or other a misuse of the biblical record. The liberals refused a part of it. Schweitzer, by inference, concluded that Jesus was in error. Dodd centered his attention only on those sayings which emphasized the present in respect to the kingdom and looked upon the future ones as following automatically. Bultmann and his followers allegorized the eschatological statements of the New Testament.

But we need to go beyond the reference to the future to discuss the overall biblical concept of history. From the biblical perspective, time is looked upon as the vehicle of God's revelation to man. It is to be thought of as a straight line that progresses from creation to consummation. The biblical concept thus sets itself up against the so-called cyclical or pessimistic philosophies of history on the one hand, and the spiral or optimistic philosophies on the other. God's decision to create man was a free decision. Of the various ways in which God could have created man, he chose that of giving him moral freedom. By the misuse of that freedom man fell, and so subsequent history has been that of the effort of God to reclaim man.

Immediately after the fall of man, God began to prepare him for redemption. The Old Testament is the story of the progressive revelation of God to man of primarily three things: (1) the nature and requirements of God; (2) the lostness of man; (3) the love of God for man.

Finally, at the midpoint of human history God himself, in the person of his Son, came to earth to provide the means of reconciliation. The events surrounding that midpoint were of crucial importance to man, so that in addition to their occurrence God provided the means whereby they might be faithfully recorded for future generations.

By the use of that record, conjoined with the work of the Holy Spirit, men today may become meaningfully related to God. Men thus coming to know him constitute his Body, the Church. The Church by its efforts will seek to further expand the number of those who come to know God's Son. It will seek to exert its influence in every area of social life both by means of constructive measures and by means of criticism of the social order.

Finally, history will one day end. Time will be swallowed up in eternity. Believers will be united forever with Christ. Unbelievers will be forever banished from his presence.

One of the finest treatments of this biblical concept of time in recent years has been the very scholarly work of Oscar Cullmann. [107] He has developed this biblical concept on the basis of exegesis of the scriptural texts. The work is a wholesome and refreshing refutation of so much of the antihistoricism of our century that has captivated biblical scholarship.

The work of Cullmann, however, has not gone unchallenged. The chief objections that have been raised against it have been of two kinds. Some have challenged it on the basis of their exegesis of the biblical texts—particularly those that have to do with time. James Barr has been one of the leaders in this movement. He maintains that the writers of the Bible were not interested in time in a philosophical or theological sense. He thus accuses Cullmann of improper procedure when the latter arrives at his concept of biblical time via lexical study. [108]

Bultmann himself has challenged Cullmann on very much the same basis. He maintains that there is no unitary New Testament concept of time, and that the work of Cullmann is a result of artificial synthesis. [109]

This cannot be maintained in light of the totality of the New Testament presentation. The linear concept of time is there. One may attribute it to non-Christian sources. One may deny its validity, but one may not successfully deny its existence.

The second objection to the conclusions of Cullmann

[107] Cullmann, *Christ and Time.*

[108] James Barr, *Biblical Words for Time* (Naperville: Allenson, 1962).

[109] Rudolf Bultmann, *Existence and Faith: Shorter Writings of Rudolf Bultmann*, trans. Schubert M. Ogden (New York: Meridian, 1960), pp. 234f.

has to do with the validity of the biblical concept of time
for us today. John Macquarrie has been most critical of
Cullmann here. He feels that it is absurd for us in our day
to demand of people that they accept the biblical ideas of
time and history in order to be real believers. [110] Into the
details of such an argument we will not go, because they
go far beyond the scope of this study. We simply note
here that the biblical concept of time and history is so
central to the Christian faith that if one discards this
concept, he has really destroyed the skeleton on which all
the flesh of biblical theology must depend for support.
From a Christian perspective, therefore, the biblical concept of time is not a dispensable feature.

Conclusion

On the basis of all the materials that we have surveyed
in this chapter, what can we say with regard to the Jesus
of history? It would appear to this writer that we have
before us mainly one of four choices: (1) One might
concentrate his study on Jesus as an historical figure and
try to separate him from any of the christological formu-
lations of the New Testament. Such a position was current very early in the history of the Church. It was then
known as Ebionitism. These people accepted Jesus as a
great prophet, but rejected him in any sense that linked
him metaphysically to the Father. Some of the critics in
the original quest, some of the members of the History of
Religions School, and some of the critics to the left of
Bultmann would be found in this group today.

(2) As opposed to the Jesus of history, one might set
up as a result of his historical investigation the Christ of
faith. According to this view it is either impossible or
irrelevant to know very much about the Jesus of history.
This position also was represented very early in the history of the Church. It was then known as Docetism. As
we have already noticed, this theology either denied or
neglected the earthly life of Jesus. The rise of the ques-

[110] John Macquarrie, *The Scope of Demythologizing* (New
York: Harper, 1962), pp. 62ff.

tion of Docetism in the historical position of Bultmann from many quarters should be enough to warn us of this danger in his position. A Jesus so conceived may be no more than the product of a wish.

(3) Either in combination with one of the above two positions or independent of it, one may decide on some basis that there are certain elements that are historical and some that are not in the Gospels. The problem with such a procedure is that most often the criteria for selection and rejection are not formulated on the basis of an examination of the record, but rather are to be found in the preconceptions of the critic. Historically the groups that have been found most often in this camp have been the advocates of a particular philosophical system. In our century this kind of approach has been used by theologians represented in the two main philosophical-theological movements. The original quest, captivated by idealism, presented us with Jesus the humanist. The new quest, captivated by existentialism, presents us with Jesus the existentialist.

(4) Finally, according to its self-witness, one may decide to take the whole record as it stands as the special revelation of God to man. In so doing he will seek to exegete it and interpret it as accurately as possible in order to understand as fully as possible the one who stands at its center. From such a study he will find Jesus not as a Jew, nor as a product of his wish, nor as the representative of any particular philosophy, but as the God-man who came to redeem men. It is our contention that this is the most natural and logical solution to the problem, and the only one that guards against excessive subjectivism and ultimate skepticism.

CHAPTER THREE

The Place of Miracle

The Nature of Miracle

There are two basic ways in which one may approach the miraculous element in the Bible, or more particularly here, the Gospels, each of which will determine how one will evaluate them. In the first place, one may ask the question in this way: Has it ever been established outside of the biblical period itself that miracles of the character attributed to Jesus have been performed by anyone else? This kind of question is apt to lead one to evaluate the past in terms of the present. Nothing of the character of biblical miracles occurs today. As a consequence, nothing of a miraculous nature could have happened in the past. It then simply becomes a question of accounting for the way in which the miracle stories were included in the Gospels. Was it pious invention? Was it competition with other religious faiths? Was it outright deception? Several other questions of similar character have been asked by those who approach the miraculous element from this perspective.

There is, however, a second way in which we may ask the question: Could God, the creator of heaven and earth, as a part of his revelation to man, use means outside of those which can be accounted for on naturalistic bases to make that revelation extraordinarily meaningful and specific? If we ask the question in this way, then if we were to answer No, we would in truth be saying that God is limited by his creation. It is our contention that the second of these questions is the proper question and that the possibility of miracles should at least be granted. The reason for the occurrence of miracles in some eras of human history and their nonoccurrence in others we shall defer to a later section of this chapter.

The term "miracle" in our day has come to be used in a very careless manner. It is used on occasion with the connotation of extraordinary or wonderful. While this might be acceptable from the point of view of English usage, it is not an adequate definition of the biblical idea. Let us therefore look at three definitions of miracles that will set them on a sounder theological basis:

> A miracle is an event palpable to the senses, produced for a religious purpose by the immediate agency of God; an event therefore which, though not contravening any law of nature, the laws of nature, if fully known, would not be competent to explain.[1]

> A miracle, therefore, may be defined to be an event in the external world, brought about by the immediate efficiency, or simple volition of God.[2]

> The name "miracles" has been given to special acts of God departing from the ordinary method, performed in the sight of men for a moral purpose.[3]

From these definitions, four characteristics of miracle, properly defined, should be obvious to us: (1) A miracle is a happening that presents itself to the senses of man. (2) A miracle cannot be accounted for on any natural basis, and it must therefore be attributed to the supernatural. (3) A miracle is a purposeful occurrence. (4) That purpose, at least in part, is to call men's attention to a special revelation of God.

If, however, one asks the question in the context of

[1] Strong, *Systematic Theology*, p. 61.

[2] Charles Hodge, *Systematic Theology* (Grand Rapids: Eerdmans, 1952), I, 618.

[3] William Newton Clarke, *An Outline of Christian Theology* (New York: Scribner, 1917), p. 133.

the present, he is apt to reject miracles on the basis that the idea implies a violation of natural law, a contradiction of it, or something in opposition to it.[4] It is in these terms that miracle is usually thought of by the majority of critical biblical scholars.

Modern Man and Miracle

Scientific objections to miracle

Of the three principal forms of objection to miracle, the primary is this scientific objection. In this connection let us notice the remarks of Bultmann:

> Now that the forces and the laws of nature have been discovered, we can no longer believe in spirits, whether good or evil . . . . The miracles of the New Testament have ceased to be miraculous, and to defend their historicity by recourse to nervous disorders or hypnotic effects only serves to underline the fact . . . . It is impossible to use electric light and wireless and to avail ourselves of modern medical and surgical discoveries, and at the same time to believe in the New Testament world of spirits and miracles.[5]

Mickelsen has pointed out that there are only two kinds of people who believe in the impossibility of miracle. The first sees no order at all in the universe, and the second sees the universe so unalterably controlled by order that God has become a virtual prisoner of that order.[6] The first group is not a significantly large or important one. Bultmann represents the second group, and it is this spirit which for the most part has captivated critical approaches to the life of Jesus.

Those who thus object to miracles on scientific bases look upon our universe as a closed causal system that will

[4] Ramm, *Protestant Christian Evidences*, p. 125.

[5] Bultmann, "New Testament and Mythology," *Kerygma and Myth*, I, 4-5.

[6] A. Berkeley Mickelsen, *Interpreting the Bible* (Grand Rapids: Eerdmans, 1963), p. 68.

tolerate no interference from the outside. There are three replies that can be made to this kind of objection. In the first place, it is highly questionable if the conception of a neat closed causal system is valid from the point of view of science. The last few decades have been characterized by a radical shift in scientific thinking. The old Newtonian physics has been largely replaced by the new atomic physics, to mention just one area of this scientific revolution. If this physics has been characterized as revolutionary from the point of view of the results it has brought us, it has also been revolutionary from the point of view of concepts. As Cairns has observed, "For many years philosophers of the first rank of eminence have been criticizing the concept of mechanical causation, and claiming that it is by no means the precise instrument in scientific research which Dr. Bultmann assumes it to be."[7] After discussing the issue at greater length, the same author concludes, "Mechanical causality, whatever its range and scope, is only one category among a number, and . . . while it does reveal certain aspects of truth, it yet has only limited applicability and value."[8] It should be obvious, therefore, that Bultmann's idea of causality, at least in the precise terms in which he thinks of it, is not in step with current scientific thought.

A second kind of reply that can be made to the scientific objection to miracles is that which questions the scope of science. The point at issue here is that science has to do with observation and classification of phenomena in the material universe. It is as a consequence only as a result of an assumption that the material world is all the world there is, that one is able to say that modern science makes the belief in miracle untenable. As Ramm says, "The categories of science are adequate within the goals of science (the quantitative, the stable, the predictable, the observable, the general), but not for the comprehension of the sum of all experience, or reality, or the universe."[9]

[7] Cairns, *A Gospel Without Myth?*, p. 125.

[8] *Ibid.*, p. 127.

[9] Ramm, *Protestant Christian Evidences*, p. 53.

Science, therefore, as it is to be properly thought of, can neither confirm nor deny the possibility of miracle. It may furnish us with data on which we will make a decision, but science cannot make it for us. The scientist either procures his data and hands it over to the philosopher for the construction of a philosophical system, or the scientist himself may become at that point a philosopher and construct the system, but he must always be aware that when he begins to construct such a system he has ceased being a scientist and has become a philosopher. No scientist is justified in making metaphyscial pronouncements and thereby inferring that these pronouncements are established via the scientific method. The realm of science and the realm of philosophy at this point must be kept distinct.

A third reply that may be made to the scientific objection to miracles is the theological. There is behind this kind of thinking a deistic mode of thought. God has somehow created our world, but now no longer has any primary interest in it. The modern appeal to "natural law" has much of this flavor to it. If, however, God created the world, the world itself is the product of the supernatural activity of God. This must be the presumption of anyone, regardless of the view of the origin of the universe he holds, with the exception of the out-and-out naturalist. If this then be the case, God is both immanent in his creation and transcendent over it. While it is an evidence of the providence of God that he set up "laws" for the governance of our world, it must not be presumed that on occasion, when there has been sufficient reason for it, he has limited himself to those laws, but, to the contrary, has revealed himself in a special way. From this we may formulate two conclusions: (1) The Christian theist as well as the scientific atheist is thankful for the regularity of nature. If this were not so, life would be made extremely difficult if not impossible. (2) The Christian theist, however, goes on to say that these laws of nature are the laws of God. One must not presume that the entire will of God is expressed in them. The possibility of God's revealing himself outside the limitations of these laws must therefore be left open.

Literary objections to miracles

This second class of objection to miracles is based on the first. If modern man had no reason to want to dispose of miracles, he would not take the trouble to try to refute the belief from a literary point of view. The literary objections themselves have been of two kinds. One is a result of the comparison of Christianity with other religions of ancient mankind; i.e., it is claimed that the miracles attributed to Jesus in the Gospels are similar to those attributed to the founders of other religions in their literature. Marcus Dods long ago exposed the weakness of any theory that attempts to dispose of the miracles of Jesus on the basis of comparative religion. He pointed out that the miracles of the Gospels differ from the miracles of any of these other religions with respect to the *occasion* on which they were wrought, the *nature* of the miracles themselves, and the *worker* who brought them about.[10]

With respect to the occasion, Dods writes, "Feeding the hungry, healing the sick, raising the dead—all these are removals of obstructions which hinder nature from being the perfect and direct expression of God's goodness to man. They are hints of an ideal state which nature will one day reach, accelerations of her slower processes." [11]

The Gospel miracles also stand on a definitely higher plane than do those of other religions with respect to their nature. Dods notes as an example that the Gospel miracles are not to be compared with the supposed account of a centaur trotting down the street. The latter account is a monstrosity and lacks all purpose. On the other hand, the Gospel miracles all occur in the natural order, and all manifest purpose.[12] The Gospel miracles stand on an entirely different level even from those miracles reported in the apocryphal gospels in this regard.

The supreme evidence for Dods, however, is to be found in their conformity with the person who worked

[10] Marcus Dods, *The Bible: Its Origin and Nature* (New York: Scribner, 1910), p. 238.

[11] *Ibid.*, p. 239.

[12] *Ibid.*, pp. 238-40.

them: "The strongest evidence in their favor is their congruity with the person who wrought them, and with the revelation in connection with which they were wrought . . . . The miracles are Christ's miracles, and that makes precisely all the difference."[13] We have here no exhibitionism, no deception, no attempt at ego inflation that so completely underlies the miracles of other religious founders. If we were to guess what God would be like if he came into our midst and lived with us, we could not devise a more desirable portrait than that which we have in the Gospels. Our decision must be, therefore, whether to accept this portrait as historical or as a literary creation. On the basis of the previous chapter, it should be apparent that the historical solution is the only adequate solution.

A second kind of literary objection is based on an analysis of the biblical literature itself. Here several things are brought to our attention. Form criticism, for example, has noticed that certain kinds of literature that we have in the Gospels show a fixed form. But form has no basic effect on the value of the content—as a matter of fact, if anything, it establishes its historical worth rather than discredits it.

Another kind of objection to miracles based on an analysis of the biblical literature is that which points out that the Gospel miracles are patterned after analogies to Old Testament miracles. This signifies to critics that the Gospel miracle stories are attempts on the part of their writers to make Jesus the complete fulfilment of Old Testament messianic expectations. Thus, as the children of Israel were provided with manna in the wilderness, Jesus provided bread for the hungry. As Elijah and Elisha healed the sick and raised the dead, so also did Jesus on a more spectacular scale. The list of parallels could be extended. What significance do all these parallels have? These parallels may be explained both from the point of view of the naturalistic critic and from the point of view of the conservative critic. From the point of view of the naturalist they may be accounted for on the basis of

13 *Ibid.*, p. 241.

invention—whether it be pious or deceitful. Once again, we must return to the results of the last chapter. There were too many witnesses to the events, both friendly and unfriendly, to make pious invention a possibility. If deceit lies at the basis of the Gospel miracle stories, we have a rare phenomenon indeed—a situation in which men created untrue stories about the life of Jesus. These same men went to the corners of the then-known earth proclaiming these fictitious stories, and finally laid down their lives for the truth of those deceitful inventions.

Is there not a more logical solution to this problem? If the Christian Scriptures are in truth the progressive revelation of God to man, is it at all surprising that Jesus should fulfil in his person the characteristics of the promised Messiah? As we noticed in the last chapter, the New Testament portrayal of Jesus is just enough different from that of the promised Messiah in the Old Testament to make us certain that it could not have been created on the basis of the Old Testament. Yet, when the Messiah came, he was to feed the hungry, give sight to the blind, restore the lame—in short, he was to care for the oppressed and the afflicted. This is precisely what Jesus did. Are we then to attribute the greatness of this person to the creativity of the early Church, or are we to see in his sayings, deeds, and life the culmination of God's revelation to mankind?

Cultural objections to miracles

The two objections to miracles that we have dealt with to this point have had to do primarily with the contemporary situation. That is, (1) miracles do not fit into the world view of modern man very well, and (2) they can be accounted for on the basis of modern man's evaluation of the sources. A third kind of objection is to be seen in modern man's analysis of the culture in which the life of Jesus was lived. It is often affirmed that the first century was a time in which belief in miracles was prevalent, as it always was in the ancient world. It therefore becomes necessary for us to discount the miraculous on the part of Jesus on the basis of the naïvete of the people. Of the authors involved in the critical quest of Jesus, it would appear that Stauffer has done the best job of handling this. He writes,

> This evidence [miracles] in the sources cannot be discounted psychologically on the ground that in those days all stories of miracles were credulously accepted and uncritically spread about. For the Jews of antiquity were extremely realistic in regard to miracles, and at least the opponents of Jesus among them were highly critical. Had that not been so, the miracles of Jesus would not have been so vehemently discussed and so gravely misinterpreted.[14]

In addition to the above, however, there are a number of other things that can be said to remove this cultural objection to miracles. For one thing, it becomes a matter of evidences from a source and documentary point of view. The exact nature of that evidence will be developed in what follows, but it may suffice here to note that we have in the Gospels, as well as in scattered sources external to them and to the Christian traditions, (1) early evidence, (2) good evidence, and (3) evidence of competent witnesses to the miracles of Jesus.

We should notice also the evidence for the performance of miracles on Jesus' part by witnesses who were hostile to the Christian point of view. Josephus, the Jewish historian of the first century, writing near the three-quarter mark of that century, refers to Jesus as a wonder-worker.[15] There is, in addition, early talmudic evidence. Rabbi Eliezer ben Hyrcanus about A.D. 95 refers to Jesus' magic arts.[16] About A.D. 110 there was a dispute among the Jews whether or not it was permissible to be healed in Jesus' name.[17] Such a discussion implies that Jesus performed miracles. Another talmudic reference not later than the above states, "Jesus practiced magic and led Israel astray."[18] Celsus, the second-

---

[14] Stauffer, *Jesus and His Story*, p. 10.

[15] Josephus, *Antiquities* xviii.3.3.

[16] Shabbath 104b; Tosephta Shabbath 11, 15.

[17] Aboda zara 27b; Tosephta Hullin 2, 22f.

[18] Sanhedrin 43a; 107b.

century critic, attributes the miracles of Jesus to sorcery.[19] While many of these references refer to Jesus' miracles in an unfriendly and derogatory light, the fact that these authors could not dismiss them is evidence that something of an extraordinary character happened.

In addition to the testimony of hostile witnesses themselves, we have the testimony of Christian writers addressing hostile witnesses. Perhaps the earliest evidence of this kind of testimony is found in Peter's Pentecost sermon in Acts 2:22. One of the strong preaching points he had was that the miracles of Jesus were well known. The early Christian apologists wrote in the same spirit. They did not need to prove that Jesus worked miracles. They only needed to point to them.

Also, we ought to notice the setting of the miracles as we have them in the Gospels. For the most part, the miracles were not performed in private. In a great many instances, there were unbelievers present when a miracle was performed. The miracles of Jesus were diverse in character and were performed in a variety of places and over a period of time. The acknowledgment of the cured should also be noticed. Finally, Ramm points out the radical difference in the purpose of Christian miracles as opposed to miracles in the other religions of the time: "Miracles are believed in non-Christian religions because the religion is already believed, but in Biblical religion miracles are part of the means of establishing the true religion."[20] We shall return to this revelatory significance of miracles later in this chapter.

The above objections can be raised against miracles from a cultural perspective as a result of the study of history. Other critics feel that they can accept the biblical records as we have them and explain the apparently miraculous in terms of the natural. These are still cultural objections to the reality of any real miraculous happening, but they are based more on our knowledge of the present than on our knowledge of the past. Sometimes, for example, it is thought that what is given the character

19 Origen, *Contra Celsum* i.38; ii.48.
20 Ramm, *Protestant Christian Evidences*, p. 142.

of the miraculous in the Gospels can be accounted for on the basis of faulty sense perception by those involved. Thus, we can account for such miracles as Jesus' walking on the water by hypothesizing that Jesus was merely walking along the misty or foggy shore, and that the disciples, due either to the stormy condition of the sea, or to their fatigue, or to a combination of both, did not realize that this was the case and thought that he was walking on the water.

In other instances what are called healings on the part of Jesus are nothing other than the release from some mental disturbance under the influence of Jesus. We have learned a great deal about the influence of the mind on the body in our day, and it is supposed by some that at least some of Jesus' healings can be accounted for on psychiatric bases. We shall return to this possibility later in this chapter.

Still others feel that a great deal of the miraculous in the Gospel records can be rationalized in other ways. There was behind each of the instances an historical occurrence, but it has been transformed into a miracle. Thus, for example, in the feeding of the five thousand, when the people saw the generosity of the lad with the five loaves and the two fish, they reached into their tunics and pulled out their "sandwiches" and were satisfied. These kinds of explanations of miracles were much more popular in the era of the liberal lives of Jesus than they are today. More critics today feel that one may either accept the miraculous or reject it, but that one is not justified in attempting to go halfway. It would appear that this is a much sounder critical opinion. It has always been a mystery to this author how twentieth-century man could feel more competent to judge what happened in a given historical instance in the first century than those who actually witnessed the event.

All of the miracles in the New Testament come to us on the same documentary evidence. The miracles of healing and the nature miracles cannot be differentiated on the basis that one is early and the other late. If this is done, it is done on some other basis than that of the sources.

Verdict depends on two things

As we have surveyed all these objections to miracles by contemporary critics, it should have become obvious to the reader that our final decision with respect to the miraculous element in the Gospels depends on two things: (1) our world view, and (2) our estimate of Jesus.[21] We have already dealt with this first item in the early part of the chapter. It becomes simply a question of deciding whether God is vitally concerned and interested in what goes on on this sphere which we call earth. If he is, then the possibility of miracle must be maintained. If he is not, then indeed man is in dire straits.

With regard to the second of these items, if Jesus was God's Son in the metaphysical sense in which he is represented in the New Testament, then the miracles cease being a real problem for modern man. If he was God incarnate there would be every reason to expect that he should give evidence of that unique nature by demonstrating his mastery over all facets of his creation. Considered from this perspective, there should be no more difficulty in accepting a nature miracle than a healing. Bruce points this out in commenting on the nature miracles:

> Here in particular our approach to the question will be dictated by our attitude to Christ himself. If He was in truth the power of God, then we need not be surprised to find real creative acts performed by Him. If He was not, then we must fall back on some such explanation as misunderstanding or hallucination on the part of the witnesses, or imposture, or corruption of the records in the course of their transmission or the like.[22]

Jesus' Attitude Toward His Miracles

If we look at the literature of the Gospels themselves, we see a double strain in the attitude of Jesus toward his

[21] Archibald Hunter, *The Work and the Words of Jesus* (Philadelphia: Westminster, 1950), p. 59.

[22] Bruce, *The New Testament Documents: Are They Reliable?*, pp. 68-69.

miracles. Generally, he tries to play them down in various ways. In Mt. 12:38-39 (cf. Lk. 11:29), the scribes and the Pharisees come to him and ask him for a sign. He replies, "An evil and adulterous generation seeks for a sign; but no sign shall be given to it except the sign of the prophet Jonah" (Mt. 12:39). In Mk. 8:11-13 (cf. Mt. 16:1-4), the Pharisees return and ask again for a sign. Here again he responds, "Why does this generation seek a sign? Truly, I say to you, no sign shall be given to this generation" (Mk. 8:12). In conjunction with the Beelzebul controversy in Lk. 11, we read, "Others, to test him, sought from him a sign from heaven" (11:16). His response to the crowd again makes it clear that he had no intention of granting their request. Finally, in the story of the healing of the nobleman's son in Jn. 4:46-54, Jesus accuses the nobleman of wanting a miracle for faith rather than the healing of his son: "Unless you see signs and wonders you will not believe" (4:48). It is only when Jesus receives assurance that it is the child's welfare that the nobleman is concerned about and not the sign, that Jesus grants his request.

There are other instances when Jesus apparently leaves the crowds to avoid performing miracles. Perhaps the primary example of this comes in the passage in Mk. 1:21-34 (cf. Lk. 4:31-41). This passage gives the narrative of a day of healing activity in Capernaum. There is no instance in the Gospels in which Jesus performs more miracles in a short space of time and does it more publicly. It will be recalled that according to the Gospel accounts, Jesus arose early the next morning and went to a secluded place to pray. When the disciples, and subsequently the crowds, found him they were anxious to have him stay, presumably to perform more wonders. His reply, however, amounted to a rejection of their request, and hence a rejection of working any more miracles in their midst.

In still other instances Jesus instructs the recipient of a healing to be quiet about it. The most notable instance of this is the story of the healing of the leper in Mk. 1:40-45 (cf. Mt. 8:1-4; Lk. 5:12-16). After Jesus heals him he instructs him to be silent: "See that you say nothing to anyone; but go, show yourself to the priest, and offer for your cleansing what Moses commanded, for a proof to the people" (Mk. 1:44). We shall notice the reason for this admonition shortly.

But the above paragraphs indicate only one of two strains in Jesus' words concerning the significance of his miracles. In other instances he regards them as revelatory and chides the people for not believing in him when he has given such clear evidence that he is from God. In Mt. 11:21 (cf. Lk. 7:13), he castigates the cities of Bethsaida and Chorazin on this very count: "Woe to you, Chorazin! Woe to you, Bethsaida! for if the mighty works done in you had been done in Tyre and Sidon, they would have repented long ago in sackcloth and ashes" (Mt. 11:21).

In Lk. 12:54 he criticizes the people for being able to read the sky and predict weather and still not being able to see the relevance of his signs to the significance of his person.

In repeated instances in John's Gospel (e.g., 5:36; 10:25, 38; 14:11), he advises the people that if they are not able to believe in him and in his relationship to the Father on the basis of his statements, they should believe in him on the basis of the works that he has performed.

The supreme example, however, of the fact that Jesus regarded his miracles as revelatory is to be found in the passage in Lk. 7:19-23 (cf. Mt. 11:2-6). In this passage John the Baptist is in prison. One can almost read his inner thoughts: "Something must have gone wrong somewhere. I was certain that Jesus was to have been the Messiah. I was his forerunner. I pointed people to him. I baptized him. But he did not take command as I expected him to. As a matter of fact he has none of those basic qualities which I thought the Messiah should have. I better check to see whether he really is the Messiah or whether I have been mistaken." Such must have been the thought of John. It will be recalled that he sent his disciples to Jesus to ask him point blank if he was the Messiah. The answer of Jesus is very significant: "Go and tell John what you have seen and heard: the blind receive their sight, the lame walk, lepers are cleansed, and the deaf hear, the dead are raised up, the poor have good news preached to them" (Lk. 7:25). Can it be doubted on the basis of this passage that Jesus regarded his works as indicating something about his person?

How are we to evaluate these two strains in the Gospels? Biblical critics have been quick to seize on the first strain we examined. Jesus' hesitancy is to be accounted for on the basis of his lack of confidence in his ability to work miracles. Some critics have even questioned whether Jesus would have attempted some of the miracles attributed to him in the Gospels, for even to have attempted them, he would have had to tempt God. They feel justified in making such an assertion on the basis of the narrative of the temptation in the wilderness.

Sometimes scholars of a more conservative bent have ignored the other strain. They picture Jesus as having been primarily a wonder-worker. His hesitancy in this regard is of no importance.

If, however, one reads the entire record carefully, the reason for this double strain appears. The temptation of Jesus in the wilderness was not primarily a temptation to satisfy hunger, to become an earthly king, and to accept divine rescue. It was a temptation to accept a cheapened, earthly, Jewish idea of the Messiah. If he had done this, the great eternal significance of his person and work would have been given up for that of a petty Palestinian kingdom. The real temptation here was not to do the deeds. The real temptation was to accept the notion of the Messiah that the doing of such deeds would imply.

As Jesus himself was tempted in this regard, so too were the Jews of his day. If he had openly performed miracles before the public for long periods of time, they too would have concluded that he was the political deliverer they had been promised. He was anxious to avoid such a characterization of his person and work.

This is the reason why in instances it appears that Jesus almost rejects people who want to believe in him. Such, for example, must be the explanation of his refusal of the people at the time of the feast of the Passover in Jn. 2:23-25. An even more explicit statement in this regard is made in the narrative in John following the feeding of the five thousand: "Perceiving then that they were about to come and take him by force to make him king, Jesus withdrew again to the hills by himself" (Jn. 6:15). A few verses later in the same chapter, when the crowds overtake him once again, he responds, "Truly, truly, I say to you, you seek me, not because you saw signs, but because you ate your fill of the loaves" (Jn. 6:26). The implication here is plain. The signs were of significance to the Jews not because of what they pointed to, but because of the benefits that accrued to the recipients in the immediate present.

In Mk. 1:45 we are told that the cleansed leper did not obey the injunction of Jesus to keep his healing silent: "He went out and began to talk freely about it, and to spread the news, so that Jesus could no longer openly enter a town, but was out in the country; and people came to him from every quarter." It is easy to see how miracles of this character could, if they were performed in large numbers openly, give rise to the Jewish materialistic idea of the messiahship of Jesus.

This also, it would appear, is the reason why in cases Jesus demands faith on the part of the recipient of a healing. Faith prior to a miracle would be evidence of genuine trust in God. Faith as a result of a miracle might only be evidence that the recipient wanted more miracles of the same character.

We may summarize Jesus' attitude toward his miracles, therefore, as follows: While Jesus did regard his miracles as revelatory in the sense that they demonstrated that he was from God and that he had come with a vital message and work from the Father, it was necessary for him to use great precaution in his performance of miracles. The chief reason for this precaution is to be found in the fact that his miracles could be interpreted in three ways: (1) To the members of the established religion, Judaism, they could be interpreted as attempts to deceive people and lead them astray. (2) To the masses, they could be interpreted as evidence that the messianic king had arrived to throw off Israel's oppressors and institute an era of unprecedented prosperity. (3) To genuine believers, they pointed to the crucial significance of his person and work.

Kinds of Miracles

Healings

Of all the kinds of miracles that Jesus performed, this class has been the easiest for modern critics to accept. This is not to say that they are accepted as bona fide miracles, but that while they are explained in other than miraculous terms, the substance of the narrative is at least preserved according to the critics' interpretation.

The recent advances in the field of psychotherapy have made some writers feel that many of the miracles of Jesus can be accounted for on this basis. Hunter gives an indication of the feeling of many critics in this regard:

> It is true to say that the healing miracles of Jesus impose no real strain on a Christian's faith. We are beginning to remember that man is "psychosomatic" and to recognize the potent part played by the mind in the cause and cure of disease. We all know something of the achievements of modern psychotherapy in cases of blindness, paralysis and various nervous disorders. And there is ever-accumulating evidence of spiritual healing. All these things conspire to bring Christ's healing miracles within the range, if not of our powers, at least of our credence.[23]

The techniques of psychological suggestion, etc. have been used by some to explain almost all the cures of Jesus. It is, consequently, possible to take at least some of the healing miracles of Jesus in one of two ways. Some tend to regard Jesus as a psychotherapist before his time. Others attribute his healings to the fact that he was a supernatural person.[24] One must avoid placing a particular theologian in a particular camp because of the way he interprets any single miracle of healing, but it is generally true that the exponents of higher criticism tend either to reject the miracles or to explain them on psychological bases, while conservative scholars feel that at least many of the cures must be explained on the basis of Jesus'

[23] Hunter, *The Work and Words of Jesus*, p. 58.

[24] Leslie D. Weatherhead, *Psychology, Religion and Healing* (Nashville: Abingdon, 1952), p. 30.

supernatural nature. We shall return to this subject later in the chapter.

There are a few other characteristics of these healing miracles that we should notice briefly. In the first place, Jesus did not equate sickness with either sin or the will of God. On occasion he gives support to the fact that sin may have an effect upon a man's body. In the story of the paralytic (Mk. 2:1-12; cf. Mt. 9:2-8; Lk. 5:17-26), he gives support to the idea that this man's sickness was due to sin. His words of healing are really words of forgiveness: "My son, your sins are forgiven" (Mk. 2:8). In another instance, however, he denies outrightly that a man's blindness is due either to his sin or to his parent's sin. When the question is asked with the presumption that the blindness must be the result of sin, he replies, "It was not that this man sinned, or his parents, but that the works of God might be made manifest in him" (Jn. 9:3).

In the ancient world, a sick person was of no interest to the gods. Only healthy people received their attention.[25] Jesus sets himself in direct opposition to this pagan notion. In Jewish thought this feeling was not nearly as pronounced as in pagan thought. The healings of Jesus were in part the kind of thing that was expected of the Messiah. This is what makes the reply of Jesus to the disciples of John the Baptist in Lk. 7:22 intelligible.

Finally, Jesus took great care to find out about the disease of the afflicted before he healed him. It is usual, for example, for Jesus to ask about the length of the illness and its precise nature before he acts. Weatherhead has noticed, interestingly, that in this connection Jesus has more in common with the modern surgeon than with the modern faith healer.[26]

Exorcisms

Reality of demon possession. As with the healing miracles, modern critics find no great difficulty in accepting the exorcisms of Jesus as essentially historical. But once

25 *Ibid.*, p. 39.
26 *Ibid.*, p. 40.

again, the cures here are not attributed to actual exorcisms, but rather to psychological techniques. Because of the nature of these miracles and their relationship to modern man, we must treat them at greater length than the other types of miracle. The first question we must ask is, Do demons exist? The contemporary disbelief in the existence of demons by so many biblical critics is difficult for this writer to understand. Almost all of them believe in God. The vast majority of them believe in angels. Unless, as Weatherhead has observed, we rule out the existence of demons a priori, it would seem that their existence must be accepted.[27] How one can deal adequately with the problem of evil in our world apart from the existence of an evil agency is difficult to understand. Pantheism has never been a widely held position in the history of the Christian Church. Both of the other two principal attempts to solve the problem—dualism and Christian theism—make provision for an evil agency. If, therefore, what we call Satan does exist, should it not be expected that he would have his aids—the demons—as well as that God would have his—the angels? We assert that at minimum this possibility must be maintained.

But even if we accept the reality of demons, we may deny the reality of demon possession. Critics have dealt with the Gospel literature in several ways that deny the reality of demon possession. Let us look at some of these. (1) There are some who feel that Jesus neither believed in demon possession nor that he practiced exorcism. What we have in the Gospels is consequently either the fabrication of the early Church or that of the Evangelists. That this cannot be maintained in light of what we have discussed in the previous chapter should be self-evident. Few hold this view today.

(2) Others feel that Jesus himself did not believe in demon possession, but that his conduct in the Gospels is a mere concession to the ignorance of the people. To this we may make two objections. In the first place, in no other area of his ministry did Jesus make an effort to support contemporary demonology. As a matter of fact

27 *Ibid.*, p. 93.

he took deliberate steps to destroy it. Weatherhead has noted some examples of this. After the feeding of the five thousand and the feeding of the four thousand he commanded his disciples to gather up the fragments. This ran directly counter to the idea that the demons lurked in the crumbs. His bypassing of the ceremonial washing of hands went against the idea that evil spirits fasten themselves to unwashed hands. His request for a drink from the Samaritan woman went against the prohibition of drinking borrowed water due to the presence of demons in it. His retiring to desert places and his fasting in the wilderness ran counter to the belief that demons frequented such places; therefore, they were to be avoided.[28]

Edward Langton has raised a second objection against this idea of concession: "Theories of accommodation do not accord well with the character of Jesus as the teacher of divine truth. They leave us with the problem of explaining why He should deliberately have strengthened about the minds of His disciples the bonds of a false theory which have never been relaxed, at least until the modern period."[29]

(3) Some critics feel that although Jesus made no general concession to the people on the idea of demon possession, he made a special concession to the afflicted much in the spirit of a modern psychiatrist who does not run the risk of alienating his patients by attributing the disease to their imagination. This theory can be disposed of even more quickly due to the fact that in some cases, e.g., that of the demoniac boy in Mk. 9:14:29, Jesus was not even dealing directly with the patient but with his father.[30]

(4) Another way in which one may approach the exorcisms of the Gospels is to assert that Jesus was a child of his day. It is difficult to explain according to this theory why a man who ran so directly counter to both

[28] *Ibid.*, pp. 90-91.

[29] Edward Langton, *Essentials of Demonology* (London: Epworth, 1949), pp. 222-23.

[30] Weatherhead, p. 90.

the religious practice and superstition of his day could at the same time be so naïve in other areas. This theory goes directly against the New Testament portrayal of Jesus and leaves all of Jesus' teachings and work open to objection or dismissal.

(5) Edward Langton has developed a variant of the last theory. He feels that Jesus' belief in demon possession was actual and that it can be accounted for on the basis of Jesus' limited knowledge in his incarnate state. He feels justified in asserting this on the basis of the Gospel accounts where Jesus asks for information, and on the basis of such things as the *kenosis* theology of Paul in Phil. 2:5-11. It therefore is not necessary for us to believe in demon possession because Jesus did during the period of his earthly life. He merely accepted the Jewish teaching on the subject.[31]

Such a conjecture runs counter to the New Testament portrayal of Jesus. Jesus' self-limitation in his incarnation did not extend to errors of fact. It merely extended to the quantity of his knowledge. As has been stated, Jesus is the only person in the history of our world who knew the precise boundaries of his knowledge.[32] If the contention of Langton is true, Jesus was subject to error, and his sinlessness is not a fact.

(6) Finally, one may take the Gospel records as they stand, and accept the reality of demon possession and along with it the reality of the exorcisms. This is the easiest solution from the point of view of the New Testament record. Weatherhead summarizes it as follows: "Our Lord clearly spoke about demons, cast them out, commanded His followers to cast them out and appeared to believe that their power over men was the cause of certain illnesses."[33] White states it more in terms of the entire New Testament: "Not only the words and actions of Christ as related in the Gospels, but also the Epistles, and still more obviously the Apocalypse, are largely unin-

[31] Langton, pp. 222-24.
[32] Boettner, *Studies in Theology,* p. 185.
[33] Weatherhead, p. 89.

telligible except on the supposition of the reality and activity of Satan and other malevolent spirits."[34]

If, however, the problem of exegesis is best solved by accepting the reality of demon possession, the reality of the existence of the phenomenon is not nearly as easily solved for many contemporary critics. Bultmann comments as precisely as anyone: "Sickness and the cure of disease are . . . attributable to natural causation; they are not the result of daemonic activity or of evil spells."[35]

The position for which we shall contend in the following is expressed in a statement by Weatherhead: "The last hypothesis to which I am driven in accounting for illness of mind and body is the hypothesis of demon-possession. Yet . . . I cannot rule it out as impossible, especially in regard to the far-off days of the Biblical narrative and the far-off places of the world where the power of Christ has yet had little chance of overcoming His enemies."[36]

What, then, is the contemporary evidence for the reality of demon possession? In the first place, as the preceding quotation would appear to indicate, some of the occurrences on foreign mission fields cannot be accounted for on any other basis than demon possession. The kind of evidence we appeal to here is not that of the ordinary missionary, but of the missionary doctor. One of the best treatments of this subject is a book by Dr. J. L. Nevius, *Demon Possession and Allied Themes*, 1892. Other works of a similar character seem to indicate that in heathen lands where the light of the Gospel has not yet penetrated, the phenomenon of demon possession is particularly frequent.

Must we, however, limit the idea of demon possession to such far-off places? If such be the case, there will always lurk the suspicion that possession may be a myth. The question is, Cannot all physical and mental abnormalities of the sort that we would attribute to demon possession in civilized lands be accounted for on psycho-

[34] Victor White, *God and the Unconscious* (London: Harvill, 1952), p. 179.

[35] Bultmann, "New Testament and Mythology," pp. 4-5.

[36] Weatherhead, p. 101.

somatic bases? Further, is it not possible for us to classify all the Gospel examples of exorcism in one of these psychological categories and thus dispose of the idea of demon possession? With respect to the biblical materials, it must be admitted that they will not admit to anything near psychological solution. Geldenhuys has noted that (1) the demons cry out or talk, (2) the demons leave the possessed person, (3) the demons possess knowledge concerning Jesus, and (4) the demons possess other supernatural knowledge, such as knowledge of their future. This leads him to assert that the phenomenon of demon possession as it is treated in the Bible can be accounted for neither on the basis of mental states nor on that of physical disease.[37]

When we come from the biblical records to an examination of modern psychiatry, we find that there is no way in which we may dispose of the problem. All too often modern psychiatry dwells in the area of symptoms rather than in that of causes. As White cautions, "We need to beware of assuming too readily that a new name necessarily involves a new explanation which refutes the old."[38] He continues, "The names whereby mental diseases are classified are purely descriptive, and in no sense at all cover etiological explanations: that is to say they are no more than labels for certain syndromes or symptoms which are commonly associated together." [39]

White also notes that the success of psychotherapy in given instances does not thereby rule out the possibility of demon possession. He notes that various techniques have been used in the history of mankind to cure such maladies, and that most of them have been effective in a measure for at least some people: "Whether by exorcism . . . or by some psychological or physical performance on or by the sufferer . . . the net result on the

[37] Norval Geldenhuys, *Commentary on the Gospel of Luke* ("The New International Commentary on the New Testament"; Grand Rapids: Eerdmans, 1960), p. 174.

[38] White, p. 187.

[39] *Ibid.*, pp. 187-188.

symptomatic level does not seem to be anything very different."[40]

It is not our intention here to create the impression that all the diseases given names by modern psychiatry are in truth demon possession. We do not even assert that any one of these categories of maladies is wholly or predominantly composed of the demon possessed. The only thing we wish to assert is that demon possession could well account for some of the instances, and that the possibility of demon possession must not be ruled out.

A particularly instructive example from a biblical perspective is the story of the demoniac boy in Mt. 17:14-20 (cf. Mk. 9:14-29; Lk. 9:37-43a). In the book of Matthew the word used by the father to explain his son's condition means "moon-struck" or "lunatic" (17:15). In the account of Mark he has a "dumb spirit" (9:39).

Many commentators, largely on the basis of Matthew's word and of the description given of the malady, have concluded that it was a case of epilepsy. We have no argument with this except to assert that if it is so named it is named on the basis of the symptoms, not the causes. The cause here, according to the biblical record, was demon possession. This is not in the least to say that every set of similar symptoms either then or now is a result of demon possession. It is to say, however, that some cases of such symptoms may be the result of demon possession.

Features of the biblical accounts. In dealing further with the accounts of demon possession recorded in the Gospels, it should be noticed that demon possession is not the cause of all types of sickness. As a matter of fact there is a clear distinction made between these two classes of ailment. Such things as insanity, leprosy, blindness, lameness, deafness, and other kinds of ailments are dealt with apart from any connection with demon possession.[41] This does not set the Gospel records in a class by themselves, for this is equally the case with contemporary

40 *Ibid.*, p. 189.
41 Geldenhuys, p. 174.

Jewish and pagan accounts. The way Jesus deals with the possessed, however, does set them off from contemporary accounts. There is none of the exhibitionism and wonder-working that so thoroughly dominate the Jewish belief. The sole object of the exorcism is to bring relief to the sufferer. Oesterley has summarized the difference between other contemporary accounts and the Gospel accounts as follows: "When the great mass of facts has been studied, the contrast between the two can be compared only to the contrast between folly and seriousness."[42]

In order to gain a proper understanding of the significance of Jesus' exorcisms, we must set them in relationship to similar phenomena in the biblical record. In the Old Testament there are only two instances of demon possession recorded. One has to do with the possession of Saul (I Sam. 16:14ff.), and the other has to do with Ahab (I Kgs. 22:22ff.). Similarly in the New Testament, apart from the Gospels there are only two recorded incidents of demon possession. One of these is the possessed slave girl who followed Paul (Acts 16:16ff.), and the other has to do with the Jewish exorcists (Acts 19:13ff.).

On the basis of all this evidence, we should be prepared to reach a conclusion with regard to demon possession in its relationship to the life of Jesus. If we accept the incarnation as a fact, then all the pieces fit nicely into the puzzle. The coming of Jesus to earth represented a real confrontation of the forces of darkness by the forces of light. Jesus was not seeking to win men merely to a new kind of thought. He sought to win men from the kingdom of darkness to the kingdom of light. But as he, a member of the Godhead, came into the world in a special and unique sense, so also did the forces of evil seek to incarnate themselves for the struggle. The instances of demon possession that we have, therefore, in the Gospel records are instances of demons attempting to incarnate themselves and thus do combat with Jesus. Jesus' exor-

42 W. O. E. Oesterley, "Demon, Demonical Possession, Demoniacs," *A Dictionary of Christ and the Gospels*, ed. James Hastings, I (1909), 443.

cisms are preliminaries to his final victory over them in his death and resurrection. This also accounts for two additional features of the demons as they are presented in the Gospels: (1) their knowledge of who Jesus is, and (2) their fear of Jesus.

It is thus to be expected that demon possession was particularly prominent during the earthly ministry of our Lord, and the total biblical record bears this out. On the other hand, the continued existence of such phenomena may not be ruled out, particularly in lands where the light of the gospel has as yet had no significant effect.

Raisings from the dead

Three of the miracles of Jesus fall into this class: the raising of Jairus' daughter (Mk. 5:21-43; cf. Mt. 9:18-26; Lk. 8:40-56), the raising of the widow's son at Nain (Lk. 7:11-17), and the raising of Lazarus (Jn. 11:1-46). Higher critics have had greater difficulty with the second than the first, and the third has occasioned the greatest difficulty of all. In the case of Jairus' daughter many have supposed that real death had not taken place, but that the girl had merely slipped into some sort of coma. This apparently gains some support from Jesus' statement, "The child is not dead but sleeping" (Mk. 5:39). The possibility of this may be retained, but it is very remote. Behind this once again lies the presumption that we are able to diagnose a matter of life and death better in the twentieth century than were people who were on the scene in the first century.

The case of the widow's son at Nain is treated similarly by many critics. The problem here is somewhat greater because death had apparently occurred at a greater distance from the event than was true of Jairus' daughter.

The resurrection of Lazarus, however, is too difficult for most critics to accept. As Howard says, "The difference between revival immediately after death, and resurrection after four days, is so great as to raise doubts about the historicity of this story."[43] In this story, at

43 Wilbert F. Howard and Arthur John Gossip, "The Gospel According to St. John," *The Interpreter's Bible,* VIII (1952), 648-49.

any rate, there can be no question about the condition of the subject, for decomposition had already begun (Jn. 11:39). We shall evaluate this kind of analysis after we mention briefly the fourth class of miracles.

Nature miracles

Miracles of this class ultimately cause modern critics the greatest difficulty. Of these miracles four are primary: the feeding of the five thousand (Mk. 6:30-36; cf. Mt. 14:13-23; Lk. 9:10-17; Jn. 6:1-15), the feeding of the four thousand (Mk. 8:1-9; cf. Mt. 15:32-38), Jesus' stilling of the storm (Mk. 4:35-41; cf. Mt. 8:23-27; Lk. 8:22-25), and Jesus' walking on the water (Mk. 6:47-56; cf. Mt. 14:24-36; Jn. 6:16-21).

Those critics who do not completely reject these stories usually attempt to rationalize them. We have already described in an earlier section of this chapter how the stories of the feedings and that of Jesus' walking on the water are dealt with and rationalized by some critics. Others deal similarly with the stilling of the storm. They point out how the Sea of Galilee is subject to sudden and violent storms, which abate just as rapidly. This, then, is what is supposed to have happened on one occasion when Jesus was with the disciples, and they attributed it to Jesus' wonder-working power.

On the basis of our survey of all this material, it should be obvious how little the narratives themselves have to do with the decision of the critics to accept or reject them. Historical evidence is not of any primary importance. The modern critic decides before he examines the record what sort of thing he will accept and what sort of thing he will not. He then proceeds to comb the record to maintain as much of it as possible with his hypothetical exegesis. Since most critics are not lacking in imagination, they are able to retain parts of most of the narratives. This, we maintain, is not honest. This writer has far more respect for the critic who on the basis of his evaluation of the Gospel records concludes that they are fairy tales and discards them, than he has for one who turns to his imagination in an attempt to make them fit nicely into his world view.

Neither of these two alternatives is desirable, however. If one holds, as we have said earlier in this chapter, that God is vitally concerned with the human race, then the great obstacle to the acceptance of the miraculous dissolves. The person and work of Christ as presented in the Gospels then becomes intelligible. If, on the other hand, we hold to some modern form of deism, the plight of modern man is sad indeed.

Significance of Miracles

While we have already dealt with this subject at some length in what has preceded, there are some additional factors which we must consider here with respect to the significance of miracles. In the first place, from the perspective of quantity, miracle occupies a large and central place in the Gospel records. Hunter tells us that 209 of the 661 verses in Mark's Gospel deal directly or indirectly with the subject of miracle. This amounts to 31 percent of the entire Gospel. Furthermore, while Q is a sayings source and not a narrative source, it contains the very important statement of Jesus to the disciples of John regarding the significance of his miracles (Lk. 7:22; cf. Mt. 11:4-5).[44] All this has led Cairns to observe, "If we remove all the miracle narratives from St. Mark's Gospel, and if we remove also the attached teaching of Christ which seems to depend necessarily on the factual reference of the miraculous stories recorded, we shall have only a very meagre relic left."[45]

Another question with which we must deal is how the miracles are to be regarded by those who accept them. Some regard them as the putting into operation of a higher form of law with which we are unfamiliar.[46] Others regard them as the products of immediate divine action.[47] The former of these two hypotheses has certain

[44] Hunter, *The Work and Words of Jesus*, p. 54.

[45] Cairns, p. 87.

[46] Weatherhead, p. 37.

[47] Dods, p. 219; Ramm, *Protestant Christian Evidences*, pp. 127-28.

difficulties about it. It is largely an argument from silence on the basis of the Gospel records. For this reason Dods calls it an unverified and unverifiable hypothesis.[48] Furthermore, the way in which Jesus related them to the Father's will and to faith in certain instances would indicate that they are products of direct divine action.

In the final analysis, however, it is perhaps possible to say that these two ideas do not present the radical antithesis that they might appear to on first glance. Anything that God decides to do, be it natural or supernatural, in the last analysis operates according to the law of God.

We have noticed the importance of the miraculous to the Gospel record from the perspective of quantity. We must also comment on it in relation to the entire biblical record. Ramm has pointed out that when one considers the length of time of the biblical period, the number of miracles contained in it is not great. Moreover, they are not evenly distributed over the biblical period, but seem to be gathered around certain persons and events.[49]

Boettner has gone further to identify the four principal periods in biblical history when miracles were the most prominent: (1) the time of the Exodus and the entry of Israel into the land of Canaan, (2) the period of the ministry of Elijah and Elisha, (3) the period of the Exile, and (4) the life and ministry of Jesus.[50]

These were four particularly crucial eras in the history of divine revelation to man. The Exodus is the greatest single event of the Old Testament. It represents the redemption of the people of God so that they could be subjects of further revelation. The period of Elijah and Elisha was one in which the worship of Jahweh was in danger of extinction. At this point Israel was in danger of accepting Baal and the other Canaanite gods and rejecting Jahweh. Similarly, the time of the Exile was a period of crisis. Had Jahweh forsaken his people? Should Israel

[48] Dods, p. 219.

[49] Bernard Ramm, "The Evidence of Prophecy and Miracle," *Revelation and the Bible*, ed. Carl F. H. Henry (Grand Rapids: Baker, 1958), p. 255.

[50] Boettner, p. 66.

worship the gods of their captors? Finally, with the coming of Christ, man received God's ultimate revelation in history. It is not surprising, therefore, that the occurrence of the miraculous should be more intense and concentrated during his life than in any other period of human history.

On the basis of this evidence, the purpose of miracles in the history of divine revelation should be clear. In the words of Boettner, they were given "to accredit a new and divinely given message."[51] The Gospels use two principal words for "miracle." The first, *dunamis* (power), is used in the Synoptics, and points to the fact that God is behind the happening. Things like this do not happen without divine agency. The second term, *sēmeion* (sign), is used by all four Gospel writers, but is particularly emphasized in the Gospel of John. It points to the fact that the message or the messenger is of divine origin.

All this should be added evidence to us why Jesus did not perform a great number of miracles before the masses. When he did this they wanted more of the miracle for its own sake. They wanted more free bread. They wanted their sicknesses healed, etc. They became attached to the sign rather than looking at what it pointed to.

For some reason this evidential value of miracles has been neglected in much of modern biblical scholarship. In fact it is even denied by many. But one who denies it does not read his New Testament carefully. The statement of Jesus to John's disciples in Lk. 7:22 clearly puts miracles on an evidential level. The concluding two verses of Jn. 20 point in the same direction. In Peter's Pentecost sermon he proclaims Jesus as "a man attested to you by God with mighty works and wonders and signs which God did through him in your midst" (Acts 2:22). The writer of Hebrews when talking about the believers' salvation says, "It was declared at first by the Lord, and it was attested to us by those who heard him, while God also bore witness by signs and wonders and various miracles and by gifts of the Holy Spirit" (Heb. 2:3-4). These are

51 *Ibid.*

only representative passages. The only conclusion that we can reach from this is that from a biblical perspective, miracles are regarded as having great evidential force, and if one denies this he does it on some other than a biblical basis.

But we may go on to press the question a step further. Why were miracles necessary? The answer is the same as the answer to the question, Why was special revelation necessary? Because of human sin and ignorance, man had been separated from God. The purpose, therefore, of miracle is the same as the purpose of special revelation itself. God had to make his revelation explicit in order to make man aware of his needs, and of God's provision for those needs.

There was also a second reason why God chose to reveal himself via miracles. The miracles themselves were a revelation of the nature of God. The miracles of healing are a great revelation of the love of God for men. He makes the blind see, the lame walk, and the dead live. These also carry intimations for the realm of the spirit. He feeds the hungry, and proclaims, "I am the bread of life." He restores the ideal state of nature and makes it a blessing to man. In every one of the miracles we learn something important about God.

Let us notice here the words of Käsemann. We do so because, in spite of his rejection of the miraculous, he gives a very fine analysis of the significance of miracle in the ancient world. With this analysis the current writer is satisfied:

> The concept of miracle current in the ancient world was not oriented primarily, as ours is, towards the suspension of causality but towards the occurrence of an epiphany. In a miracle there is an encounter with the divinity and its power, which, in its self-manifestation, is reaching out to take hold of me. It is not merely that something *extraordinary* is happening but that I encounter *someone*, be it deity or demon . . . . because a power is reaching out for us, we are being summoned to make a decision which may express itself either as faith or as unfaith (hardness of heart).[52]

[52] Käsemann, *Essays on New Testament Themes*, p. 52.

This conception of miracles as evidence of a new and vital revelation of God helps us to understand two things. In the first place, it helps us understand why they occurred with such frequency in certain eras of human history. God had a message for those particular eras which he wanted to make explicit. As we have said, of all these eras the period of the life and ministry of Jesus was the most important; therefore, we should expect that miracles would be greater in number and magnitude than they have been at any other time.

In the second place, however, it helps us understand why miracles do not occur today. Throughout Scripture miracles accredit the messenger and authenticate his message. But the era of special revelation through events has now passed; therefore, we should not expect biblical miracles to recur in our day. For this reason many movements to the theological right are as much in error as movements to the left. Healing campaigns, etc., find no adequate theological justification in the New Testament. This is not to say that God will not hear our prayers for the sick in accordance with the prescription of Jms. 5:14-15, but when great public demonstrations are made in connection with healing meetings, the participants are in effect trying to duplicate the signs that accompanied God's supreme revelation in Jesus Christ.

The thing that makes a miracle of revelatory value is its uniqueness. If we could accomplish today what Jesus did during the time of his earthly life, the significance of what he did would sink into oblivion. Boettner has summarized the matter excellently:

> Revelation and miracles go together. While the former remained in the Church, the latter remained also; but when the process of revelation had been completed with the work of Christ and the explanation of that work by the apostles, miracles also ceased. A new era of miracles would indicate a new era of revelation. We believe, however, that with the closing of the New Testament Canon revelation was completed and that we are to expect no more such works until the end of the world.[53]

53 Boettner, p. 56.

At various points in this chapter the question of the relationship of the miracles of Jesus to modern psychiatry has come up. We must now address ourselves briefly to this question. The possibility, or even the probability, must be maintained that some of the cures effected by Jesus could be accounted for on the basis of psychotherapy. But to say that all of the cures may be accounted for on this basis is absurd from a physical point of view and impossible from a revelatory point of view.

Let us consider first the physical aspect. Weatherhead points out the inadequacy of the psychological approach: "While the mental mechanisms which He used can sometimes be identified through our modern psychological knowledge, the miracles certainly cannot be regarded merely as psychotherapeutic treatments."[54] It would appear that in some instances Jesus' emphasis on the nature and length of the illness would be evidence that he applied techniques similar to those of a modern doctor. But in many cases, such analysis of the miracle is not possible. Such physical ailments as congenital blindness, among others, cannot be accounted for on psychological bases. In addition we have such phenomena as raisings from the dead, healing at a distance where there is no contact between Jesus and the subject, and the nature miracles, which fall completely beyond the scope of psychological explanation. Furthermore, in such instances as the raising of Lazarus, Jesus directs himself in prayer to the Father before the astonishing miracle. All this evidence weighs against any attempt to put all the miracles of Jesus on a psychological basis.

There is in addition an objection against this kind of complete solution from the point of view of special revelation. While to people living in the first century who did not know the techniques of modern psychology, the miracles of Jesus may have been revelatory, if on the basis of our knowledge today we could account for them rationally, they would lose their revelatory character for us. As a result, Jesus would be merely a skilled psychiatrist ahead of his day. He would thus bear no necessary or

54 Weatherhead, p. 69.

important relationship to the Father, and he would take his place along with the other great men of history. Against the background of the Gospel miracles, however, such an assertion cannot be made.

Miracles and Faith

While some critics have felt that the miracles of Jesus bear no evidential value, others have felt that the miracles, if established, would bear too much. This particular strain of thought can be traced back to Kierkegaard and is found recurring in the work of Bultmann and his successors. The line of thought here is somewhat as follows: If we could prove conclusively that the miracles of the New Testament did happen, faith would no longer be a necessity for us. We would have a demonstration of God's presence. This kind of construction is strongly reminiscent of something we discussed in the previous chapter. Then, if we could construct a critical history of Jesus, that would make faith a work and be the end of faith. Now, if we can demonstrate the actuality of the miracles, it will destroy faith.

There are two fundamental errors in this theory. In the first place, the mere establishment of a miracle neither compels nor destroys faith. There were those who witnessed Jesus' miracles at the time of his life here on earth who did not believe. Some attributed them to demonic agency. Some became so completely wrapped up in the miracle that they failed to see what it signified. Cairns comments in terms of the present: "The need for the leap of faith remains. But the man who can accept the miracles may find that he can make the leap of faith to better advantage, for he is at liberty to believe . . . that God is a God who does mighty works."[55]

The second error in the theory that the establishment of miracle destroys faith is seen in a nonbiblical conception of faith. As we noted in the last chapter, faith is not a product of human decision based on historical evidence. The believer comes to faith through the work of the Holy

[55] Cairns, p. 144.

Spirit. The Spirit may use a number of means to bring this about. An historical record may help. As a part of that record the evidence of miracle might be of particular importance. But neither history nor miracle in and of itself is sufficient to bring about faith. As Ramm insists, "The priority of the work of the Spirit excludes the adequacy of a purely 'intellectual' faith stimulated by Christian evidences in isolation."[56]

[56] Ramm, "The Evidence of Prophecy and Miracle," p. 259.

CHAPTER FOUR

The Resurrection of Jesus

Approach to the Subject

As in the previous chapter we examined the miraculous element in the biblical record from two perspectives, so here we may approach the subject of the resurrection in two basic ways each of which will determine the manner in which we will evaluate it. Here, too, we may ask the question, Has it ever been known outside the biblical period that anyone who was certainly dead has been raised from that state of death to a life that showed no effects of the ordeal that preceded? If the question is asked in this way, a negative answer would be expected.

But we may ask the question in a second way: Would it be possible for God, the creator and sustainer of our universe, in his plan of redemption for mankind, to send his Son to suffer and die as a part of that plan, and to raise him from death as an evidence of that plan to mankind? If we were to give a negative reply to this question, we would be putting the same limitation on God that we spoke of in the previous chapter. As it was impossible for us to do it there, so it is impossible for us to do it here.

As Ladd has noticed, it all boils down to the way in which one looks at God in his relation to the world. If God is deistically removed from our world, then it would be impossible for him to intervene in its workings. If this be the case, the resurrection must be rejected in the same way as miracle and all special revelation. If, on the other hand, God is identified with our world in a pantheistic sort of way, he loses any existence separate from it, and any "interference" with it is automatically ruled out. If, however, God is at once actively involved in our world, and yet maintains an existence separate from it, the possibility of the resurrection as well as that of miracles may be retained.[1]

Bruce appears to have discerned the way in which the question should be asked: "The question is not, 'Can a man rise from the dead?' but 'Did *Jesus* rise from the dead?' "[2]

There is a sense in which the previous chapter and this one should not have been divided, for their subject matter is largely the same. While we have chosen to divide them from the point of view of analysis of the material, we do not feel that the two subjects should be treated in isolation from each other. The resurrection is central. Apart from it the miracles lose their significance. In light of the resurrection, however, the entire life of Jesus has meaning for us.

Importance of the Resurrection

We will deal with this subject at some length because until recently it has been neglected by contemporary critics.[3] While the self-sacrifice of Jesus in his death is

[1] Ladd, "The Resurrection of Christ," *Christian Faith and Modern Theology*, p. 267.

[2] F. F. Bruce, *The Spreading Flame* (Grand Rapids: Eerdmans, 1961), p. 61.

[3] In comparatively recent years there has been renewed interest in the resurrection in certain critical circles: (1) Some writers continue to see the source of the resurrection in the faith of the early Church, e.g., Bultmann, Bornkamm, Käsemann, Ebeling, R. Fuller, E. Brunner, Tillich, etc. (2) Others are convinced that in the resurrection "something" happened, but lack confidence in our ability to determine "what" happened, e.g., Marxsen, S. H. Hooke, etc. (3) Others see the resurrection either as transcending history, or as an historical anomaly, e.g., K. Barth (later), Künneth, G.

dealt with at great length, the idea of his resurrection has been more or less an embarrassment to these critics; as a result it either has been ignored, or has been given a most inadequate treatment. While we shall deal briefly with some of these inadequate treatments at a later point in this chapter, we here look at the centrality of the resurrection from a biblical perspective. While it is necessary to read the New Testament itself to gain a total impression of the importance of the resurrection, the following facts are particularly significant: (1) When the primitive Christian community selected a successor for Judas Iscariot, there were two requirements for such a candidate. He had to be a witness to the public ministry of Jesus, and to his resurrection (Acts 1:22). It is interesting in this connection that the resurrection is mentioned in addition to the public ministry. The only reason for this is that this event gave meaning to the rest of his life.

(2) The repeated emphasis that the resurrection of Jesus received in Peter's Pentecost sermon (Acts 2:24, 31, 32) can only be explained in light of the importance he attached to it.

(3) Paul has a great number of things to say about the importance of the resurrection. His general statement in this regard is found in I Cor. 15:14: "If Christ has not been raised, then our preaching is in vain and your faith is in vain." The reason for this emptiness appears in other Pauline passages which we shall now examine.

(4) When writing to the Romans, Paul explains that the justification of the Christian is dependent upon the resurrection of Jesus (Rom. 4:25).

(5) In keeping with this, in the previously referred to Corinthians passage Paul notes that not only is one's preaching in vain, but his faith is in vain and he remains in sin if the resurrection of Christ is not a fact (I Cor. 15:17).

Koch, R. R. Niebuhr, etc. (4) Pannenberg sees its truth as lying in an eschatological conception of history.

Even among those authors who accept the resurrection as an event in or above history, however, there remain many doubts as to the historicity of much of the material in the Gospels that comes after the resurrection.

(6) In light of this, Paul's insistence on belief in the resurrection as a prerequisite to salvation becomes intelligible (Rom. 10:9).

(7) For Paul, not only one's earthly salvation was dependent on the resurrection of Jesus, but any hope for a more glorious life thereafter depended on it equally (I Cor. 15:18).

(8) Finally, the resurrection of Jesus transformed the disciples from regarding Jesus' life as a tragedy, and gave rise to the most dynamic faith in the history of mankind (Lk. 24:21; cf. v. 32).

In light of evidence like this Fuller concludes, "The New Testament conceives of the resurrection of Jesus as the basis for all of the events of redemptive history."[4]

Comparative New Testament Accounts

Before we examine the nature of the resurrected body of Jesus on the basis of the biblical materials, it is necessary for us to deal with certain purported discrepancies in the resurrection narratives as we have them in the biblical materials. Critical scholarship has made a great deal of these supposed differences in its attempt to arrive at something other than a literal resurrection.

It is noted, first of all, that there is a basic difference in the Gospels themselves. The source of the difficulty here lies in two sets of facts. All four Gospels are relatively close in the account they give of the passion narrative. There are, however, considerable differences in the Easter narratives and subsequent appearances of Jesus. Here we may trace at least three kinds of tradition: (1) In the Gospel of Mark, nothing is made of any appearances of Jesus subsequent to the first Easter morning. The section composed of Mk. 16:9-20 is an attempt to fill in this gap, but this section cannot be regarded as an original part of the Gospel. It must be left out on textual grounds. (2) Mt. 28:16-20 tells of a subsequent appearance only in Galilee. (3) Luke and John emphasize appearances in or near Jerusalem; however, John contains the story of the

---

[4] Daniel Fuller, *Easter Faith and History*, p. 19.

appearance to Thomas (20:26-29), which, because it occurred a week after the resurrection, has caused some
critics to feel that it occurred in Galilee. Be that as it
may, Jn. 21:1-24 does give an account of appearances to
the disciples in Galilee. The question of whether this
chapter is an original part of the Gospel must await our
investigation in a subsequent chapter.

Do the differences in these resurrection appearances
pose any real problem? When one stops to think about it
for a moment, the differences between the passion narrative and the resurrection narrative are precisely what
one should expect if both accounts are historical. The
passion narrative was a well-defined historical sequence
observable to all who were in any way involved in it,
either as spectators or participants. It began with the
triumphal entry on Sunday; moved through a series of
conflicts with the Jews during the early part of the week;
continued into Jesus' final conversations with his disciples on Thursday; and culminated in Jesus' agony in
Gethsemane, betrayal, arrest, trial, crucifixion, and burial. These events all occurred in a week's time at a sequence of geographical locations.

On the other hand, the appearances of the risen Christ
occurred at a variety of geographical locations over a
period of forty days (Acts 1:3), and to groups of varying
sizes ranging from more than five hundred (I Cor. 15:6)
to one (I Cor. 15:5). Under these circumstances it is
understandable that the accounts of the appearances
should be more fragmentary in nature than connected. It
should be noted that for the entire period of forty days,
Matthew includes just one chapter of twenty verses; Mark
has an even briefer eleven-verse account which does not
deal with anything after Easter morning itself; Luke similarly gives us one chapter of fifty-three verses; and John
gives us but two brief chapters.

On the basis of these observations, any difficulty we
incur in attempting to construct an historical sequence of
the appearances of Jesus is primarily due to the inadequacy of the sources from a quantitative perspective rather
than from a qualitative one. We have only three brief
accounts. They come from sources or witnesses who were
only partially involved in the totality of the appearances

during that forty-day period. Not a single person, outside of Jesus himself, was involved in all those appearances.

A second kind of discrepancy that is sometimes pointed out by modern critics in an attempt to show the unreliability of the resurrection narratives sets the writings of Paul against the Synoptics. It has been claimed that while Paul writes of a kind of spiritual resurrection in which the substance of Jesus' body was completely different from his earthly body, the Synoptics talk only of the revivification of a corpse. As a consequence, because Paul's writings are earlier than those of the Synoptics, it is to be supposed that the latter are an attempt to make concrete a less objective kind of experience.

Our criticism of this alleged antithesis in these two sets of writings may await our discussion of the nature of the resurrected body itself, but we need to comment here that any such opposition is based on a partial reading of either set of writings. Thus in the Synoptics, writings which supposedly tell us of the resurrection of a corpse, we have the narrative of the walk of the two disciples to Emmaus with Jesus. Their nonrecognition of Jesus is inexplicable if his resurrection had been merely the revivification of a corpse.

On the other hand, in Paul's Areopagus speech, it appears that the real offense to the Athenians was his emphasis on the resurrection of the body (Acts 17:32). We could multiply the illustrations to demonstrate that there is no such thing as a neat division into a physical resurrection in the Synoptics and a spiritual resurrection in Paul.[4a]

A third kind of difference that critics sometimes note is the difference between the appearances to the other disciples and the appearance to Paul. The difficulty here has arisen over three lines of evidence: (1) Paul, in describing his confrontation with Jesus in Acts 26:19, uses

[4a] Recently, redaction critics have attempted to explain the divergent characteristics in the Gospels on the basis of their discipline, e.g., Reginald Fuller, *The Formation of the Resurrection Narratives* (1971), but here too the analysis of the resurrection narratives in the Gospels is carried out with the presumption that they are composed of early (spiritual) and late (physical) portions that have been brought together.

the word "vision" to describe the appearance of Jesus to him. (2) The word "vision" is nowhere used in the Synoptic accounts to describe the experience of the disciples when Jesus appeared to them. (3) Yet, in the summary of the appearances of Jesus given by Paul in I Cor. 15:5-8, he links himself to the other disciples with no apparent differentiation as to the mode of the appearance.

This has led some critics to hypothesize that all the appearances of Jesus must be classified as visions, and that the reason why the Synoptics speak of them as physical appearances rather than visions must be found in their attempt to make concrete what had previously been regarded as less substantial.

Here we do not feel it necessary to assert that the appearance to Paul was of the same kind as that to other disciples. There are good reasons for saying this. In the first place, the appearance to Paul is to be differentiated from that to the other disciples by the character of the recipient of the experience. Paul had been, up to the time of this experience, an extreme antagonist of all that Jesus and his followers represented. In the case of the disciples, the appearance to them resulted in the glorious realization that their devotion to Jesus of Nazareth had not been in vain. God had raised him up for their justification. In the case of Paul, the appearance entailed a conversion from a militantly anti-Christian determination, and resulted in incidents that were pronouncedly more violent than was the case in Jesus' appearance to the other disciples. He was arrested by the bright light, stricken to the ground, and led blind into Damascus. Only three days later was his sight restored. This is completely different from the experience of any of the other disciples that we have preserved for us.

Second, the fact that Paul includes himself in the list of those who had seen the risen Christ in I Cor. 15 does not in itself necessitate the assumption that his experience was the same in kind as theirs. Paul's experience must have come a year or more after Jesus' resurrection. If the ascension that occurred forty days after the resurrection means anything, it must be taken as an indication that the appearances that had characterized that forty-day period had now come to an end. If the appearance to Paul was the same in kind as were those to the other apostles, it must have involved a "descension" of the living Christ. This, of course, is possible, but in our view highly unlikely.

Third, visions appear to have played a major part in the ministry of Paul subsequent to his conversion experience. In Acts 18:9 Paul receives a vision of the Lord in Corinth, giving him reassurance about his mission to that city. In Acts 23:11 he receives similar reassurance from the Lord after his arrest in Jerusalem. And in Acts 27:23 Paul tells of an angelic visitor he had at the time of the storm in his voyage to Rome.

Visions are one of the modes of special revelation. In the Old Testament they are more numerous than in the New Testament, but they find their place also in the New Testament. This has been the position of the orthodox Church from earliest days down to the present. It is not therefore necessary to insist that the experience of Paul was precisely the same as that of the other disciples.

The one problem that remains for this kind of interpretation is the passage in I Cor. 15. But here we are against no insurmountable obstacle. Would it not be possible to say in light of Acts 26:19 that Paul felt that he had come into vital contact with Jesus (a vision) without therefore assuming that his experience was precisely the same as that of the other apostles? We maintain that such a possibility is not only tenable, but the most logical solution to the problem.

Paul includes his experience with the others because he regards it as a "last of all" experience (I Cor. 15:8). No longer are men to expect appearances and visions of this sort. They now have the collective experience of the early Church on which to base their faith. This is sufficient.

Nature of the Resurrected Body

It should be emphasized immediately that the New Testament makes no profession of being a treatise on chemistry or physics—ancient or modern. This being the case, it does not speculate on the precise nature of Christ's body after the resurrection. We may take the statement of Ramm here as minimal: "It is generally agreed that the New Testament belief in the resurrection is belief in the *physical* transformation of the crucified body of Jesus."[5] We may go beyond this, however, to make several additional observations on the basis of New Testament materials.

There is, in the first place, some sense in which the resurrected body of Jesus resembled the body of his previous earthly life. In Lk. 24:39 Jesus calls attention to his hands and his feet, apparently to demonstrate who he is by means of his wounds. In Jn. 20:20 Jesus calls attention to his hands and his side in a similar demonstration, and in Jn. 20:27 he even asks Thomas to touch the wounds in order that he might be convinced.

In the second place, there are indications in the Gospels that the resurrected body of Jesus partook of physical characteristics. We mention here just three passages of several that could be included: (1) His body could be touched. In Mt. 28:9 the disciples "took hold of his feet and worshiped him." (2) He indicates on another occasion that his body is physical: "A spirit has not flesh and bones as you see that I have" (Lk. 24:39). This passage should not be taken out of its context, however, as an indication that Jesus' body was precisely the same as it had been prior to his passion. As Ladd says, "The context indicates . . . that no 'scientific' analysis of the body is intended here; Jesus only meant to prove that He was not a disembodied spirit but possessed a real body."[6] (3) Similarly, in Lk. 24:42, 43 Jesus eats a piece of fish in the company of the disciples. Here again the words of Ladd are instructive: "The words 'before them' . . . would indicate that He did this to manifest the bodily nature of His resurrection."[7]

In the third place, there are other indications in the Gospels that the resurrected body of Jesus was different from his previous earthly body. Of special significance here is the way his body could be materialized or demate-

5 Ramm, *Protestant Christian Evidences*, p. 193.

6 Ladd, p. 277.

7 *Ibid.*

rialized at will. Thus, he suddenly appears before the disciples (Lk. 24:36, 37; Jn. 20:19, 26); just as suddenly he disappears from their sight (Lk. 24:31). Also as an indication of the transformed body of Jesus are those passages in which Jesus confronts his followers and yet for a period of time they do not recognize him. We have already mentioned the instance of the disciples on the road to Emmaus (Lk. 24:16). Also of the same general character is the instance of the nonrecognition of Jesus by Mary Magdalene on Easter morning (Jn. 20:14), and the instance of his appearance before the disciples on the shore of the Sea of Galilee (Jn. 21:4).

What can we say about the nature of Jesus' resurrected body on the basis of all this evidence? I believe that Ladd has seen it clearly when he says that the nature of the resurrected body can best be described in two words: continuity and discontinuity.[8] That is, there was in an important sense a continuity between Jesus' physical body and his resurrected body. On the other hand, there was another sense in which the resurrected body was radically different and thus represented a discontinuity with all that had preceded it.

Paul lends weight to this position in I Cor. 15. In that chapter he uses the resurrection of Jesus as an indication of what will be true for all believers in him in the future. Therefore, what he says about the resurrected body of believers would also presumably be true of the resurrected body of Christ. From this passage as well as from other writings of Paul, we are warranted in drawing three conclusions with respect to the nature of Jesus' resurrected body and hence the resurrected body of all believers in the future: (1) Christ's body before the resurrection may be best described as a "physical body" while after the resurrection it is called a "spiritual body" (v. 44). (2) The change in the composition of the body was necessary to prepare it for a new mode of existence (v. 50). (3) Any attempt to go beyond this to describe the composition of that body is beyond the reach of the New Testament. Paul himself classifies it as a mystery (v. 51).

On the grounds of all this evidence it would appear

8 *Ibid.*, p. 276.

that Stauffer has summed up the matter as well as anyone:

> In these various accounts the Gospels aimed at conveying three
> facts. In the first place, the risen Christ was a vital personality
> who acted according to a definite plan, bearing witness to
> himself by appearing whenever, wherever, however, and before
> whomever he pleased. In the second place, the risen Christ
> existed in a new form of existence whose character was neither
> spiritualistic nor materialistic. . . . The Evangelists and their
> authorities could not explain this; they could only state it as a
> fact, only "testify" to it.[9]

In the light of this investigation, it should at once be
evident how completely Bultmann misses the point of the
resurrection of Jesus when he writes of that resurrection
in terms of the "resuscitation of a dead person."[10] This
was not the restoration of life to a physical body. It was a
breakthrough of eternity into the realm of time. It was
the introduction of a new and wholly different order of
life. If the resurrection were only the raising of a corpse,
we would agree with Bultmann that it would have no
profound significance, but this is not what the New
Testament represents it to have been.

Attempts at Rationalization

Since large segments of the critical movement cannot
accept a literal resurrection of Jesus from the dead, it has
become necessary for these critics to account for what we
have in our Gospels in some other way. These rationalizations range all the way from outright deception by the
disciples on the one extreme, to gullibility on the other.
We shall deal with these features in connection with each
theory, but with respect to the idea of gullibility we must
clear the ground by a preliminary observation. Karl Jaspers has approached this issue as honestly as anyone. He
writes, "The Resurrection . . . was just as implausible to

[9] Stauffer, *Jesus and His Story*, pp. 151-52.

[10] Bultmann, "New Testament and Mythology," *Kerygma and
Myth*, I, 8, 39, 40.

the contemporaries of Jesus as it is to modern man." [11] The point here is that we may not dispose of the resurrection of Jesus by attributing it to the naïve belief of a prescientific era. If we attempt to do this, we demonstrate our naïveté more than that of a past age.

In dealing with specific theories, we must first mention two theories that no longer claim the allegiance of any large group of critics. The first of these is a theory developed by some members of the History of Religions School. It was felt by these critics that the idea of the resurrection was an invention by primitive Christianity in order to place itself on a firmer competitive basis with other religions that had a god who died and rose again. The inadequacy of this theory, however, has been demonstrated by two observations: (1) None of these other deities with whom Christianity was supposed to have been in competition is to be located either historically or geographically as is Jesus. (2) Most of these deities functioned in relation to the annual calendar. That is, they died in the fall and rose in the spring. They were thus basically fertility cults. Jesus' resurrection, on the other hand, was a once-for-all event.[12] When these factors are considered, it becomes obvious that there is no basis for comparison.

A second theory, of lesser importance, attributes the idea of the origin of the resurrection to the fact that the disciples went to the wrong tomb. How something like this could have occurred is beyond the imagination of all but a few contemporary critics. But even if this were true, as Bruce has said, "The simplest thing for the Sanhedrin to do when the apostles began to proclaim the resurrection of Jesus was to organize conducted tours to the real tomb and show His body still lying there."[13]

Of theories that are more widely held, there are princi-

[11] Karl Jaspers, "Myth and Religion," in Karl Jaspers and Rudolf Bultmann, *Myth and Christianity* (New York: Noonday, 1958), p. 5.

[12] Howard Clark Kee and Franklin W. Young, *Understanding the New Testament* (Englewood Cliffs, N.J.: Prentice-Hall, 1960), p. 180.

[13] Bruce, *The Spreading Flame*, p. 65.

pally three. The first attempts to account for the resurrection on the basis of the idea that Jesus had not really died. He had merely slipped into a coma or some other such physical state, and after he was placed in the tomb he revived and subsequently left it. There are a number of objections that can be raised against any such theory: (1) It was the business of the Roman soldiers to make sure that death had occurred before they removed the victim from the cross. The piercing of Jesus' side recorded in Jn. 19:34 was to insure that death had taken place. Roman soldiers were accustomed to this technique and knew how to do it efficiently.[14]

(2) According to the record of Jn. 19:39-40, Joseph of Arimathea and Nicodemus embalmed the body of Jesus in accordance with the Jewish custom. (3) The stone in front of the tomb was not only of considerable size (Mk. 16:3), but was sealed to prevent any movement either from within or outside the tomb. (4) In addition to the stone itself a guard was placed before the tomb (Mt. 27:65-66). (5) The nature of the appearances of the risen Christ is another obstacle to this theory. As we have noted previously in this chapter, there were some characteristics of the body of Jesus after the resurrection that radically differentiated it from his prepassion body. If he had merely been revived, how are these differences to be accounted for? (6) Finally, what happened to Jesus after the forty days of his appearances? If the ascension is not an historical occurrence, as it would not be for those who deny the resurrection, how did Jesus completely disappear from the scene after this period? This is a great unanswered question for any theory of revival apart from resurrection.

A second theory attempts to rationalize the resurrection by stating that the body of Jesus was removed from the tomb either by friends or enemies. Of those who have held that the body was stolen by Jesus' friends, perhaps the most noteworthy is H. S. Reimarus. This theory

[14] R. V. G. Tasker, *The Gospel According to St. John* ("The Tyndale New Testament Commentaries"; Grand Rapids: Eerdmans, 1960), pp. 212-13.

shares with the previous theory the problem of the guard placed before the tomb. Furthermore, the agreement between the guards and the chief priests recorded in Mt. 28:11-15 indicates the bankruptcy of any attempt by the Jewish authorities to account for the resurrection on naturalistic bases. In addition, it must be questioned whether the early Church would have allowed a passage like the aforementioned to remain in its canon, were it not self-evident to all that such an explanation was perfectly ridiculous.

There is, however, an even greater obstacle to the theory that the body of Jesus was stolen by his friends. Here, as we have noticed earlier in connection with the question of the invention of miracles in the Gospel narratives, it would be necessary to suppose that the same disciples who stole the body of Jesus and invented the idea of the resurrection went to the corners of the then-known world proclaiming the message of his resurrection and finally died for their belief in it. Men have often been deceived and died for causes in the name of religion. But no considerable group of men has ever invented a religious tale and then laid down their lives for a belief in the historical truth of the tale.

The idea that the body of Jesus was taken from the tomb by his enemies has even less to commend it. The problem of getting the body out of the tomb would have been as great for them as for Jesus' friends. Furthermore, the only enemies that could possibly have done this would have been representatives of Judaism. If for some reason they could have stolen his body, and if they had desired to steal it—either possibility is difficult to imagine—any claim of Jesus' resurrection would have been quickly silenced by the production of the body.

The greatest number of critics who attempt to rationalize the resurrection, however, are found in the group that attempts to explain the resurrection on the basis of the subjective experience of the disciples. There are various names given to this class of rationalizations: vision, spiritual resurrection, the continuing impact of Jesus' personality, hallucination, etc. While there are shades of difference between these various theories, what we have to say here with regard to the vision theory bears equally on them all.

First of all, visions themselves may be conceived of in two senses. Some think of them primarily as due to the expectation of the recipient of the vision. By this sort of theory they are put primarily in the category of wish fulfilment. There is nothing supernatural about them. This is the way visions are thought of by the majority of critics who explain the resurrection in terms of vision. Others think of visions as one of the modes of God's special revelation. It is in this sense that visions are usually thought of in the Bible. They come not because of any precondition on the part of the recipient, but because God chooses to make known something of his will. On the grounds of what we have said earlier in this chapter in relation to Jesus' appearance to Paul, we feel justified in asserting that he had this latter kind of experience.

In the case of biblical critics who attempt to account for the visions on the basis of the subjective experiences of the disciples, however, there are a number of objections that may be raised: (1) None of the psychological conditions for the occurrence of such a phenomenon were present. In spite of Jesus' preparation of the disciples for his death, the idea of a suffering Messiah remained repulsive for them. Jesus' death was also the death of the hopes of the disciples. The comment of the disciples to Jesus on the road to Emmaus sums up their despair perfectly: "We *had hoped* that he was the one to redeem Israel" (Lk. 24:21). That hope was now gone.

(2) The idea that the spirit of Jesus could exist apart from his body is foreign to Jewish thought. As Kee and Young observe, "Jewish thinking rarely, if ever, portrays a separate, immaterial part of man, such as we usually mean when we speak of *soul* or *spirit*, as the enduring part of man in contrast to his mortal body. Except among the Essenes, it did not conceive of man as existing apart from his body."[15]

(3) The nature of the experiences of the disciples in

15 Kee and Young, p. 181.

their interaction with the risen Christ in the New Testament rules out the possibility of visions. Hepburn points this out: "If you are confronted with form, human facial expressions, gestures, a voice responsive in conversation (and the detailed resurrection narrative provides all these with respect to the risen Christ), then the possibilities of illusion . . . are enormously diminished."[16]

(4) The vision theory fails to account for the fact that the disciples touched Jesus' body, and it similarly fails to account for the fact that Jesus ate in their presence.

(5) The vision theory fails to account for the fact that on occasion Jesus holds conversations with some of his followers when they yet regard him as someone else. Thus the disciples on the road to Emmaus (Lk. 24) simply regard him as another traveler. And in Jn. 20, Mary regards him as the gardener and has conversation with him before his true identity is revealed.

(6) Then, of course, the problem of the empty tomb remains for any advocate of the vision theory. If the disciples had started to proclaim the resurrection of Jesus on the basis of their subjective experience, it would have been a simple matter for the Jewish authorities to go to the tomb and produce the body. This would have stopped all such proclamation, but obviously they could not do this.

(7) Finally, the resurrection appearances occurred to an ever widening group of people for a period of forty days, and thereafter they did not recur. If they were subjective experiences, why did they not continue?

On the basis of our examination of all these attempts at rationalizing the resurrection, it must be concluded that not one of them may be maintained without doing violence to the New Testament accounts as we have them. We find ourselves back in precisely the condition we described in the first chapter of this study. What justifies picking and choosing? If we refuse to take the self-witness of the record with all seriousness, why not give it up and adopt a position of absolute skepticism?

Most of these attempts at rationalizing the resurrection

16 Hepburn, *Christianity and Paradox*, p. 101.

are based in part on the Gospels. We should also look briefly at the book of Acts and the writings of Paul as a demonstration that nothing other than a literal resurrection can account for the phenomenon of the early Church. Daniel Fuller has done much to establish this fact. He writes,

> A consideration of Luke's argument for the resurrection of Jesus shows that it is just as impossible to deny his resurrection as it is to deny the existence of Julius Caesar. How can the historical fact of Christianity's mission to the Gentiles and its origin in Judaism be explained unless we include the resurrection of Christ? Apart from Christ's resurrection, these two historical facts remain an insoluble riddle, for how could the Jews of that day admit Gentiles to a place of equal standing apart from supernatural intervention? To try to explain this without reference to the resurrection is as hopeless as trying to explain Roman history without reference to Julius Caesar.[17]

Similarly, elsewhere in his book Fuller points out that Paul's leadership of the mission to the Gentiles cannot be explained on the grounds of either (1) his continued loyalty to Judaism apart from any connection with Jesus, for then there would have been no motivation for him to go to the Gentiles; or (2) his revolt against Judaism, for then he would not have remained a loyal Jew as the New Testament pictures him to have done. It therefore turns out that the only explanation sufficient to account for Paul's leadership in the mission is that Christ appeared to him.[18]

We shall consider one other matter here in connection with rationalizations of the resurrection. While Bultmann shows no primary interest in attempts at rationalization due to his interest in the kerygma, he admits the possibility of such attempts and then proceeds to allegorize the resurrection. A paragraph from his thematic essay is particularly significant here and for that reason we quote it in full:

> The real Easter faith is faith in the word of preaching which brings illumination. If the event of Easter Day is in any sense

17 Daniel Fuller, pp. 258-59.
18 *Ibid.*, p. 245.

an historical event additional to the event of the cross, it is nothing else than the rise of faith in the risen Lord, since it was this faith which led to the apostolic preaching. The resurrection itself is not an event of past history. All that historical criticism can establish is the fact that the first disciples came to believe in the resurrection. The historian can perhaps to some extent account for that faith from the personal intimacy which the disciples had enjoyed with Jesus during his earthly life, and so reduce the resurrection appearances to a series of subjective visions. But the historical problem is not of interest to Christian belief in the resurrection. For the historical event of the rise of the Easter faith means for us what it meant for the first disciples—namely, the self-attestation of the risen Lord, the act of God in which the redemptive event of the cross is completed.[19]

The critical school has thus resorted to two techniques to dispose of the resurrection of Jesus—rationalization and allegory. While we have dealt at greater length with the former here, we shall treat the latter in the next chapter. It is sufficient here to note that neither from the perspective of interpretation nor from that of theology is either one of these devices acceptable to the conservative theologian.

Resurrection and History

The real question we must face here is, Was the resurrection of Jesus an historical event? Our answer will depend in part on the way we define "historical." Considered from certain perspectives it cannot be considered historical. The reader who has traveled with us this far in our study will realize that the term "historical" has a rather definite meaning to modern students of history. It has to do with the critical reconstruction of the events of the past—with the process by which the historian separates truth from error in arriving at what really happened. In his attempt to arrive at these facts the historian has two chief principles by which he operates. The first of these is continuity. By this the historian means that history must be explained on the basis of cause and

[19] Bultmann, "New Testament and Mythology," p. 42.

effect. Difficult and complex as this may become, the historian will not rest until he has arrived at the interpretation of an event that makes sense from the perspective of causation. The other chief principle at the disposal of the historian is analogy. He attempts to interpret the event on which his attention is concentrated in terms of similar events in the history of mankind about which he knows more.

Ladd has pointed out that if this is the perspective from which we consider the historicity of the resurrection, our answer will be negative. We cannot arrive at a positive answer to the question of the historicity of the resurrection via the means of historical causation or historical analogy, for the resurrection considered from either of these perceptives is absolutely unique.[20]

There is a second sense in which the historicity of the resurrection may be denied. Cairns has pointed this out: "If the word 'historical' be defined in the quite singular sense that an event cannot be declared historical unless it was public to all, and demonstrable even to the sceptic, then the resurrection was not historical."[21]

If, however, by "historical" we simply mean a happening of the past that took place in time and space, the resurrection of Jesus may certainly be classified as historical. There is a great deal of evidence to support this contention. The biblical and extrabiblical evidence at our disposal points uniformly to its occurrence. The inability of critics to offer a defensible alternative to its occurrence which would adequately explain all the New Testament evidence points to its occurrence. The only basic reason for denying it from this perspective is to be found in a metaphysical presupposition that such an event is impossible.

To avoid a conflict over the meaning of the term "historical," it is perhaps best to adopt the term "suprahistorical," as Ladd does, to describe the resurrection. By this he means that in the resurrection we have the entrance into the realm of human history of a new mode of

[20] Ladd, p. 279.
[21] Cairns, *A Gospel Without Myth?*, p. 159.

existence. It cannot be explained in terms of continuity and analogy. Ladd writes, "The resurrection is an objective event which took place *within history;* but, in the modern definition of the term, it is not an 'historical' but a supra-historical event."[22]

It may not be obvious to all why it is important that we insist that the resurrection was an event that occurred within human history. Simply put, the reason is the same as that which causes us to insist on the historicity of the entire life of Jesus. Yet, while many modern theologians are willing to accept the historicity of the largest portion of that life, they hesitate with respect to the resurrection. No one has pointed up the fallacy of this position better than James Stewart: "What some present-day theologies do not understand is this—that the docetic tendency which they themselves would disown as heresy when it touches the Cross cannot suddenly become respectable as an interpretation of the Resurrection."[23]

Resurrection and Faith

As we have studied the relationship of history to faith and miracles to faith in the last two chapters, we must now study the relationship of the resurrection to faith. Braaten asks the crucial question in the introduction to Kähler's book: "When the apostles proclaimed the resurrection event, was the primal datum of their preaching something which had happened to Jesus, or was it something which had happened to themselves?"[24] To ask the question in a slightly different form, Was the resurrection an objective fact of past history, or was it an evidence of faith on the part of the disciples? Bultmann takes the position that it is an article of faith:

> Cross and resurrection form a single, indivisible cosmic event which brings judgment to the world and opens up for men the

[22] Ladd, p. 279.

[23] James S. Stewart, *A Faith to Proclaim* (New York: Scribner, 1953), p. 109.

[24] Kähler, *The So-Called Historical Jesus and the Historic Biblical Christ*, p. 15.

possibility of authentic life. But if that be so, the resurrection cannot be a miraculous proof capable of demonstration and sufficient to convince the sceptic that the cross really has the cosmic and eschatological significance ascribed to it.

. . . .

The resurrection is itself an article of faith, and you cannot establish one article of faith by invoking another.

. . . .

We cannot buttress our own faith in the resurrection by that of the first disciples and so eliminate the element of risk which faith in the resurrection always involves.[25]

But while the above construction may be desirable from a philosophical perspective, it is diametrically opposed to the New Testament presentation. Bultmann is saying the same thing here that he says in relation to miracles and the history of Jesus in general. If the resurrection could be demonstrated as an historical fact, faith would be made impossible. There would be no longer any need to believe. But Paul says, "If Christ has not been raised, your faith is futile and you are still in your sins" (I Cor. 15:17). Thielicke has observed, "The encounter with which Bultmann is concerned does not cause faith in the resurrection: the resurrection is the cause of an encounter with Christ. . . . Just as the Old Testament can only be understood and can only become an encounter in the light of the fact of Christ, so too the life of Jesus makes sense only in the light of the resurrection, and only so can it become an encounter."[26]

Here, once again, we must consider the significance of the resurrection in the New Testament from an evidential point of view. As Jesus used his miraculous powers sparingly and with a certain amount of reticence, so it is with the resurrection appearances. He did not go to the temple court after his resurrection to proclaim his significance. He appeared to enough people to erase any doubts

[25] Bultmann, "New Testament and Mythology," pp. 39, 40, 42.

[26] Helmut Thielicke, "The Restatement of New Testament Mythology," *Kerygma and Myth*, I, ed. Hans Werner Bartsch, trans. Reginald H. Fuller (London: S. P. C. K., 1964), p. 154.

that he had really risen, but, with the exception of Paul (and, as we have previously noted, this appearance has certain unique features about it in the history of divine revelation), the appearances of Jesus were limited to those who had known him and fellowshiped with him. As in the case of the miracles in general, so in the case of the resurrection, Jesus showed no desire to bludgeon anyone into faith in him.

So it is in the New Testament era itself. Men are presented with the evidence of Jesus' resurrection and still will not believe. Can it be supposed, for example, that King Agrippa in Acts 26 was in doubt about the historical truth of the resurrection? He not only had the testimony of Paul, but he was in the very area where the event had transpired, and certainly could have checked the truthfulness of the occurrence of the event. So also the Jews did not lack evidence for the occurrence of the event, but they were determined not to believe.

The presentation of the evidence is one thing, but its acceptance is another. Here again the New Testament position is that one's ability to accept the evidence is the result of a special work of the Holy Spirit. To some people in the New Testament era, the mere proclamation of the message was all that the Holy Spirit needed to bring them to faith. To others, the evidence of the resurrection was the means the Spirit used to arouse that faith. Does not Paul have in mind this latter kind of appeal as he writes I Cor. 15?

The remarks of Bruce form a fitting conclusion to our discussion not only of the resurrection, but also of the entire life of Jesus as we have discussed it in this and the two preceding chapters:

> That a man should rise from the dead after three days is, as we have said, certainly improbable; but we are not concerned here with *a* man, but with *this* man. There are many other things recorded of this man which in isolation are equally improbable—His virginal conception, His life and works—but in Him all these improbabilities coincide. Does the coincidence of improbabilities amount to sheer impossibility, so that we conclude the picture is a cunningly wrought invention? Or is the picture that of God incarnate, in whom the "improbabilities"

coincide like a threefold cord that is not quickly broken? That
God incarnate should enter human life by a unique way
("conceived of the Holy Ghost and born of the Virgin Mary,"
as the ancient creed says) is not improbable, but perfectly
fitting. That God incarnate should live a life of perfect holiness, marked by works of miraculous power and teaching of
pre-eminent wisdom, is not improbable, but just what we
should expect. That God incarnate should *die*—there is something in the highest degree amazing. Die he did, none the less;
but this was not the end. When we have seen this act in the
drama of our salvation, we wait breathlessly for the sequel,
and greet it as something divinely natural: this is the one
"whom God raised up, loosing the bonds of death, because it
was not possible that death should hold him fast."[27]

[27] Bruce, *The Spreading Flame,* p. 69.

CHAPTER FIVE

The Importance of Mythology

Biblical Language and Science

While the word "myth" had been used by many in biblical studies prior to the time of Bultmann, were it not for his work the term would never have achieved the importance that it has in contemporary critical thought. It is, as a consequence, with the thought of Bultmann that we shall have to deal primarily in this chapter.

Of the many statements by Bultmann that could be taken to illustrate his position, the following is only representative: "All our thinking to-day is shaped irrevocably by modern science. A blind acceptance of the New Testament mythology would be arbitrary...."[1] Bultmann's thinking in this regard could perhaps be summarized in three statements: (1) Modern man's view of the world is determined by modern science; (2) the world view of the New Testament is determined by mythology; (3) therefore, if modern man is to accept the New Testament in any sense, he must accept it minus the mythology contained therein.

Although we have discussed the question of modern science in our chapter on miracle, we need to press the issue a step further by an analysis of the biblical language as it relates to what we call science. Only after we have

[1] Bultmann, "New Testament and Mythology," *Kerygma and Myth*, I, 3-4.

done this will we be able to evaluate the importance of mythology as it relates to the New Testament. Of all the works that have appeared in the past few decades relative to the question of biblical language and science, one of the finest, in our opinion, is the book by Bernard Ramm.[2] In his book Ramm makes four observations relative to biblical language in its reference to natural things: (1) "The language of the Bible in reference to natural matters is popular, not scientific."[3] He notes that the word "popular" means "of the people," while the word "scientific" refers to the technical speech developed by scientists whereby they may communicate with one another more efficiently. Because the Bible is a book directed to all the people, it is illegitimate for us to find the particular scientific view of any age or any people in its contents. One must not expect "a popular treatise to speak the language of science,"[4] and one must not ask the Bible to "speak that which it does not propose to say."[5]

(2) "The language of the Bible is phenomenal. By phenomenal we mean 'pertaining to appearances.' "[6] He goes on to illustrate this by showing how the biblical writers describe things from the point of view of their observation. We do the same thing in our day when we refer to "every corner of the earth," the rising and setting of the sun, etc.[7]

(3) "The language of the Bible is non-postulational in reference to natural things. By this we mean that the Bible does not theorize as to the actual nature of things."[8] Here, once again, the biblical view is confined to the popular and phenomenal view of things.

(4) "The language of the Bible employs the culture of

2 Bernard Ramm, *The Christian View of Science and Scripture* (Grand Rapids: Eerdmans, 1954).

3 *Ibid.*, p. 66.

4 *Ibid.*, p. 67.

5 *Ibid.*

6 *Ibid.*

7 *Ibid.*, pp. 67-69.

8 *Ibid.*, p. 69.

the times in which it was written as the medium of revelation."[9] Ramm feels we need to guard against two kinds of errors here. One is the view of the radical critic who feels that the Bible is filled with the errors of its cultural period. An adequate view of inspiration guards against this. A second kind of error is that of those who expect the Bible to contain modern science. It makes no pretension in this regard.[10]

After he has developed this third observation at greater length, Ramm notes for us three advantages that result from this view of the Bible with reference to natural things:

(1) Because the language is popular and non-postulational it forms a *meaningful* revelation. . . . (2) Although the Bible is not in scientific language it is not *anti-scientific* language. It is *prescientific* language. . . . (3) Because the Bible uses pre-scientific terms it is a Bible for all ages and is adapted to all stages of human progress.[11]

The relationship of thought similar to this to the question of mythology has led George Ernest Wright to observe, "The revelation of God occurred within the conceptual life of the people then. Yet the absence of a modern scientific view of the universe scarcely makes the literature in itself mythology."[12]

In light of these observations, it is questionable whether Bultmann's setting up of the "modern world view" against the "New Testament world view" has any validity. We need only review what the critics of Bultmann have pointed out. Jaspers levels two criticisms at Bultmann here: (1) He challenges his implied assertion that there is *a* modern world view; and (2) he notes that if Bultmann is talking in the more restricted sense of modern science, he still is in trouble, because if modern science says anything in this regard, it says that such a

[9] *Ibid.*, p. 70.

[10] *Ibid.*

[11] *Ibid.*, pp. 76-77.

[12] G. Ernest Wright, *God Who Acts* (London: S.C.M., 1952), p. 128.

comprehensive world view as Bultmann pretends to present us with is impossible.[13]

Just as Bultmann has been attacked from his left with respect to his idea of the modern world view, so also he has been attacked from his right. Walter Künneth has criticized Bultmann for the confusion of a "world view" with a "world picture." Thus the same world picture is subject to being interpreted in terms of a number of world views.[14] We might put his criticism in terms of the description that Ramm has given us by saying that what the New Testament gives us as popular, phenomenal, and nonpostulational, Bultmann interprets as being scientific and theoretical. Künneth's second criticism of Bultmann is that the three-storied world which Bultmann pictures at the base of the biblical representation is nonexistent when one examines the records more carefully.[15]

Myth in Contemporary Theological Thought

We now come more specifically to the question of mythology on the contemporary theological scene. It would appear that there are three main positions in this regard. Let us look at each of them.

Myth is contained in the New Testament, and it must be eliminated

This, of course, is the position of Bultmann. The New Testament is constructed on the basis of the mythology of Jewish Apocalyptic and Gnosticism. As a part of this mythology we have such things as a three-storied world with heaven above and hell beneath, miracles, angels and demons, orthodox Christology, the biblical idea of sin, temporal eschatology, etc. These ideas are completely alien to the modern mind; therefore, if the kerygma of the

[13] Jaspers, *Myth and Christianity*, pp. 5-6.

[14] Walter Künneth, "Bultmann's Philosophy and the Reality of Salvation," *Kerygma and History*, ed. and trans. Carl E. Braaten and Roy A. Harrisville (Nashville: Abingdon, 1962), p. 103.

[15] *Ibid.*

New Testament is to be made acceptable to modern man, it must be stripped from this mythological framework.

Our evaluation of this conception of the biblical record must await our analysis of the third position. We merely note here the concern of the new quest with respect to the position of Bultmann. It has been one of its basic concerns that a connection be established between the Jesus of history and the Christ of faith in order that the whole New Testament may not be dissolved into a myth.[16] There is real danger that this is where the position of Bultmann might ultimately lead.

Myth is contained in the New Testament, and it must be retained

Karl Jaspers is perhaps the most noteworthy representative of this position. Critics who hold this position usually base their contention on one or a combination of three observations: (1) Some of these critics feel that scientific language is inadequate to express what the language of myth gives us. The language of science has to do with empirical data. It deals with historical facts and tends to organize things in terms of sequence and causality. For these reasons, it tends to view reality in a mechanistic way. It cannot deal with the question of metaphysics or, as Wright says, with "the dimension of depth in human experience, of beginning and ending, and of the 'beyond' which transcends experience. The only way the human mind has to deal with these deeper meanings in and beyond present experience is to draw upon intuition and imagination and present pictures, use metaphors, and tell stories."[17]

(2) This leads to a second observation by those who insist that myth must be retained. Although scientific language is not equipped to handle the deeper issues of human experience, mythical language is. As Jaspers observes, "It is the language of a reality that is not empirical, but existential, whereas our mere empirical existence

[16] Daniel Fuller, *Easter Faith and History*, p. 140.
[17] Wright, p. 118.

tends continually to be lost in the empirical, as though the latter were all of reality."[18] Myth, therefore, from this point of view, is the language of experience. It is the means by which the truths of faith are communicated. But even those who advocate the necessity of myth from this point of view argue that myths must not be interpreted as historical and scientific truths, but only as existential truth.

(3) A third observation by those who insist on the necessity of myth is one that asserts the necessity of myth for men of any age. Critics who argue this point out that there is behind the argument of Bultmann the implication that modern man can exist solely on the basis of the rational and the scientific. Yet, as Wright has pointed out, mythmaking has been just as characteristic of our age as it has been of any other. He points to the mythology of communism and its great idea of a classless society. And for those of us who like to look on it with disdain, there is the necessity that we look at the great Western myth and its idea of progress. Behind it lies the naïve faith that man will redeem himself in the historical process.[19] These three observations cause some contemporary critics to argue for the presence and necessity of myth in the New Testament record.

There is an element of truth, we believe, in what these writers are saying, but it is unfortunate that they have retained the word "myth" to describe the element for which they contend. The real inadequacy of this term will fully appear when we consider the third position with respect to the place of mythology in the New Testament. Here we merely make some observations from the point of view of terminology. Later we shall deal more fully with the concept of myth.

If God was to give man a meaningful revelation of his person and will, it was necessary for him to condescend to the level of man's understanding. Inasmuch as special revelation, if it was to have any effect upon man, had to be intelligible to him, God chose to reveal himself via

18 Jaspers, p. 17.
19 Wright, p. 122.

concepts and ideas that could be understood by man. This is what Ramm refers to as the anthropic character of special revelation.[20]   God used man's vocabulary and man's conceptual framework. Sometimes the anthropic character of that revelation becomes very specific, in which case we have anthropomorphisms. In other instances it becomes more abstract. Since this is so, it would be far better for us to speak of the language of the New Testament as being metaphorical, analogical, or figurative than it would be for us to call it mythical. The word "myth" has an origin and connotation that is far different from these other terms, as we shall soon see.

The figurative language of the Bible is thus designed to give man a glimpse of the transcendent. Is this not what Paul was thinking of when he wrote I Cor. 13? "For our knowledge is imperfect and our prophecy is imperfect; but when the perfect comes, the imperfect will pass away" (vv. 9-10). And later in the same chapter, "Now we see in a mirror dimly, but then face to face. Now I know in part; then I shall understand fully, even as I have been fully understood" (v. 12).

We may make both a negative and a positive observation with regard to this metaphorical language. Negatively, we should be warned against taking any given metaphorical expression and wringing it dry, so to speak, to the exclusion of other metaphors. Positively, we may be assured of the truth any particular metaphor presents us with by comparing it with other metaphors. If Jesus had only called himself "the door," for example, contemporary man would have been in great doubt as to what feature or characteristic of a door Jesus compared himself to. But in addition to calling himself the door, Jesus called himself the vine, the good shepherd, the bread of life, the water of life, etc. When we take all of these metaphors in combination with his more literal statements and his life as it is portrayed for us in the Gospels, what Jesus was talking of when he called himself the door becomes much more evident to us.

Thus metaphorical language is the only way in which

[20] Ramm, *Special Revelation and the Word of God*, p. 36.

God could have given man a meaningful revelation. We cannot do without these metaphors. Our endeavor should be to make clear what they mean. The real task for the contemporary biblical scholar is therefore one of translation, not one of demythologization. As Künneth says, "The concepts and pictorial ideas of the New Testament are indissociably connected with what they express. They do not need demythologizing, but only translation into the language and conceptual world of any given time." [21]

If Bultmann had considered this feature of New Testament language and expression, he would never have run into the trap he did in his thematic essay and subsequent works where he points to the "contradictions" in the New Testament as an illustration of its need for demythologization. [22] How any serious Bible student, for example, can regard the fact that in some places the New Testament interprets Jesus as the Messiah, and in other places interprets him as the Second Adam as an evidence of contradiction, is difficult to imagine.

Myth is not found in the New Testament

Those who hold this position assert that myth in its essence is something completely foreign to the New Testament. That this is the proper position can be demonstrated by the nature of myth itself. We shall develop our position here on the basis of three observations about the idea of myth: (1) Myth is characteristic of polytheistic religions and nature worship. Here nature, man, and the gods all form part of a continuum on which life is acted out. We have not in the New Testament the folk-literature of such a society in which all of nature is alive. It is therefore with great justification that Wright complains of the appropriation of this term, rooted in polytheism as it is, by modern theologians as a description of what we have in our Bible. [23]

(2) Myth in these polytheistic religions has no basic

---

[21] Künneth, p. 115.
[22] Bultmann, "New Testament and Mythology," p. 11.
[23] Wright, p. 125.

interest in history. It is connected either to the annual cycle of life, or in certain instances to a cyclical view of history which is a mere extension of the idea of the annual cycle. In this kind of society myth could offer some interpretation of what went on. This, however, is not true of the biblical faith.

(3) Myth, in its connection with polytheism, is man's effort to understand God. It is man's quest for an expression of the meaning of God. In the New Testament the emphasis of the thrust moves in the other direction. It is the effort by God to make himself known to man.

When these features of myth have been carefully considered, it should at once be obvious that the New Testament cannot possibly be put in the same class with the literature of mythology. Here, once again, the biblical view and presentation of history sound the death knell of any attempt to interpret it as mythology. Human history is taken seriously in the Bible. It is the vehicle through which God has chosen to reveal himself to man. History had a beginning. It has moved through a series of meaningful epochs in which God has progressively revealed more of himself and of his requirements to mankind, climaxed in the offering of his Son. It moves toward a culmination in which time will be no more. This is as diametrically opposed to the idea of myth as it can be.

In addition to this general incompatibility of the idea of myth with that of the historical presentation of the New Testament, the word "myth" itself is used on four occasions in the New Testament, always in the sense of an untruth or fancy in comparison with what has been received from God in Christ (I Tim. 1:4; 4:7; II Tim. 4:4; II Pet. 1:16).

Hughes makes a significant observation on this use of myth in the New Testament: "This is in complete harmony with the classical connotation of the term which from the time of Pindar onwards always bears the sense of what is fictitious, as opposed to the term *logos*, which indicated what was true and historical."[24]

[24] Philip Edgcumbe Hughes, "Myth," *Baker's Dictionary of Theology*, ed. Everett F. Harrison (Grand Rapids: Baker, 1960), p. 368.

Bultmann and his supporters are not ignorant of this judgment of myth by the New Testament writers. They do not accept this, however, as a final verdict on the question of mythology in the New Testament. Born-kamm is quick to come to Bultmann's defense in this regard:

> The New Testament message itself can be and is understood as a kind of demythologizing, but the problem remaining for us is obviously rooted in the fact that not even the demythologizing carried out in the New Testament encounters us apart from a mythological mode of conception. Where this fact is over-looked, it is difficult to see how one can avoid the danger of changing the sphere of biblical revelation into a kind of shelter and quarantine which must be a priori set off limits, which no longer allows critical observation. In that case, our quest for truth, as the destiny and task of thought, can no longer be seriously undertaken, and the believer or the one called to faith would also have to doff everything which otherwise belonged to his ordinary equipment of life lest the objects of his observation suffer harm.[25]

In reference to statements like the above we make three comments: (1) There is here, as well as in other writings of similar character, the use of the terms "myth" and "mythological" apart from any specific definition of what the word means. If the word were carefully ana-lyzed as to its origin and meaning, its tangency to the biblical record would be demonstrated to be nonexistent. (2) The New Testament statements on myth are not seriously taken. The presence of these passages is admit-ted, but their force is denied. (3) Here, as has so often been the case in our study, special revelation is effectively disposed of. The intellect of man is sufficient.

Mythology and Existentialist Interpretation

Let us here take a step back to the era of the liberal lives of Jesus in order to understand the rise of demythol-

[25] Günther Bornkamm, "Myth and Gospel: A Discussion of the Problem of Demythologizing the New Testament Message," *Keryg-ma and History*, ed. and trans. Carl E. Braaten and Roy A. Harrisville (Nashville: Abingdon, 1962), p. 180.

ogization. The liberal scholars were confident that they could separate the kernel from the husk in the biblical record and thus arrive at what was of lasting significance in its account. It will be recalled that the Jesus they presented us was similar to a nineteenth-century humanist gentleman. On the basis of the observations of some of the critics, of whom Schweitzer and Kähler were particularly important, it was demonstrated that such attempts to trace Jesus' life were based more on current idealist philosophy than on the Gospel records. It thus became obvious to large segments of the critical school that such a quest ought to be abandoned.

With the rise of form criticism and existentialism, a new approach to the Gospel records was undertaken. As we have contended elsewhere in this study, form criticism should be understood in its relationship to existentialism. To be sure, Bultmann, to take the primary example, developed his existentialist thought to greater lengths after he had undertaken his form-critical investigation, but at the roots of form criticism itself lies existentialism. The basic difference therefore between the liberal lives of Jesus and the work of Bultmann and his successors is to be found not primarily in historical techniques or in improved methods of literary analysis, but in a different point of philosophical departure. The liberals were idealists; Bultmann and his disciples are existentialists. Neither of these philosophies goes well with the biblical record from an historical point of view. Idealism had a naïve view of progress in human history. Existentialism has no concept of history in the linear, biblical sense at all.

Because a literal interpretation of the New Testament did not go well with existentialist philosophy, it was necessary to view it in some other than a literal, historical sense. At this point the idea of myth was seized upon. The wedding of mythology and existentialism was a very happy one. Neither of these modes of thought had any interest in the linear concept of history. Both of them allowed the interpreter to pour into the biblical message such content as he desired. Let us notice some of the results of this alliance.

Pre-eminence of modern man

While the unaided competence of man in matters of religion has been assumed by large segments of the critical school ever since the time of the Enlightenment, the confidence in his ability to know the truth apart from special revelation has never been more confidently expressed than in the work of Bultmann and his followers. The "event of Christ" is necessary, to be certain, but beyond that nebulous event man has all he needs. Thus Bultmann's prior understanding becomes the basis of the construction of his hermeneutical system. One's own experience becomes the infallible guide to what is possible. Let us notice the result that this has on Bultmann's treatment of the New Testament in his thematic essay:

> There is no longer any heaven in the traditional sense of the word.[26]

> We can no longer look for the return of the Son of Man on the clouds of heaven or hope that the faithful will meet him in the air.[27]

> Now that the forces and laws of nature have been discovered, we can no longer believe in spirits, whether good or evil.[28]

> The miracles of the New Testament have ceased to be miraculous, . . . [29]

> To attribute human mortality to the fall of Adam is sheer nonsense, . . . [30]

> The same objections apply to the doctrine of the atonement. How can the guilt of one man be expiated by the death of another who is sinless—if indeed one may speak of a sinless man at all?[31]

> The resurrection of Jesus is just as difficult for modern man. . . . Quite apart from the incredibility of such a miracle,

[26] Bultmann, "New Testament and Mythology," p. 4.
[27] *Ibid.*
[28] *Ibid.*
[29] *Ibid.*, p. 5.
[30] *Ibid.*, p. 7.
[31] *Ibid.*

he cannot see how an event like this could be the act of God, or how it could affect his own life.[32]

This is only representative of the way in which Bultmann in this essay and elsewhere decides what may be accepted—or rather, what must be rejected. Only what modern man can accept may be retained. Everything else must be treated as mythology and disposed of. The depraved human intellect is put on the throne of God.

Biblical and theological results

The first and basic result of this approach to the New Testament is that history ceases to be important. The consequences of this for the gospel are catastrophic, for if we strip the gospel of its history we strip it of its substance.

As a corollary of the elimination of history in the usual biblical sense, there is the elevation of the individual to the place of supreme importance. Everything is viewed in terms of man's existential experience. Now, to be certain, the history of divine revelation has been vitally concerned with man—otherwise what was its purpose? But to place the experience of the individual over and above that history, or rather to replace that history with the experience of the individual, is not in any sense biblical. As Ellwein says, "As certain as it is that all the theological and christological statements of the Bible are oriented to the *pro me*, it is equally certain that this *pro me* rests upon the rock of the *extra me*."[33]

Because of Bultmann's extreme emphasis on the individual, elements in the New Testament that are not commodious to existentialist interpretation are in effect eliminated. We shall speak of two large blocks of this material in a moment, but here we may notice the absence of such doctrines as the providence of God, the corporate idea of the Church, the significance of redemption in any other than a highly individualistic sense, etc.

[32] *Ibid.*, p. 8.
[33] Ellwein, "Rudolf Bultmann's Interpretation of the Kerygma," *Kerygma and History*, p. 38.

The two large blocks of material that are the most violently handled in this regard are the doctrines of creation and eschatology. Everything is poured into the present in this mode of interpretation. The past and the future are effectively eliminated except for a certain allegorical sense in which they are retained. At this point we feel that Ellwein asks the important question: "Is it not a matter of concern when the past and future references of the biblical proclamation are so nullified, emptied, and dissolved by an existential-dialectical interpretation of the aorist and future tenses that they coincide to the point of virtual identity with the event of preaching and with the decision of faith, and only exist in that manner and place?"[34]

When the subjectivity of the interpreter is allowed such a range of freedom, the end result will be precisely what he desires. We shall discuss this feature of demythologization at greater length shortly.

The raising of individual experience to the place of supreme importance and the attendant degradation of history has resulted in the replacing of theology with anthropology. The doctrine of God and the doctrine of man both have their proper place in any theological system, but as the word "theology" suggests, any system of beliefs with respect to the relation of the human to the divine must properly start with God. While we cannot and must not deny the interrelationship of these two entities, we must never forget which of the two is the primary. From this perspective it must be seriously questioned whether Bultmann's demythologization and existentialist interpretation is not in itself an elaborate myth. It is an effort on his part to get control of God rather than to understand God—or to create God after the image of man.

If we are to place the credit for this reversing of the order of importance in the anthropology of Bultmann, we must place it at the door of the biblically alien philosophical system that gave it birth—existentialism. Walter Künneth makes four important points in this regard:

34 *Ibid.*, p. 40.

(1) There is in Bultmann the preservation of Christian terminology, but a completely different content is given to this terminology. Christ becomes an ideogram. The cross, the resurrection, the atonement, etc. express only processes going on in the individual consciousness. [35] (2) Further, Bultmann divorces Christian terminology not only from its traditional meaning, but also from its historical setting. Künneth writes, "For example, what does sin mean for Bultmann? It is philosophical knowledge concerning the lostness, the fall from authenticity, from the authentic being of man."[36] (3) Because of the rationalistic and philosophical point of departure of Bultmann's theology, his system, like most others that are philosophically based, becomes a collection of timeless truths with no necessary historical connection: "The Christian words and concepts such as 'Christ,' 'love,' 'faith,' 'forgiveness,' 'eschatology,' et cetera, become timeless symbols of a universal truth."[37] Such an interpretation, while it might do for a rationalistic philosophical system, is manifestly unsatisfactory from the point of view of an historically based revelation of God. (4) As a consequence, the stage has been set for the complete divorce of anthropology from any Christian connection at all. This is precisely what has happened in the case of Bultmann's student, Wilhelm Kamlah.[38]

It cannot be too strongly emphasized how far-reaching an effect the theology of demythologization has on the orthodox doctrines of the New Testament. Hughes summarizes it for us: "He [Bultmann] accordingly finds it necessary to discard such obviously (on his premises) mythical elements as Christ's pre-existence and virgin birth, his deity and sinlessness, the substitutionary nature of his death as meeting the demands of a righteous God, his resurrection and ascension, and his future return in glory, also the final judgment of the world, the existence of spirit-beings, the personality and power of the Holy

[35] Künneth, pp. 110-11.
[36] *Ibid.*, p. 111.
[37] *Ibid.*, pp. 111-12.
[38] *Ibid.*, p. 112.

Spirit, the doctrines of the Trinity, of original sin, and of death as a consequence of sin, and every explanation of events as miraculous."[39]

In various places in the New Testament the gospel is referred to as an "offense" or "stumbling-block" (*skandalon*). Bultmann interprets this as meaning that the events there contained are subject to historical investigation and yet for faith are at the same time "eschatological phenomena."[40] But on at least one occasion Paul has in mind the very kind of inventiveness and unwillingness to take Gospel history at face value that characterizes the theology of demythologization: "We preach Christ crucified, a stumbling-block to Jews and folly to Gentiles, but to those who are called, both Jews and Greeks, Christ the power of God and the wisdom of God" (I Cor. 1:23-24).

In our introductory chapter we discussed briefly the subject of interpretation of the text. The conclusion we reached there with respect to interpretation was that both from the point of view of sense, and from that of the history of the Church, the only method of interpretation that has proved its worth has been the literal method. One would have thought that this issue would have been settled for all time in theological circles. But the invasion of modern existentialism into the biblical field has resulted in the rebirth of one of the oldest and least adequate means of interpretation known—allegorical interpretation. Most writers do not have the courage to face the issue as honestly as Jaspers does: "True piety, as a matter of course, eliminates the materialistic, magical, and utilitarian misuse of literal interpretation."[41]

There is even an attempt to avoid the use of the word "allegory." Yet it cannot be denied that much of what goes by the name of existentialist interpretation is allegory pure and simple. Bultmann even deals with the subject of allegory in a disparaging way in his thematic essay: "This method spiritualizes the mythical events so that they become symbols of processes going on in the

39 Hughes, p. 369.
40 Bultmann, "New Testament and Mythology," p. 44.
41 Jaspers, p. 19.

soul. This is certainly the most comfortable way of avoiding the critical question. The literal meaning is allowed to stand and is dispensed with only for the individual believer, who can escape into the realm of the soul."[42]

Yet in the same work in which he makes this statement, we find statements like the following:

> The old quest for visible security, the hankering after tangible realities, and the clinging to transitory objects, is sin, for by it we shut out invisible reality from our lives and refuse God's future which comes to us as a gift.[43]

> The last judgment is no longer an imminent cosmic event, for it is already taking place in the coming of Jesus and in his summons to believe.[44]

> The Spirit does not work like a supernatural force, nor is it the permanent possession of the believer. It is the possibility of a new life which must be appropriated by a deliberate resolve.[45]

> The resurrection itself is not an event of past history. . . . For the historical event of the rise of the Easter faith means for us what it meant for the disciples—namely, the self-attestation of the risen Lord, the act of God in which the redemptive event of the cross is completed.[46]

> Through the word of preaching the cross and the resurrection are made present: the eschatological "now" is here, . . . [47]

It is difficult to see how the above citations can escape the charge of allegory.

We have thus in existentialist interpretation the return of a device which Philo did so much to popularize, which through Origen and his successors entered into Christian biblical interpretation, and which shackled biblical interpretation to a very large degree until the era of the Reformation. The great fault of this kind of interpreta-

[42] Bultmann, "New Testament and Mythology," p. 13.
[43] *Ibid.*, p. 19.
[44] *Ibid.*, p. 20.
[45] *Ibid.*, p. 22.
[46] *Ibid.*, p. 42.
[47] *Ibid.*

tion has been pointed out by Ramm: "The fallacy of allegorical interpretation is that it is reading into Scripture the views already held by exegetes, rather than the discovery of the world view and system of values held by the writers of Scripture."[48]   Allegory is thus the means whereby the New Testament is made into a textbook of existentialism by those who would demythologize the New Testament.

Because we have already touched on the subject of interpretation in Ch. 1, and because the subject of biblical interpretation as a whole is beyond the scope of our study here except insofar as we encounter it in views that we discuss, we shall not deal with this subject at greater length here. We shall, however, make a few observations that, in addition to the general objections raised against allegory, demonstrate even further the futility of the application of this method to the New Testament.

Bernard Ramm criticizes Bultmann for making the New Testament such a book of mythology that if what he says is true, there would be left no possibility of understanding it. He notes that in any writing in which we find mythology, such as the writing of Plato and Aristotle, the myths are understandable to us because there is a common core of language at their base. That is, there are ideas and conceptions in that particular language which are characteristic of every language. We may then interpret these writers on the basis of the common elements in their language and ours. If, however, the New Testament is mythological to the extent that Bultmann claims, the possibility of our ever understanding it would be removed. We would have no common core of language on the basis of which we could proceed.[49]

Barth criticizes Bultmann from the perspective of the thought of the writers of the biblical books. If what Bultmann says is true, it would be necessary to assume that the existentialist interpretation with which he pre-

48 Bernard Ramm, *Protestant Biblical Interpretation* (Boston: Wilde, 1956), p. 83.

49 Ramm, *The Christian View of Science and Scripture*, pp. 121-22.

sents us was in the minds of the original writers. The impossibility of such a hypothesis is driven home by Barth: "However much the New Testament writers borrowed their imagery and language from the surrounding world, it could hardly have occurred to them to produce their message as the proclamation of general cosmic truths disguised as a tale about the gods and their doings."[50]

We will raise one other objection against existentialist interpretation and demythologization from the point of view of hermeneutics. The study of hermeneutics has usually been divided into two parts: general hermeneutics and special hermeneutics. As the terms themselves suggest, general hermeneutics deals with those principles of interpretation which are to be applied to all parts of the Bible, while special hermeneutics deals with those principles which are to be applied to special literary forms or special topical areas. We have included in this last category such things as figurative language, for example, metaphor, parable, typology, and symbols. Included also in the class of special hermeneutics would be such topics as prophecy.

The biblical interpreter should always be clear as to the kind of literature with which he is dealing. He should accordingly apply the appropriate set of hermeneutical principles to his text. If it were to be demonstrated that there were myths in the New Testament literature, then it would be necessary for us to develop a set of special hermeneutical principles for their interpretation. At this point we would level two criticisms at existentialist interpretation as represented by Bultmann: (1) He has assumed, against both the direct and indirect testimony of the New Testament itself, that we have in it a special kind of literature called "myth," and he has developed a set of special hermeneutical principles to deal with it. The suitability of any device of interpretation depends in part on whether it is applied to literature for which it was designed. We do not deny that demythologization and existentialist interpretation may have some value if they are applied to mythical material. But the New Testament is not composed of polytheistic, ahistorical myths. It is in its essence historical.

(2) Bultmann in principle has made out of this special hermeneutical system a general hermeneutical system. Even if it could be argued that myth plays a part in the New Testament, which possibility we have here consistently denied, it cannot be argued that Bultmann is justified in treating the New Testament as comprehensively as he does as a mythological treatise and therefore applying his hermeneutical technique to its entirety. This is the whole problem with the existentialist interpretation of the New Testament. It is applied to the wrong kind of literature.

We may perhaps summarize everything we have been saying in this chapter in two statements: (1) Any attempt to interpret the Bible accurately must begin by taking seriously its self-witness to being the special revelation of God; and (2) in accordance with the divine purpose of special revelation, the Scriptures must be interpreted literally. For the exact meaning of this kind of interpretation we refer the reader to Ch. 1. This is what we should expect if God wished to make himself known to man. He did not conceal that revelation in allegories and myth. To be sure, the communication of divine truth to man had its problems. The necessity of figurative language, metaphor, analogy, etc. could not be avoided. But these devices were used to clarify, not to obscure the message.

The relevance of all this for the study of the Jesus of history has been well expressed by Hughes: "The Christ of the Bible is *The Logos*, not a *mythos;* he needs no demythologization at the hands of human scholars."[51]

_____
51 Hughes, p. 371.

CHAPTER SIX

The Gospel of John and History

It will be recalled that in our chapter on history we dealt almost exclusively with the Synoptic Gospels. We left the consideration of the Gospel of John for this chapter. We did this, not because we felt that this was the only way to approach the subject, but because this is the way John has been handled by the majority of the exponents of criticism. As a consequence, in this chapter we shall not consider at any length the historical element in the Synoptics—we have already done that. We shall look at the element of history from the standpoint of John, and bring in the Synoptics only at such places as they are related to that subject.

Critical Preference of the Synoptics

It would be well for us to summarize briefly the positions of various members of the critical school before we proceed to our analysis. We may begin by noting that, with very few exceptions, the vast majority of critics hold that the Synoptics are much to be preferred from an historical point of view. The liberal authors, while they did not discount John entirely from an historical point of view, felt that its historical worth was much less than that of the Synoptics. There were a number of reasons for this. Most of them felt that the Gospel was more of a theological or philosophical nature than it was of an historical nature, and that it was written at a much later

date than the Synoptics. Also, since it traced the life of
Jesus mainly on a Judean background in contrast to the
Galilean provenance of the Synoptics, it was regarded as
suspect.

Bousset, the chief representative of the History of
Religions School, also had a preference for the Synoptics.
In certain instances he preferred certain elements in John
as against the Synoptics, but his overall preference remained with the Synoptics.

Beginning with Martin Kähler there was a new approach to the whole subject. Now the entire Gospel
literature was looked upon with even greater suspicion
than formerly. This being the case, all the Gospels suffered a decline in estimate at the hands of biblical critics.
There was, however, no tendency to look more favorably
upon John from an historical point of view.

Bultmann pushed this development even further. He
concluded that while the Synoptics had little interest in
history, John had none. In spite of this, however, he
preferred John to the Synoptics because he felt that in
John's book the process of demythologization had already begun. History in the sense of facts has little
importance for Bultmann.

There is no significant shift on the part of critics to the
left of Bultmann from what preceded Bultmann's work.
Jaspers, as a consequence, prefers the Synoptics to John.

The new quest, to the contrary, continues in the line
of Bultmann. Due, however, to their concern for history,
these critics deal more directly with the question of
history in the Gospels. There is no general statement that
will encompass all the critics in this school. They range
from those who like Robinson now feel that all the
Gospels stand pretty much on the same level in regard to
history, to those who like Käsemann regard the departure
of John from the Synoptics as a willful departure from a
more serious historical intention.

Of all the writers engaged in the current quest, Stauffer
is somewhat unique in his preference for John over the
Synoptics from the point of view of history.

Before we direct ourselves to the question of history
itself in the Gospel of John, we must seek to understand

more fully the reasons for the general historical mistrust on the part of critics of the Gospel. There are two broad classes of reasons for this mistrust. One class is found in the divergences of this Gospel from the Synoptics. A second is found in the independent analysis of the Gospel itself. Let us direct our attention to these two areas.

Comparison with the Synoptics

We begin here on a positive note. There are a number of narrative incidents in which all the Gospels share. Materials concerning John the Baptist are found in all four Gospels. All of them similarly deal with the call of the disciples, Peter's confession, the triumphal entry, and several events of passion week. In addition there are what some have thought to be common narratives put in different settings. The primary one is the cleansing of the temple. Finally, there is similarity in some of the sayings of Jesus, but on the whole there is little verbal agreement.[1] It is to the differences that we must now direct our attention.

One of the great differences that has been noticed is the absence of a large quantity of the Synoptic material from John's Gospel. Guthrie has noticed the main omissions: "John does not record the virgin birth, the baptism, temptation or transfiguration of Jesus, the cure of any demoniacs or lepers, the parables, the institution of the Lord's supper, the agony in the garden, the cry of dereliction or the ascension."[2]

The omission of Synoptic material is accompanied, as we should expect, by the inclusion of much material not found in the Synoptics. Let us notice again the comments of Guthrie: "The main material consists of the early Judaean ministry including the miracle at Cana, the encounters of Jesus with Nicodemus and the Samaritan woman, the healing of the cripple and the blind man in Jerusalem, the raising of Lazarus, the washing of the disciples' feet, the farewell discourses and parts of the

[1] Guthrie, *New Testament Introduction: The Gospels and Acts*, p. 263.

[2] *Ibid.*

passion narrative. John's Prologue (1:1-18) is also unique."[3]

A third kind of difference that is often pointed to is the way in which the material is presented in the two classes of literature. Here several things are brought to our attention. There is, for example, a great deal more discourse material in John than there is in the Synoptics. It is greater in quantity and also more lengthy in individual units than in the Synoptics. The semiphilosophical prologue differentiates it from anything we find in the Synoptics. Jesus is presented as a popular teacher in the Synoptics. In John he is cast more in the role of a Rabbi. This in turn has had two effects upon the presentation of him in the Fourth Gospel. His sayings and the discussions that center around his person are more deeply theological in nature. In this connection Reginald Fuller has pointed out that while the Q material in the Synoptics represents Jesus as proclaiming the kingdom of God, the Gospel of John presents him as proclaiming himself.[4] And while we have the secret messiahship of Jesus in Mark, we have the open messiahship of Jesus in John. Finally, we have a great deal more controversy of Jesus with the religious authorities in John than we do in the Synoptics.

A fourth kind of difference that is often noticed by critics of the Gospel of John has to do with the supposed difference in the length of Jesus' ministry there portrayed from that of the Synoptics, and with the apparent disagreement on the time when certain events in his career occurred. While it is possible from the point of view of the Synoptics to confine the public ministry of Jesus to about one year, the Gospel of John apparently describes a public ministry of at least three years.

Furthermore, while the Synoptics place the cleansing of the temple on the part of Jesus early in passion week, the Gospel of John places the incident very early in the ministry of Jesus, immediately after the miracle at Cana.

Finally, there is the chronological problem with the

[3] *Ibid.*, pp. 264-65.

[4] Reginald H. Fuller, *The New Testament in Current Study*, p. 144.

Last Supper as it is presented in the Synoptics and John. Mark definitely identifies the Last Supper with the Jewish Passover (Mk. 14:12, 16). On the other hand, according to John, at the time of the trial of Jesus before Pilate the Passover was still future (Jn. 18:28; 19:14). All of this evidence has led a great number of critics to suppose that the Gospel of John is composed of bad history at best when compared with the Synoptics.

Other Johannine problems

There have been a number of objections raised as to the historical reliability of John apart from those that are based on a comparison of it with the Synoptics. One of these has to do with the authorship of the Gospel. It is claimed that the Gospel comes from the hand of one in whose mind it must have undergone considerable development. This is in keeping with the theological and philosophical character of the Gospel we noticed earlier. From all that is known of the entourage of Jesus' disciples, it is considered unlikely that anyone from this group could produce such a work. If the work purports to be from John the son of Zebedee, the disciple, the truth of the assertion is even further reduced for certain critics, since he is presented as a simple Galilean fisherman in the Synoptics.

Along with this general objection against the historical accuracy of the Gospel from the point of view of authorship is that of date. Partly as a result of the developed theology which we have just mentioned, and partly because of the Gospel's alleged combat with Gnosticism which we shall soon discuss, some have thought that the date of the writing of the Gospel must be placed very late. It was characteristic of many critics about the turn of the century to date the Gospel about A.D. 150 or later. If the Gospel was written so long after the events, its claim to historical accuracy would indeed be slight.

One of the reasons why the Gospel was dated so late, as we have just mentioned, had to do with its supposed connection with Gnosticism. Gnosticism was not a uniform movement, but was rather a group of heretical

Christian sects that rose to prominence in the second century. The word "Gnostic" comes from the Greek word for knowledge, *gnosis*. As such, the movement emphasized secret knowledge that Jesus had passed on to his followers in addition to that contained in the Gospels. Actually, this was only a pretext for the combination of pagan philosophical thought with Christian thought. Among other features of these sects one finds the rejection of the entire Old Testament and of anything in the New Testament to which its advocates objected. There was also at the core of most of the Gnostic systems a dualistic conception of the universe. Now it has been thought by many of the exponents of criticism that the Gospel of John directly confronts such teaching. If Gnosticism is then in view, and it did not rise to prominence before the mid-second century, it stands to reason that the Gospel could not have been written before that date.

A further reason for the doubt of the critics as to the historical accuracy of John is to be found in an analysis of the composition itself. The Synoptics give evidence of very careful composition on the basis of sources. We are of course aided in reaching this conclusion because we have three records on the analysis of which we may base our conclusion. But despite the fact that we have no parallel records with which to compare John, many critics feel that the writing itself gives evidence of free composition, and due to this they feel that it cannot lay claim to historical accuracy.

In the earlier part of this century it was usual for many critics to question the unity of the Gospel of John. There were many explanations of how the book reached its present state. Some felt that the book as originally written had undergone several revisions or redactions. If this was so, it could not possibly lay claim to accuracy from an historical perspective. While this tendency has lessened considerably among critical treatments, there is still some tendency to regard parts of the Gospel as later additions. Ch. 21 in particular is often mentioned as having been a later addition.

Theories of dislocation were also for a time very popular in connection with the Gospel of John. These might not reflect quite as much on its historical accuracy as do some other points mentioned, but if the book as we have it does contain dislocations—that is, portions that have been removed from their original sequence in manuscript transmission—then at minimum we do not have those events in their chronological sequence.

Finally, biblical critics have sometimes felt that the Gospel of John is so steeped in Paulinism that it could not possibly have been written with any basic historical intention in mind.

Necessity of Reassessment

One would have thought fifty years ago, on the grounds of evidence such as we have outlined above, that the question of the historical accuracy of the Gospel of John had been settled in its disfavor. However, some discoveries have been made in our century that have forced critics to re-examine the issue. The primary discovery in this regard has been one that has necessitated the much earlier dating of the Gospel.

Date of the Gospel

In 1917 there was discovered in Egypt a fragment of the Gospel of John, which has since come to be known as the Roberts fragment. This fragment contains Jn. 18:31-33, 37, 38.[5] On the basis of the palaeography of this text, it has been dated sometime between A.D. 100 and 150. It is likely that a date of about A.D. 130 for the fragment, if we attempt a more specific date, would be very close to being accurate.[6]

The significance of this find becomes apparent when one realizes that this is the oldest fragment we have of the New Testament. There is nothing that has been un-

[5] C. H. Roberts, *An Unpublished Fragment of the Fourth Gospel in the John Rylands Library* (Manchester: Manchester University, 1935).

[6] Bruce, *The New Testament Documents: Are They Reliable?*, p. 17.

covered from either the Synoptics or Paul, all of which were by common consensus written before John, which is within fifty years of this Roberts fragment.

But we are warranted in drawing some further conclusions on the basis of this fragment. The almost universal tradition of the Church is that the Gospel of John was written in Ephesus. If this be the case, then if the Gospel was to attain a wide enough circulation so that it would be found in the form of a papyrus copy in Egypt by about the year A.D. 130, it would almost necessarily be a product of the first century.

While the finding of the Roberts fragment should certainly be regarded as the key evidence that has forced an earlier dating of the Gospel, certain other facts have come to light that have confirmed this evidence. Chief among these are some investigations relative to the origin of Gnosticism. There is no uniformity here among biblical critics, but we may at least trace the main lines of investigation that have gone on in order that we might see what relevance they have for our study here. Reginald Fuller outlines five main theories that have attempted to account for the Gnostic or anti-Gnostic character of the Gospel of John: (1) The oldest view, which caused critics to date the Gospel very late, stated that Gnosticism was a second-century Christian heretical movement. Gnosticism was thus a perversion arising within Christianity in the second century.[7] (2) Later it was felt that some of the other New Testament writings, for example, the Pastoral Epistles, Jude, and Colossians, were doing combat with this Gnostic tendency. This had no revolutionary effect upon its point of origin. It was still a perversion originating in Christianity itself. It only forced the date of its origin somewhat earlier.[8] (3) With the History of Religions School and with Bultmann, the origin of Gnosticism was found elsewhere. It was believed to be a product of oriental syncretism, which came into Judaism via such groups as the Qumran community, the John the Baptist sect, etc. The New Testament, and John in particular,

7 Reginald H. Fuller, pp. 131-32.
8 *Ibid.*, p. 132.

both combat this Gnosticism and use its terminology. (4) There are those who feel that Gnosticism came into Judaism via Iranian religion. K. G. Kuhn has demonstrated what he believes to be significant parallels between the Dead Sea Scrolls and Iranian religion. The contrasts between good and evil, light and darkness, truth and perversity, etc. are examples of this. Others have gone on to express the feeling that this is the source of the thought of the Gospel of John.[9] (5) Fuller himself feels that the Gnostic type of thought came into the Church via a sect of John the Baptist.[10]

The origin of Gnosticism and its precise relation to the Gospel of John is not our primary consideration here. Our whole point has been to demonstrate that it is no longer necessary to date the Gospel of John late because of its relationship to Gnosticism. As Fuller concludes, "We are ready to agree, as all indications now are increasingly tending to suggest, that gnosticism or whatever we choose to call it is a widespread phenomenon antedating the beginning of Christianity. . . ."[11]

On the basis of the Roberts fragment and a closer analysis of Gnosticism, the critical movement has been forced to adopt some new opinions with regard to the Gospel: (1) It is now generally agreed among critics that the Gospel was written sometime in the period A.D. 90-110. A date near the beginning of this period is distinctly to be preferred, and there are some critical scholars who feel that a date near A.D. 80 is best. [12] (2) The earlier date of the Gospel makes it much more possible that it contains reliable history. (3) The other objections that have been raised against the Gospel's authenticity are now subject to thorough review.

History in the Gospel

Synoptic and Johannine corroboration. While the comparison of the Synoptics with John causes some prob-

9 *Ibid.*, pp. 137-39.
10 *Ibid.*, p. 141.
11 *Ibid.*, pp. 135-36.
12 *Ibid.*, p. 143.

lems, it also offers some solutions to problems if one allows the possibility that both records are reliable. The greatest problem is perhaps the presentation of the scene of Jesus' ministry in the two sets of writings. The ministry of Jesus in the Synoptics occurs in Galilee. His ministry in the Gospel of John occurs in Judea. It must not, however, be thought that either set of writings infers that the ministry occurred exclusively within the geographical area in which it sets it. Thus there is mention of a Galilean ministry in Jn. 7:1. Similarly, there is evidence that Jesus had previous acquaintance in Jerusalem before the time of his final visit. Bruce has reminded us that Jesus apparently knew the owner of the colt (Mk. 11:3-6; cf. Mt. 21:3; Lk. 19:31). The owner of the room in Jerusalem apparently expected him for the Passover (Mk. 14:12-16; cf. Mt. 26:17-19; Lk. 22:7-13).[13]

In addition certain statements of Jesus with respect to the city of Jerusalem are inexplicable apart from a rather extended ministry there. His lament over the city is an illustration of this: "How often would I have gathered your children together as a hen gathers her brood under her wings, and you would not!" (Mt. 23:37; cf. Lk. 13:34). Likewise the statement of Jesus on the occasion of the triumphal entry is inexplicable apart from the identification of "the time of your visitation" with a previous ministry of Jesus in the city (Lk. 19:44).

The problem of the chronology of Jesus' life is also best solved by a combination of the Synoptics with John. As we have previously noted, the Galilean ministry of Jesus, which we have pictured in the Synoptics, lasted about one year. John apparently deals with an earlier Judean ministry before the Galilean ministry of the Synoptics. The Galilean ministry of the Synoptics can be fitted into the Johannine chronology of the section Jn. 6:1-7:2. John then tells us of other Judean activity that is not contained in the Synoptics (7:3-ch. 8).

The Gospel of John also casts light on other incidents in the Synoptic Gospels that are difficult to explain apart

13 Bruce, *The New Testament Documents: Are They Reliable?*, p. 55.

from his account. The call of the four disciples (Mk. 1:16-20; cf. Mt. 4:18-22; Lk. 5:1-11) appears to be very abrupt, and the response of the disciples unnatural, according to the Synoptic account. When, however, we read of Jesus' previous acquaintance with these disciples in Jn. 1:35-42, the reason for their quick response is much more evident.

Tasker has pointed out that the opposition to Jesus in Jerusalem in the final week of his life before the crucifixion is inexplicable apart from previous contact between Jesus and the Jewish authorities. If we take the Johannine record as being accurate, however, such a difficulty is removed. Such opposition had been developing throughout his ministry.[14]

Bruce has shown that a comparison of John with the Synoptics throws light on the events that occurred after the Galilean ministry. The Synoptics by themselves are obscure at this point. Thus Bruce feels that Jesus completed his Galilean ministry in the autumn of A.D. 29; that he went to Jerusalem for the Feast of Tabernacles and remained there until December and the Feast of Dedication (Jn. 10:22); that he then retired to the Jordan valley (Jn. 10:40); and that he returned to Jerusalem a week before Passover in A.D. 30 (Jn. 12:1).[15]

Similarly, the fact that John in his writings makes mention of the Jewish feasts and festivals is an aid in attempting to construct a chronology of Jesus' life. This has led Bruce to observe, "Several scholars who decline to accept as historical John's portrait of Christ are quite willing to accept his chronological framework."[16] We shall return to a few of the historical problems as they relate to the comparison of John with the Synoptics shortly. First let us look at other evidence that would support the Gospel's trustworthiness from an historical perspective.

Other evidence of historical trustworthiness. That a

14 Tasker, *The Gospel According to St. John*, p. 33.

15 Bruce, *The New Testament Documents: Are They Reliable?*, p. 56.

16 *Ibid.*

given account gives evidence of having been written by an eyewitness may be very difficult evidence to weigh, but that a scholarly historian like A. T. Olmstead will vouch for the eyewitness character of the stories of the raising of Lazarus and the empty tomb of Jesus should give one confidence that he is not dealing in the Gospel of John with the creative fancy of its author.[17]

There are also a number of places where archaeology has demonstrated that the writer of the Fourth Gospel has remarkable geographical and topographical knowledge. The location of Aenon near Salim (Jn. 3:23) has been substantiated as a result of archaeological investigation. John's statement in the same verse that "there was much water there" similarly has been vindicated.[18]

In like manner the author's knowledge of the Hebrew name of the pool near the Sheep Gate in Jerusalem, the fact that it had five porches, and the fact that healing properties were attributed to the water there have all been substantiated by the recent excavation of the pool and its inscriptions (Jn. 5:2ff.).[19]

Reginald Fuller writes that recent excavations at Shechem have substantiated the identification of Sychar in Jn. 4:5 with that place.[20]

Finally, we may group a number of other topographical details that suggest accurate knowledge on the part of the author of the Gospel. Two Bethanys are mentioned (1:28; 12:1), as is Cana in Galilee (2:1; 4:46; and 21:2); Tiberias is used as the proper alternative for the Sea of Galilee (6:1; 21:1); Mount Gerizim is placed near a well (4:21); and Ephraim is located near the wilderness (11:54). The author gives the Hebrew name of the pavement outside the Praetorium (19:13), and he

[17] A. T. Olmstead, *Jesus in the Light of History* (New York: Scribner, 1942), pp. 206, 248.

[18] Archibald M. Hunter, *Teaching and Preaching the New Testament* (Philadelphia: Westminster, 1963), p. 62.

[19] Joachim Jeremias, *Die Wiederentdeckung von Bethesda* (Göttingen: Vandenhoeck und Ruprecht, 1949).

[20] Reginald H. Fuller, p. 142.

identifies the pool of Siloam (9:7) and the brook Kidron (18:1) by name.[21]

Evidence like this has led Bruce to observe:

> The evangelist was evidently a Palestinian. Although he may have been far from his native land when he wrote his Gospel, his accurate knowledge of places and distances in Palestine, a knowledge which appears spontaneously and naturally, strongly suggests one who was born and brought up in that land, not one whose knowledge of the country was derived from pilgrim-visits. He knows Jerusalem well; he fixes the location of certain places in the city with the accuracy of one who must have been acquainted with it before its destruction in A.D. 70.[22]

While earlier in our century theories of an Aramaic origin of the Gospel were circulated in some groups, most contemporary critics no longer regard this as a possibility. However, there are a number of scholars who hold in a less inclusive form the idea that there are Aramaic elements behind the Gospel. Thus A. T. Olmstead held that the narratives of the Gospel were composed in Aramaic.[23] Tenney, on the basis of research by Albright, has concluded that the author was familiar with the data about Jesus as it circulated in Palestine in Aramaic,[24] and Black has discovered what he believes to be Aramaic logia in the discourses of the Gospel.[25] This Aramaic character of the Gospel pushes us in the direction of an early date for its materials, and suggests the possibility of greater historical accuracy.

Re-examination of problems. If on the basis of manuscript and other archaeological evidence it becomes obvious that the Gospel of John was written much earlier

[21] Guthrie, pp. 225-26.

[22] Bruce, *The New Testament Documents: Are They Reliable?*, p. 49.

[23] Olmstead.

[24] Merrill C. Tenney, "Reversals of New Testament Criticism," *Revelation and the Bible*, ed. Carl F. H. Henry (Grand Rapids: Baker, 1958), p. 361.

[25] M. Black, *An Aramaic Approach to the Gospels and Acts* (Oxford: Clarendon, 1967), pp. 273-74.

than critics formerly thought, and if on the basis of a
closer examination of the Gospel it becomes obvious that
from the perspective of such things as geography, language, etc. it deserves more serious consideration as an
historical record, then it would seem apparent that we
should look again at the main factors that have caused
critics to set it in opposition to the Synoptics.

The first of these opposing factors has to do with the
length of Jesus' public ministry. Do we have a one-year
ministry in the Synoptics as opposed to a three-year
ministry in John? Harrison has shown that the entire
Gospel record of Jesus' life gives us only about thirty
days of activity.[26] It therefore becomes apparent that
they make no pretense to being exhaustive accounts.
Furthermore, as we have already noticed, there are both
hints of a more extensive Judean ministry in the Synoptics and indications of a Galilean ministry in John. All
this has led Guthrie to conclude: "The major difference . . . is one of impression rather than of fact, owing
mainly to the omission of the Judean ministry from the
Synoptics and their lack of data concerning the Jewish
festivals."[27] It is difficult, therefore, to see how the
Synoptics can be set against John in an antithetical way
in relation to the length of Jesus' public ministry.

The most clear-cut opposition of the two sets of writings at first glance would appear to be the placing of the
incident of the cleansing of the temple in different portions of Jesus' public ministry. Modern criticism has all
too often fallen into a disjunctive type of reasoning here
which insists that either/or account must be correct, but
not both/and. Yet if we maintain both cleansings we are
aided in understanding the Gospel narratives as they are
developed. What was it that caused the Jewish religious
leaders to oppose Jesus so violently throughout his public
ministry? We may be certain it was not a mild ethical
code that he admonished his followers to accept. There
must have been some incident early in Jesus' public

26 Harrison, "The Phenomena of Scripture," *Revelation and
the Bible,* p. 246.

27 Guthrie, p. 270.

ministry that caused them to oppose him in a systematically vehement way thereafter. Would not the incident of the Johannine cleansing have done this?

That Jesus escaped any immediate consequences from the Johannine cleansing may be accounted for partly on the basis that both the religious authorities and the people knew that the business as carried on was not right, and partly on the basis of shock at the audacity of this new, zealous reformer. It is similarly not unlikely that the practice was revived in short order. It was too profitable to be discontinued unless it had been prohibited by some authority that had and desired to use more political or religious backing than Jesus did. By the time of the second cleansing, however, the Jews had ample time to formulate their plan of attack.

A third difficulty with respect to the relationship of John to the Synoptics has to do with the date of the Last Supper and its relationship to the Jewish Passover. The Synoptics definitely identify the Last Supper with the Jewish Passover (Mk. 14:12; cf. Mt. 26:17, 18; Lk. 22:7, 8, and Mk. 14:16; cf. Mt. 26:19; Lk. 22:13). In John, however, at the time of Jesus' trial before Pilate, the Passover had not yet been celebrated (18:28; 19:14). Critics who feel that an either/or position must be adopted in relation to these two accounts, have in general preferred the account of John. The reason for this is simple. It would be contrary to Jewish law to carry out a trial and crucifixion after the feast had begun. It is interesting to note that in this instance critics, who generally look down on John from an historical perspective, accept his record against the Synoptics.

It has become increasingly evident, however, that it is not at all necessary to accept one of the two records. Mlle. Annie Jaubert has raised the possibility that certain segments of the Jewish community followed a different calendar from that which was followed in Jerusalem. Evidence for this is found in the Book of Jubilees, and it is now thought that this calendar was used in the Qumran community. This calendar apparently always placed the Passover on the same day of the week, while the Jerusalem calendar fixed the date via lunar calculations, and as a consequence it could occur any day of the week.[28]

As a result, the strong possibility must be entertained that Jesus and his disciples celebrated the Passover (Lord's Supper) earlier in the week, following a calendar like that of the Book of Jubilees, and that the Jerusalem Passover was still future at the time of his trial. One need not accept this particular theory, however, to admit the possibility that both sets of records might be accurate historically.

A final difficulty that has been raised in any attempt to hold the Synoptics and John together has to do with the difference in the nature of the discourses. As we have noted previously, in the Synoptics Jesus proclaims the kingdom of God; in John he proclaims himself. But here again the difficulty in accounting for both sets of discourses is by no means as formidable as some critics would lead us to believe. The difference in the subjects to whom the discourses were delivered will go a long way toward the solution of this problem. In the Synoptic discourses Jesus is speaking mainly with the simple folk of Galilee. They lack education, and in particular they lack knowledge of all the intricacies of the Jewish religion. It would not be expected that in such an environment Jesus would immediately launch into a profound discussion of his metaphysical significance.

The discourses in the Gospel of John, on the other hand, are of an entirely different character. Here the main recipients of his discourses are the Jewish religious authorities and Jesus' disciples. Needless to say, the Jewish authorities were well educated, particularly in the area of their religious beliefs. In such a situation Jesus' teaching was not merely received, it was disputed. It would be expected, therefore, that the dialogue would be much more profound and much more argumentative, and this is precisely the kind of thing we have in the Gospel of John. It would be expected also that, as Jesus drew

[28] Annie Jaubert, *The Date of the Last Supper*, trans. Isaac Rafferty (New York: Alba, 1965).

near the end of his earthly life, he would have something more profound to say to those who had followed him for the period of his earthly ministry. This is precisely the kind of thing we have in the farewell discourses of Jn. 14-16.

There is another feature about the two localities in which Jesus delivered his discourses that should not escape our attention. Bruce has contended that the political atmosphere of the two localities might have had something to do with the way in which Jesus proclaimed his message.[29] As compared with Jerusalem and Judea, Galilee was always a place of political unrest. There were always ideas of revolt there. We noticed in our chapter on history that it was necessary for Jesus to guard the proclamation of his messiahship in such an atmosphere. A political revolt early in his ministry would have defeated his purpose in coming. The picture in Jerusalem was completely different. The Sadducees, for example, were quite content with Roman rule. They controlled the political power that the Romans had given to the Jews, which, by the way, was considerable. The institutionalized life of Judaism was also very profitable to them. Jesus' speaking of his person in this setting would not involve the dangers that it would in Galilee.

Guthrie has noted a further difficulty in adopting an either/or approach to the Synoptic and Johannine discourses. If the discourses in John were not delivered by Jesus himself, it would be necessary to assume that a personality greater than Jesus composed them.[30] What advantage there could be in such a position is difficult to imagine.

It is interesting to note that on the subject of the discourses in John, Jewish scholars have been quicker to accept the record in many cases than have Christian scholars. Israel Abrahams, for example, has expressed the belief that "the Gospel enshrines a genuine tradition of

[29] Bruce, *The New Testament Documents: Are They Reliable?*, p. 59.

[30] Guthrie, p. 268.

an aspect of Jesus' teaching which has not found a place in the Synoptics."[31]

Relation to the Synoptics. If, then, we are justified in assuming that John's Gospel merits serious consideration as an historical source for the life of Jesus, we must next consider the relationship that its author had to the Synoptics. Did he know them? Did he use them, etc.? H. Windisch has given us the four possibilities with respect to this problem.[32] He expresses the possibility that the Gospel of John might be either supplementary to, independent of, interpretive of, or a substitute for the Synoptics. Let us consider these possibilities in reverse order.

The idea that John was a substitute for the Synoptics was the theory Windisch himself held. This theory gains no support either by an examination of the Gospel or by a review of Church history. While a large part of the Gospel traces an independent course from that of the Synoptics, there is no evidence of any attempt to refute them that it would be necessary for such a theory to demonstrate. Neither can it be shown that any section of the Church ever held John in opposition to the Synoptics. If, therefore, this was the purpose of the author in his writing, he was completely unsuccessful in attaining his goal.[33]

The idea that John is an interpretation of the Synoptics has two main obstacles against its acceptance: (1) It carries with it the assumption that John had no basic historical objective in writing his book.[34] On the basis of the historical investigations we have conducted thus far in this chapter, the likelihood of such a possibility is remote. (2) This theory cannot explain why, if John's purpose was to interpret the Synoptics, we find so few parallels to them incorporated in his book.[35]

[31] Israel Abrahams, *Studies in Pharisaism and the Gospels* (Cambridge: The University Press, 1917), I, 12.

[32] H. Windisch, *Johannes und die Synoptiker* (Leipzig: Hinrichs, 1926).

[33] Guthrie, pp. 274-75.

[34] *Ibid.*, p. 274.

[35] *Ibid.*

The idea that John is independent of the other Gospels has claimed the support of a larger number of contemporary critics. Earlier in the twentieth century many felt that John used Mark, and some even felt that he used Luke. Critical opinion, however, has undergone a considerable shift since that period. Erwin R. Goodenough has expressed belief that John was ignorant of the Synoptic tradition.[36] Reginald Fuller observes that the current trend is to say that John did not know the Synoptics. [37] Finally, Robert Grant, on the basis of his literary investigation, holds that it is impossible to demonstrate that John is either earlier or later than the Synoptics.[38]

There are two fundamental objections against this theory: (1) It is unlikely that if John had not known the Synoptics, his record would have avoided the segments of Jesus' ministry contained in the Synoptics to such an extent; and (2) if the theory is valid that John was the last of the Gospels written, it is unlikely that its author could have been in possession of such material as he had relative to the life of Jesus and at the same time have been so ignorant of previous accounts of his life.

The idea of supplementation has the most to commend it. There are a number of factors that support this theory. While the difference of plan of the Gospel of John is inexplicable from the point of view of the independence theory, it is perfectly natural from the point of view of supplementation. John wrote with the others in mind. The same is true of omissions. John knew the other Gospels and wanted to avoid unnecessary duplication. The availability and cost of writing materials, the time needed for production, the peculiar materials that he had at his disposal, all may have been factors in his omission of Synoptic materials. Furthermore, the fact that he had so much additional material to present was in itself reason enough for his writing. That he had some interpretive

[36] Erwin R. Goodenough, "John, a Primitive Gospel," *Journal of Biblical Literature*, LXIV (June 1945), 145-82.

[37] Reginald H. Fuller, pp. 123-24.

[38] Robert M. Grant, *A Historical Introduction to the New Testament* (New York: Harper, 1963), p. 155.

ambition is not to be ruled out. All the Gospel writers had this.

Unity of the Gospel

Whether or not the Gospel is a unity as we have it would, of course, reflect on its historical worth. The early twentieth-century tendency to partition the Gospel and ascribe it to several authors has undergone a significant change. The earlier date that must now be ascribed to the Gospel has necessitated this. The part of the Gospel that is most frequently mentioned as being by another hand is ch. 21. This chapter was supposedly added by someone to attribute the authorship of the book to John. If, however, the Gospel was written before the end of the first century, any attempt to authenticate the work under false pretenses is highly unlikely.[39] It is thus true that today most critics accept the work as an essential unity.

Dislocations in the Gospel

This subject may appear to have even less bearing on the historical element in the Gospel. If, however, it can be demonstrated that the original manuscript has been significantly altered in transmission, our assurance regarding its accuracy would be seriously affected. The tendency to rearrange the Gospel has, however, also lessened. Rudolf Bultmann is the notable exception to this trend. Some critics find it desirable to reverse chs. 5 and 6. Others feel that chs. 15 and 16 should follow 13:31 in order that Jesus' statement, "Rise, let us go hence" (14:31), not be followed by sixty verses of discourse. Still others feel that the incident of the cleansing of the temple (2:13-3:21) should be placed after 12:36 in order to harmonize the account of John with the Synoptics; but as we have already noticed, such a theory is based on the assumption that there was only one cleansing.

The words of Hunter would appear to be a good warning for all who would rearrange the order of the Gospel: "All such reshuffling implies that the twentieth-

---

39 Hunter, *Interpreting the New Testament 1900-1950*, p. 86.

century critic knows what John really intended—a big assumption. We must not confuse our 'feelings' about the right order with 'proof'. It is significant that a number of recent scholars (Hoskyns, Dodd and Lightfoot) are sceptical about dislocations."[40]

Authorship of the Gospel

While it would have been logical from some points of view to have considered this question first, we felt it advisable to defer our consideration of it until we had some of the information considered above at our disposal. The traditional answer to the question of authorship has been that it was written by John the son of Zebedee, the disciple. There can be little doubt that this is the claim of the book itself. In 21:7, 20 we are told of "the disciple whom Jesus loved," and in 21:24 the same individual is shown to be the author of the book. Earlier in the book we find this same beloved disciple at the Lord's Supper (13:23) and at the crucifixion (19:26), among other places.

Bruce has reminded us that of the twelve disciples, three were admitted to a more intimate fellowship with Jesus on occasion,[41] for example, at the healing of Jairus' daughter, at the transfiguration, in Gethsemane, etc. It must be supposed that "the disciple whom Jesus loved" was one of these three. This beloved disciple is distinguished from Peter in 13:24; 20:2; and 21:20. We know that James was martyred no later than A.D. 44 (Acts 12:2). This leaves us with John as the only possibility for "the disciple whom Jesus loved."[42]

While the other Gospel writers always identify John the Baptist by his full title, the author of the Fourth Gospel merely identifies him as John. In giving an account of two individuals with the same name, writers are usually careful to distinguish them. If, however, the

40 *Ibid.*, p. 87.

41 Bruce, *The New Testament Documents: Are They Reliable?*, p. 48.

42 *Ibid.*

author of a given work gave an account of another individual with the same given name as his own, such a distinction would not be necessary, particularly if the author designated himself as he entered into the narrative in another way, i.e., "the disciple whom Jesus loved."[43]

The authorship of the Gospel by the disciple is also supported by other evidence, some of which we have discussed previously in this chapter. The features of the account that indicate it was prepared by an eyewitness strengthen the case for authorship by the disciple. The same can be said of the excellent geographical and topographical information contained in the Gospel. The Aramaic flavor of much of the material points in the same direction.

Bruce has observed that the author must have been a Jew because of his thorough knowledge of Jewish customs. He mentions such things as the Jewish purification rites (2:6) and the Jewish manner of burial (19:40). He makes mention of the Passover, the Feast of Tabernacles, and the Feast of Dedication. He is familiar with the attitude of the educated in Judaism toward the uneducated (7:49). All this would indicate that the author of the Gospel was someone thoroughly conversant with the situation in first-century Palestine, as John doubtless was.[44]

Guthrie has pointed to the author's knowledge of Jewish history. He knows of the time element in the construction of the temple (2:20). He knows of the attitude of the Jews to the Samaritans (4:9). He is aware of the contempt of the Palestinian Jews for the Jews of the dispersion (7:35), and he is acquainted with the hierarchy and relationship of the high priests (11:49; 13:13ff.).[45]

The external evidence for the authenticity of John is as strong as it is for any of the other Gospels. We cannot go

[43] *Ibid.*

[44] *Ibid.*, pp. 49-50.

[45] Guthrie, p. 225.

into a detailed analysis of this evidence here, but we refer the reader to treatments of this subject in other works.[46]

That the Gospel gained apostolic authority must also be accounted for. If it was indeed a first-century work, its acceptance by the Church and its attribution to John are very difficult to understand apart from the accuracy of that attribution.

The main difficulty in accepting the disciple John as the author of the book in addition to those factors which differentiate it from the Synoptics, has been in ascribing a book of its character to a Galilean fisherman. This difficulty, however, is not very great when one stops to realize that fifty or more years might have passed between the time when the events occurred and the time when he wrote the book. Motivation has always been a tremendous factor in learning, and what greater motivation could one have had than that which must have urged John to communicate the Gospel? The possibility of an amanuensis would dispose of this problem in an even simpler fashion.

We must also look briefly at the two main alternative suggestions to authorship of the Gospel. One theory is that the Gospel was written by a different John, John the elder of Ephesus. This theory takes its rise from a quotation of Papias, bishop of Hierapolis c. A.D. 130-140, preserved in the writings of the church historian Eusebius. In this work of Papias, entitled *An Exposition of the Oracles of the Lord*, we read,

> I shall not hesitate to set down for you, along with my interpretations, all things which I learnt from the elders with care and recorded with care, being well assured of their truth. For, unlike most men, I took pleasure not in those that had much to say but in those that teach the truth; not in those who record strange precepts, but in those who relate such precepts as were given to the Faith from the Lord and are derived from the Truth itself. Besides, if ever any man came who had been a follower of the elders, I would enquire about the sayings of the elders; what Andrew said, or Peter, or Philip,

[46] Guthrie, pp. 233-38; Bruce, *The New Testament Documents: Are They Reliable?*, pp. 50-54.

or Thomas, or James, or John, or Matthew, or any other of the Lord's disciples; and what Aristion says, and John the Elder, who are disciples of the Lord. For I did not consider that I got so much profit from the contents of books as from the utterances of a living and abiding voice.[47]

Although some would dispute the claim that the elder John is to be distinguished from John the disciple in this passage, it is most natural to assume that two individuals are in view here and that the elder John had probably also seen Jesus during his earthly life. This being the case, some writers have felt that the author of the Fourth Gospel is this John the elder. The possibility that he was the independent author of the Gospel apart from John the son of Zebedee would be very difficult to maintain. The external evidence to which we referred earlier is completely against such a presumption. Irenaeus in particular identifies its authorship with the disciple. The most that could be maintained would be that John the disciple and John the elder were close companions and that the latter served as a copyist and editor for the former. But even this is a precarious argument from silence.[48]

Early in the twentieth century many critics were convinced that the Gospel of John was written by an unknown Hellenistic mystic about the middle of the second century. This view has been dealt a serious blow in light of the discoveries made in this century which have necessitated an earlier dating of the Gospel. In addition, it has the liabilities of accounting for the apostolic authority of the book, the features that mark it as the product of an eyewitness, the Aramaic flavor of the book, the excellent Palestinian geography contained in it, and the strong external evidence to its apostolic authorship. As Tenney has said, "There is . . . less objection to ascribing the Fourth Gospel to the disciple of Jesus . . . than to the 'great unknown' hypothecated by Biblical criticism a century ago."[49]

[47] Eusebius, *Ecclesiastical History* iii.39. Translation here is from Bettenson, p. 27.

[48] Bruce, *The New Testament Documents: Are They Reliable?*, p. 54.

[49] Tenney, p. 361.

We may conclude this discussion of the authorship of the Gospel of John with the well-written words of Tasker: "Just as the value of the Gospel of Mark for the early Church, and for ourselves today, lies in the fact that it embodies the witness of Simon Peter, so what we need to be assured about is that the Fourth Gospel contains not the imaginative reflections of some second-century mystic, but the testimony of one of the original apostles to the life and teaching of Jesus."[50]

Theology of the Gospel

As we have noticed previously, some have discounted the historical value of the Gospel of John because of its theological characteristics. It is claimed that the Christology of John removes his treatment from the realm of history, and that we have here the theology of Paul, which is not primarily based on history. Such a theory is, however, not based on a careful analysis of any of the three sets of writings—the Synoptics, John, or Paul. Bruce has shown that Jn. 20:31 and Mk. 1:1 approach the subject from the same perspective.[51] Furthermore, in addition to the high Christology of John, we have many references that point equally to Jesus' humanity.[52] Finally, we must call the reader's attention to what we have noticed earlier in this chapter. The statements of Jesus relative to his person must be understood in relation to the people to whom they were made. This in itself is enough to account for the more developed theology of John.

With respect to the question of Pauline theology in John, it would appear that Reginald Fuller represents the contemporary critical mood: "Much that used to be thought specifically Pauline has turned out to be common apostolic Christianity, whether Palestinian or Hellenistic."[53]

50 Tasker, p. 11.

51 Bruce, *The New Testament Documents: Are They Reliable?*, p. 58.

52 *Ibid.*

53 Reginald H. Fuller, p. 128.

Conclusion

When all the evidence we have surveyed in this chapter has been taken into account, it would appear that a more serious look must be taken at the Gospel of John from the point of view of history. The words of Donald Guthrie express well what this writer feels should be our conclusion:

> Once the basic historicity of the narratives is granted, it would seem reasonable to assume the historicity of the whole until historical improbabilities can be demonstrated. In other words, an interpretation of the relationship between John and the Synoptics which preserves the historicity of both, where that is possible, is to be preferred to any hypothesis which presupposes some unhistorical strata in one of them. This is not a plea for harmonization at all costs, but a plea for an examination of the possibility of harmonization as a first essential, instead of excluding it without serious consideration, as sometimes happens. In any such consideration it will be recognized that each Gospel has its own distinctive purpose both in the selection and in the employment of the historical material.[54]

[54] Guthrie, p. 300.

CHAPTER SEVEN

The Significance of Jesus

The Biblical World View

Any attempt to offer an estimate of the importance of the life of Jesus must do so from the perspective of the entire biblical revelation. If one approaches his life as an isolated phenomenon and divorces the setting of that life from all that preceded it and all that succeeded it, he will of necessity arrive at a distorted conception of what significance that life had. It therefore follows that our task in this chapter shall of necessity be one of going from the broader scope of history to the narrower one. We shall as a consequence begin by dealing with the entire range of biblical history. We shall next narrow our scope to the life of Jesus itself. Finally, we shall deal with the principal events of that life and their significance.

In the first place, then, it will be necessary for us to discover what the biblical or Christian world view is. At this point, the history of the critical movement has been a particularly deficient one, for it has been a history of inadequate dealing with this subject. Of the many sorts of errors that have crept in at this point two have been primary. The most apparent of all is that of Bultmann. He approaches the New Testament as he would a twentieth-century scientific treatise and concludes at once that it is mythological; therefore, we must get rid of the mythology. In so doing he makes two grave mistakes: (1) He fails to understand properly what science is, and the relationship of the Bible to science. By way of review, he fails to see that science deals with "the quantitative, the stable, the predictable, the observable, the general." [1] To the contrary, when the Bible comments on natural things, it comments from the point of view of the popular, the phenomenal, the nonpostulational, the culture of the day in which it was written.[2] What Bultmann thus does is in effect to apply the criteria used to evaluate a modern scientific treatise to the New Testament and to conclude that the New Testament is largely mythological. The only way he would be justified in doing this would be if the New Testament claimed to be a scientific treatise, which it does not.

(2) The second mistake of Bultmann is his failure to see what comprises a world view. Science is only one factor that goes into the construction of a world view. When one attempts to construct a world view on the basis of a scientific perspective alone, he is little better off than the proverbial blind men who attempted to describe the elephant on the basis of the particular part of the animal they happened to touch. Science is certainly a factor in the construction of a world view, but it is only *a* factor, not *the* factor. A world view results from the comprehension and assimilation of all experiences. It deals with cosmology to be sure, but it also deals with metaphysics. What is the ultimate nature of reality? What is the ultimate nature of the universe? What is the source of good and evil? Questions like this cannot be adequately answered by science. This is the province of metaphysics.

To Bultmann's credit, however, he has at least seen the problem more clearly than have many of his predecessors in the critical school. For while he has seen the problem and handled it poorly, many of the liberal scholars have merely ignored the problem. They have simply approached the Bible with their idealistic philosophy at hand and picked from it data that would support

[1] Ramm, *Protestant Christian Evidences*, p. 53.

[2] Ramm, *The Christian View of Science and Scripture*, pp. 66-70.

their theory of the inevitability of human progress, and ignored the rest of it.

Neither of these approaches is acceptable from a biblical point of view. One is not justified in ignoring the totality of the biblical world view in order that he may rest on his philosophical presuppositions. One is not justified in allegorizing the biblical record in order to harmonize it with his philosophical presuppositions.

One should instead look at the entire biblical record, listen to what it has to say, formulate a world view based on that record, and then decide whether or not that is an adequate world view. We have done this briefly in an earlier chapter when dealing with the subject of time. [3] We shall now approach the subject both from the perspective of metaphysics and from that of human redemption, for it is to be assumed that the place of man in the metaphysical construction that is developed would be of particular interest and importance.

Of the many fine treatments of this subject that would merit our attention at this point, we here cite that of James Orr. He states the Christian view in the form of nine propositions:

> I. The Christian view affirms the existence of a Personal, Ethical, Self-Revealing God. It is thus at the outset a system of Theism, and as such is opposed to all systems of Atheism, Agnosticism, Pantheism, or mere Deism.
> II. The Christian view affirms the creation of the world by God, His immanent presence in it, His transcendence over it, and His holy and wise government of it for moral ends.
> III. The Christian view affirms the spiritual nature and dignity of man—his creation in the Divine image, and destination to bear the likeness of God in a perfected relation of sonship.
> IV. The Christian view affirms the fact of sin and disorder of the world, not as something belonging to the Divine idea of it, and inhering in it by necessity, but as something which has entered it by the voluntary turning aside of man from his allegiance to his creator, and from the path of his normal development. The Christian view of the world, in other words, involves a Fall as the presupposition of its doctrine of Redemption; . . .

[3] See above, pp. 114-19.

V. The Christian view affirms the historical Self-Revelation of God to the patriarchs and in the line of Israel, and, as brought to light by this, a gracious purpose of God for the salvation of the world, centering in Jesus Christ, His Son, and the new Head of humanity.

VI. The Christian view affirms that Jesus Christ was not mere man, but the eternal Son of God—a truly Divine Person—who in the fulness of time took upon Him our humanity, and who, on the ground that in Him as man there dwells the fulness of the Godhead bodily, is to be honoured, worshipped, and trusted, even as God is.

. . . .

VII. The Christian view affirms the Redemption of the world through a great act of Atonement—this Atonement to be appropriated by faith, and availing for all who do not wilfully withstand and reject its grace.

VIII. The Christian view affirms that the historical aim of Christ's work was the founding of a Kingdom of God on earth, which includes not only the spiritual salvation of individuals, but a new order of society, the result of the action of spiritual forces set in motion through Christ.

IX. Finally, the Christian view affirms that history has a goal, and that the present order of things will be terminated by the appearance of the Son of Man for judgment, the resurrection of the dead, the final separation of righteous and wicked— final, so far as the Scriptures afford any light, or entitle us to hold out any hope.[4]

The Importance of the Life of Jesus

Even a superficial look at the nine propositions we have just listed should impress one with the central place of importance of the life of Jesus. As a matter of fact, it would be almost impossible to place the life of Jesus in this biblical world view without the employment of the adjective "central."

Why is this true? It would appear that there are two main reasons for it. In the first place, both the biblical materials preceding the life of Jesus and those succeeding it gain their meaning and substance from that life. The

[4] James Orr, *The Christian View of God and the World* (Grand Rapids: Eerdmans, 1947), pp. 32-34.

Old Testament is a book of anticipation. It is incomplete without its fulfilment in the New Testament. As Reid writes, "The Old Testament awaits something like what is provided in the New Testament as a crime and detection story awaits its final chapter."[5] What is true of the Old Testament by way of anticipation is true of the New Testament by way of retrospection. It is a meaningless book apart from the life of Jesus. Cullmann has summarized the central significance of the life of Jesus in the biblical record: "Jesus' earthly activity as the central event consequently became the temporal centre of a line of salvation running both forward and backward. Since it represents the highest form of God's self-communication, all other divine revelations must be related to it, for there can be no revelation of God essentially different from the revelation in Christ."[6]

A second reason for the insistence on the life of Jesus as being the central event of all history is that it is in this life alone that we find an adequate historical basis for faith. The necessity of this historical basis, as well as the danger of its absence, is equally well stated by Cullmann:

> Whatever particular function may be under consideration, the identity of the pre-existent, present, or coming Christ with Jesus of Nazareth is certain only when it is recognized that the real centre of all revelation is the Incarnate One. Without this relationship there would be nothing at all to prevent degeneration into Docetism and syncretism. Jesus would become a philosophical-religious principle, his historical life a mythological cloak.[7]

Cullmann goes on to dispute the idea that the offense of the gospel lies in its "mythological cosmology." The advancement of scientific procedures has not been the factor that has made faith difficult for modern man. Rather, he observes, "The *skandalon*, the foolishness, lies

[5] J. K. S. Reid, *The Authority of Scripture* (New York: Harper, 1957), p. 243.

[6] Oscar Cullmann, *The Christology of the New Testament*, trans. Shirley C. Guthrie and Charles A. M. Hall (Philadelphia: Westminster, 1959), p. 321.

[7] *Ibid.*, pp. 323-24.

in the fact that historically datable events ('under Pontius Pilate') are supposed to represent the very centre of God's revelation and to be connected with all his revelations. That was just as hard for men of that time to accept as for us today."[8]

If, then, the Jesus of history is important to the biblical or Christian world view, how much of that life presented to us in the Gospels must we insist on as being historical? There has been considerable difference here among the critical scholars. We may summarize each position via a diagram and a few comments.

We could present the liberal picture of Jesus as follows:

| Life and Teaching | Passion | Resurrection-Ascension |
| semihistorical | historical | semihistorical |

From the point of view of these scholars there was a large historical element in the Gospels. Items such as miracles and prophecy were of course to be ruled out as actual occurrence, but even at the base of many of these one could see a certain minimum of history.

With Bultmann there is a significant shift in opinion. We might diagram his position in this way:

| Life and Teaching | Passion | Resurrection-Ascension |
| semimythical | historical | mythical |

We use "semi-mythical" here as opposed to "semi-historical" in the previous diagram as an indication that Bultmann has far less confidence in the historical accuracy of the Gospels than had the liberal scholars. Although he feels that there may be historical elements in the life and teaching of Jesus included in the Gospels, because of the nature of the Gospels it is not possible for us to be absolutely certain about the historicity of any single

8 *Ibid.*, p. 327.

word or event. The historical is confined to the cross, "the event of Christ." The resurrection and the ascension are to an even greater degree mythical.

The critics to the left of Bultmann push his thought even further:

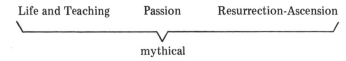

Life and Teaching   Passion   Resurrection-Ascension

mythical

For these critics there is no necessity of retaining any of the Gospel record as historical. It is mythological in its entirety. Man's religious history has presented other mythologies of a similar character.

The new quest swings back once again from the position of Bultmann toward the position of the liberal lives:

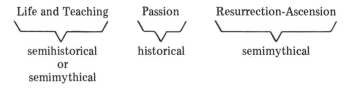

Life and Teaching   Passion   Resurrection-Ascension

semihistorical   historical   semimythical
or
semimythical

The position of these scholars with respect to the historical element in the Gospels is neither as optimistic as that of the liberals nor as pessimistic as that of Bultmann. They go to greater pains attempting to discover what is historical, but always in view of the work of Bultmann.

If, however, the conclusions we have reached in our chapter on history are sound, then it should be apparent that the only proper way to diagram the life of Jesus is as follows:

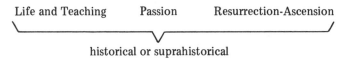

Life and Teaching   Passion   Resurrection-Ascension

historical or suprahistorical

The New Testament presents us not with an event, nor merely with the cross, but with a life. Each part of that life is important from an historical perspective. Baillie criticizes Bultmann for ignoring the life of Jesus that preceded that event:

> Bultmann does indeed keep hold of the idea of the decisive incursion of the Word of God into history in one concrete event, the Cross of Christ. But apart from the whole story of Jesus as an historical human figure, with a teaching and character and career of his own, leading up to the passion, it is difficult to see how we could hear God speaking to us through the cross at all.[9]

What Baillie has insisted for what preceded the cross, we here would insist in like manner for what succeeded the cross in the New Testament, i.e., the resurrection and ascension.

We used both the terms historical and suprahistorical in our diagram. We did this not because we feel that part of the narrative is objective and part is not, nor because we feel that part of the narrative occurred in time and space and part did not, but solely because of the technical sense in which the word "historical" has come to be used. The resurrection and the ascension cannot be arrived at as historical events via the techniques of historical causation or historical analogy. There is, however, good evidence for believing that these were both objective events that occurred within the realm of time and space. Both events occurred within history, but they occurred apart from either historical causation or historical analogy. This made them particularly significant as evidences of the special revelation of God.

The entire life of Jesus must therefore be the subject of our investigation. It follows that any attempt to fathom the significance of that life must look at it as a whole, for we are not warranted in drawing our own conclusions as to what in it was important and what was not. Christianity is incurably an historical faith, and of that great expanse of history from creation to consummation, the history of the life of its founder is of supreme importance. There can be no adequate theology without

[9] D. M. Baillie, *God Was in Christ* (New York: Scribner, 1948), pp. 221-22.

an adequate Christology, and there can be no adequate Christology except that which is based on the life of Jesus. It is consequently to the principal events of that life that we must now direct our attention.

The Principal Events and Their Significance

What we shall attempt to do in this section of our study will be very modest. The reader is referred for fuller treatment to the sections of various orthodox theologies on the person and work of Jesus.[10] What we attempt here is only a sketch.

Pre-existence

It is the universal testimony of the New Testament that Jesus did not begin his existence in a cradle in Bethlehem in the first century of our era. He merely assumed a different form of existence for a specific purpose. In the Synoptic Gospels Jesus does not as a rule make abstract statements about his pre-incarnate state. He does, however, make very frequent comments about "coming" and "being sent" that of necessity imply such a state. Thus in Mark's Gospel when Jesus is criticized for eating with tax collectors and sinners he replies, "Those who are well have no need of a physician, but those who are sick; I came not to call the righteous, but sinners" (Mk. 2:17). Similar statements are found in Mk. 1:38 and 10:45.

In Matthew's Gospel Jesus comments on the effect that response to his person might have on the closest of relationships: "Do not think that I have come to bring peace on earth; I have not come to bring peace, but a sword" (10:34). This may also be compared with statements like those in Mt. 5:17 and 15:24.

In Luke's Gospel, in conjunction with the Zacchaeus account, Jesus makes his familiar pronouncement, "For

[10] See in particular Berkhof, *Systematic Theology*; Boettner, *Studies in Theology*; Edgar Young Mullins, *The Christian Religion in Its Doctrinal Expression* (Philadelphia: Williams, 1917); Strong, *Systematic Theology*.

the Son of Man came to seek and to save the lost"
(19:10).

In John's Gospel Jesus makes more open statements
about his relationship to the Father. Part of the reason
for this diversity must be seen in the variety of the people
to whom Jesus addresses himself. In Jn. 8:58 he makes
the remark that incites the Jews to attempt to stone him:
"Truly, truly, I say to you, before Abraham was, I am."
In his last discourse with his disciples Jesus says, "I came
from the Father and have come into the world; again, I
am leaving the world and going to the Father" (16:28).
Statements of a similar nature may be discovered in Jn.
3:13, 31-34; 6:62; 8:14-16, 23; 17:5, 24, etc.

Paul, too, makes most explicit statements about the
pre-existence of Jesus. Perhaps the most explicit statement of this is found in the great christological passage of
Phil. 2:5-11: " . . . though he was in the form of God,
[he] did not count equality with God a thing to be
grasped, but emptied himself, taking the form of a servant, being born in the likeness of men" (2:6-7). Paul
refers to the same thing elsewhere (e.g., Gal. 4:4-5; II
Cor. 8:9, etc.).

Finally, at the close of the New Testament, Christ
himself proclaims, "I am the Alpha and the Omega, the
first and the last, the beginning and end" (Rev. 22:13).

Boettner has pointed out very well the significance of
this pre-existence of Jesus:

> In all the history of the world Jesus emerges as the only
> "expected" person. No one was looking for such a person as
> Julius Caesar, or Napoleon, or Washington, or Lincoln to
> appear at the time and place that they did appear. No other
> person has had his course foretold or his work laid out for him
> centuries before he was born. But the coming of the Messiah
> had been predicted for centuries.[11]

Anyone who has even a superficial acquaintance with
the New Testament will realize that a multiplicity of
titles are ascribed to Jesus. In addition to our sketch of
the principal events of the life of Jesus, we shall select at

[11] Boettner, p. 160.

least one of these titles for consideration which relates in particular to his work and significance at each particular time. His real significance, of course, can be seen only in the totality of the ascriptions.

The title that we shall discuss briefly here is "Word." This title is applied directly to Jesus only in the Johannine writings. We find it in the prologue to the Gospel of John, in I Jn. 1:1, and in Rev. 19:13. The idea is used frequently, however, in both the Old Testament and in Hellenistic literature. The Hebrew equivalent *dabar* is used 394 times in the Old Testament for a communication that comes to men from God. The avenue by which the word comes is diverse. It may be a commandment, a prophecy, a warning, or an encouragement.[12]

In Hellenistic thought the term has to do more with the reasonable force that rules the world. In Stoicism it is used of both divine reason in and of itself and that reason as it is manifested in the world. In the Jewish Alexandrian philosopher Philo, the word becomes a Divine Principle between transcendent God and the world. Even here, however, the emphasis remains on the rational. The *logos* is not personal.

In the Johannine literature of the New Testament, the title is applied directly to Jesus: "And the Word became flesh and dwelt among us, full of grace and truth; we have beheld his glory, glory as of the only Son from the Father" (Jn. 1:14). The title "Word" as it is used in John thus tells us two things: (1) It informs us that Jesus, who came to reveal God, did not begin his existence at his birth; but, beyond this, (2) it informs us that the one who came is of the very nature of God himself.

Birth

That Jesus is represented as having been virgin-born is clear from the early part of both Matthew's and Luke's Gospels. One's acceptance or rejection of the accounts given there will depend largely upon the same two things that determine one's attitude to the miraculous in the

12 J. B. Taylor, "Word," *The New Bible Dictionary*, ed. J. D. Douglas (Grand Rapids: Eerdmans, 1962), p. 1337.

New Testament as a whole: (1) one's world view; (2) one's estimate of Jesus. It is possible to lose sight of the significance of an event like the virgin birth and to degenerate into a kind of argument for argument's sake. We disdain this sort of enterprise. While a great deal could be said here regarding the theology of the virgin birth, we shall limit ourselves to three observations that for us demonstrate its absolute necessity: (1) If Jesus was the supernatural person the New Testament represents him to have been, it is only logical to suppose that his birth was supernatural. The idea of a virgin birth may be difficult to understand, but any attempt to account for his life on purely naturalistic bases is even more difficult to understand. (2) Jesus was a human and divine person. We shall develop this further shortly, but the divine element is difficult to account for apart from a supernatural birth. The only other alternative of adoptionism has never been held by any large segment of the Church. The reason for this is evident. It is not the New Testament position. (3) In order to accomplish human redemption Jesus had to be a sinless person. It is the testimony of the Scriptures as well as of the consciousness of every other man that such a possibility does not exist for naturally born men.

The significance of Jesus at the time of his birth is best expressed by the title "Emmanuel." The great revelatory significance of the birth of Jesus is clarified in the Gospel of Matthew as it quotes the words of Isaiah: "Behold, a virgin shall conceive and bear a son, and his name shall be called Emmanuel (which means, God with us)" (Mt. 1:23). We have thus in the incarnation of Jesus the actual appearance of God on the human scene.

Life and teaching

In his book on evidences, Bernard Ramm makes some hypotheses as to what we should expect if God became a man. These hypotheses may serve as a background against which we may study the life of Jesus:

A. If God became a man we would expect His human life to be sinless.[13]
B. If God were a man we would expect Him to be holy.[14]
C. If God were a man we would expect His words to be the greatest words ever spoken.[15]
D. If God were a man we would expect Him to exert a profound power over human personality.[16]
E. If God were a man we would expect supernatural doings:
   (1) Being God alone would involve some tokens of the supernatural;
   (2) Certainly God owes it to man that there is no possible mistake at such a tremendous point.[17]
F. If God were to become a man we would expect Him to manifest the love of God.[18]
G. If God were to become a man, He would be the most divine man that ever lived.[19]
H. If God were a man we would expect His personality to be true humanity.[20]

Now out of this list of hypotheses two things immediately come to our attention. If God were to become a man we would expect (1) that he would give clear-cut and adequate evidence that he was not just another man but that he was really God, and (2) that the life of that man would be a perfect human life. When we bring these expectations to the New Testament, this is precisely what we see reflected. Jesus is both God and perfect man or, as theologians customarily put it, Jesus is the God-man. In a discussion of the significance of the life of Jesus, therefore, we must deal with both his deity and his humanity.

Deity of Jesus. A good place to begin would be with the literature of the New Testament. When we have discussed that, we may turn to certain supplementary

[13] Ramm, *Protestant Christian Evidences,* p. 167.
[14] *Ibid.,* p. 169.
[15] *Ibid.,* p. 170.
[16] *Ibid.,* p. 171.
[17] *Ibid.,* p. 173.
[18] *Ibid.,* p. 175.
[19] *Ibid.,* p. 176.
[20] *Ibid.,* p. 177.

evidence. In the first place, there are numerous places in the New Testament where Jesus himself makes direct and indirect claims to his deity. The Gospel of John contains the greatest number of these. We have already seen that the likely reason for this is to be found in the class of people with whom Jesus has his conversations. For the most part they are either the religious authorities of Judaism or his own disciples. "I and the Father are one" (Jn. 10:30) and "He who has seen me has seen the Father" (Jn. 14:9) are two of the most explicit. With this one might compare 3:13; 5:17, 18, 19-27; 6:37-40, 57; 8:34-35; 10:17, 18, 35, 36, etc.

The Synoptics, too, give strong indication of Jesus' realization of his metaphysical unity with the Father. In Matthew Jesus comments, "All things have been delivered to me by my Father; and no one knows the Son except the Father, and no one knows the Father except the Son and any one to whom the Son chooses to reveal him" (Mt. 11:27; cf. 7:21; 10:32, 33; 12:50; 15:13; 16:17; 18:10, 19, 35; 20:23; 21:37, 38; 22:41-46; 24:36; 25:34; 26:29, 53; 28:19, etc.).

Immediately after Peter's confession in Mark's Gospel Jesus begins to tell the disciples of his anticipated suffering. He definitely identifies himself as the Son of Man in connection with those sufferings (Mk. 8:31). Then he comments, "For whoever is ashamed of me and my words in this adulterous and sinful generation, of him will the Son of man also be ashamed when he comes in the glory of his Father" (Mk. 8:38; cf. 12:6; 13:32, etc.).

In Luke the same tendency of Jesus to refer to the Father in terms of the first person singular possessive is seen (cf. Lk. 2:49; 22:29; 24:29). In addition he shares with Matthew and Mark some of the passages formerly mentioned (cf. Lk. 10:22; 20:13, 41-44).

On the basis of all this evidence it cannot be denied that the Gospels uniformly present Jesus as one who was conscious of union with the Father and the Spirit in the Trinity of the Godhead.

The testimonies to the deity of Jesus are not to be limited to his own proclamations. The apostles bear frequent witness to their evaluation of his person. The

Gospels close with the realization by the disciples of who this Jesus really is. The book of Acts is a story of the proclamation by the early Church of God's Son and his work. We are told that immediately after his conversion Paul began to proclaim this message: "And in the synagogues immediately he proclaimed Jesus saying, 'He is the Son of God' " (Acts 9:20). Constantly in his letters Paul refers to Jesus in the most extravagant terms. If Jesus were not God, it would be necessary for us to charge Paul with the most crude blasphemy (see in particular Rom. 1:7; 9:5; I Cor. 1:1-3; 2:8; II Cor. 5:10; Gal. 2:20; 4:4; Phil. 2:5-11; Col. 2:9; I Tim. 3:16). The Epistle to the Hebrews is equally emphatic in its ascription of deity to Jesus (cf. Heb. 1:1-3, 5, 8; 4:14; 5:8). To put it briefly, we may say that every New Testament book attributes deity to Jesus either by direct statement or by inference.

In addition to these direct and indirect assertions of his deity, many of the characteristics or attributes of deity are ascribed to him. Boettner has compiled a list of these attributes along with the scriptural references. Such a list includes holiness, eternity, life, immutability, omnipotence, omniscience, omnipresence, creation, authority to forgive sins. Jesus is the author of salvation and the object of faith. To him prayer and worship are to be offered, and also to him is ascribed the judgment of all men.[21]

Numerous divine titles are ascribed to Jesus. We shall notice in particular one of these shortly.

In addition to this direct New Testament evidence there is certain supplementary evidence that should be brought to our attention in support of the deity of Jesus. It was popular in the era of the liberal lives of Jesus to suppose that one could separate the early from the late in the Gospels and thus arrive at an earlier nonsupernatural Jesus as compared with a later supernatural Jesus. Bruce has pointed out that form criticism has done much to destroy that thesis: "Perhaps the most important result to which form criticism points is that, no matter how far back we may press our researches into the roots of the

21 Boettner, pp. 161-72.

gospel story, no matter how we classify the gospel material, we never arrive at a non-supernatural Jesus."[22]

But we may press our investigation a step further. If a supernatural Jesus is at the roots of the earliest Gospel material, it must have come from one of two sources. It could have come from Jesus himself, or it could have been an invention by the disciples. We have already in earlier chapters raised the issue of invention on the part of the disciples in connection with the miracles and the resurrection. We felt that it had to be discarded because it would necessitate our believing that the disciples laid down their lives for something they knew to be false.

If the source for the idea of the deity of Jesus is Jesus himself, it may be accounted for on one of two bases. Either he was God's Son in the metaphysical sense, or he made a false claim to such significance. If the second of these alternatives is true, then we have a curious circumstance indeed. Ramm observes, "If we impugn the person of Christ, we must admit that what on the one hand appears to be the holiest, godliest, divinest man that ever lived is also guilty of the grossest misrepresentation in all of human history."[23] As others have put it, "If Jesus is not God, he is not good." The idea that Jesus was deluded has even less to commend it.

Our inability to account for the divine portrait of Jesus in the Gospels on psychological grounds is matched by a similar inability to account for it on sociological grounds. In our chapter on history we noted how closely related the Gospel records are to the actual events and to the persons involved in those events. In the heyday of the liberal lives and the succeeding form criticism, it may have been possible to visualize the evolution of a supernatural Jesus from a nonsupernatural Galilean teacher, but in the light of the latest manuscript and archaeological evidence such a possibility no longer exists.

We should also observe that great sayings and great movements are the products of individuals, not communi-

22 Bruce, *The New Testament Documents: Are They Reliable?*, p. 33.
23 Ramm, *Protestant Christian Evidences*, p. 179.

ties. Communities are not to the slightest degree productive in this regard. It thus becomes necessary for us to hypothesize a figure of greater stature than Jesus, if the Christian movement did not take its rise from him. In summary, history has not given meaning to Jesus; Jesus has given meaning to history.

Ramm has put his finger on the real issue as it relates to twentieth-century critics:

> If we deny the divinity of Christ and the presence of the supernatural, where do we get the picture of the Jesus we think actually existed? We get it out of our own heads dictated by our own metaphysical and religious convictions; we do not get it out of the Gospels. . . . The Christ of these men is a hybrid combination of accepted segments of the Gospel narrative patched together with religious and metaphysical opinions. The documentary evidence weighs like lead against the unbeliever at this point.[24]

Some may entertain the notion that we may retain the Gospel portrait of Jesus and still account for his life on humanistic bases. Such a possibility, however, may be quickly disposed of. For one thing, the tremendous authority Jesus claimed and exercised was outside the possibility of any human teacher. The thing that impressed the masses was that the teaching of Jesus was differentiated from that of the scribes by its innate sense of authority (Mk. 1:22; cf. Mt. 7:29; Lk. 4:32).

That authority also characterized his actions. The religious leaders of Judaism were offended and insulted by that unique authority. They could not deny that he performed exorcisms (Mk. 1:27; cf. Lk. 4:36), but on the occasion of his triumphal entry they challenged the authority that his actions implied (Mk. 11:28; cf. Mt. 21:23; Lk. 20:2). He even claimed authority to forgive sins (Mk. 2:10; cf. Mt. 9:6; Lk. 5:24), and his authority was vindicated by the visible physical results in the paralytic. That any mere human could claim such authority and back it up with his actions is beyond the remotest possibility.

24 *Ibid.*, p. 180.

Jesus' entire life and ministry was conducted in such a way that any attempt to account for it on purely humanistic bases is doomed to failure. There was a perfect correlation of character and conduct which neither before nor since has been equaled in the history of the human race. When the temple police were denounced for not arresting Jesus, as they had been directed to do by the chief priests and the Pharisees, their only reply was, "No man ever spoke like this man!" (Jn. 7:46). Boettner has summarized the matter well when he writes, "There can be no doubt but that in His teaching Jesus presented Himself not as one needing salvation but as the Saviour of men, not as a member of the Church but as the head of the Church, not as the example but as the object of faith, not merely as a suppliant praying to God but as the one to whom prayer is to be made, not merely as a teacher of men but as their sovereign Lord."[25]

Since we have already devoted a chapter to the subject of miracles in the life of Jesus, we need not reintroduce the subject here at any length. But the same things that have been said of his teaching and conduct in general may be said of his miracles. No mere man, no matter how splendid his character, could have done the things that Jesus did. One may deny his miracles. One may attempt to rationalize them. When critics do this however, one is left with the gnawing feeling that it is done not on purely critical grounds, but rather as a last-ditch effort to escape the significance of his person.

No successful estimate of his person can be made which does not hold his words and his works together. Many liberal scholars have centered their attention on his words, and many conservative scholars have delighted themselves with the miracles. But one can arrive at a fair appraisal only when he holds these two facets of Jesus' life together. What is the result of such an investigation? Boettner sees it clearly:

> He differs from all other men not only in degree but also in kind. He is, of course, the central figure in the New Testament, and also in the Old when it is read in the light of the New. No

[25] Boettner, p. 176.

explanation other than that He was Deity incarnate is sufficient to account for the majesty of His person and the uplifting influences that have followed wherever His Gospel has been made known.[26]

If we were to choose a title that indicates more clearly than any other Jesus' significance as deity, it would perhaps be the title "Son of God." Vos has noticed that this name occurs in four senses in the biblical record: (1) It is sometimes used in a general moral and religious sense, and thus it is virtually equivalent to "child of God." (2) It is sometimes used to refer to the Messiah. Used as such it refers to the office of the Messiah and not his nature. (3) It is sometimes used in the nativistic sense ascribing the Messiah's human nature "to the direct, supernatural paternity of God." (4) It is sometimes used in "the Trinitarian sense, which affirms the sonship as existing in eternity before the world was, as something not merely antedating but absolutely transcending His human life and His official calling as Messiah."[27]

That all four of these senses of the term as they apply to Jesus are used in the New Testament is evident. It is in the last sense, however, that his metaphysical union with the Father and thus his deity is pointed out. Into a lengthy treatment of this title we cannot go. That has been done elsewhere.[28] Cullmann has summarized well the meaning of the title in the New Testament: "While 'Son of God' does indeed point to the divine majesty of Jesus and his ultimate oneness with God, it also essentially implies his obedience to the Father."[29]

The significance of Jesus as God's Son and its effect on mankind is well stated in the last two verses of Jn. 20: "Now Jesus did many other signs in the presence of the disciples, which are not written in this book; but these are written that you might believe that Jesus is the Christ,

[26] *Ibid.*, pp. 266-67.

[27] Geerhardus Vos, *The Self-Disclosure of Jesus* (Grand Rapids: Eerdmans, 1953), pp. 141-42.

[28] Cullmann, *The Christology of the New Testament*, pp. 270-305; Vos, pp. 141-226.

[29] Cullmann, *The Christology of the New Testament*, p. 270.

the Son of God, and that believing you may have life in
his name" (20:30-31).

Humanity of Jesus. There is as much danger in stressing the deity of Jesus to the exclusion of his humanity as
there is in stressing the humanity of Jesus to the exclusion of his deity. The problem here does not lie in the
fact that in our day the humanity of Jesus is usually
denied, although the docetic tendency on the part of a
critic like Bultmann may result in virtually the same
thing. The problem lies in the fact that we devote so
much of our attention either to the demonstration of or
the significance of his deity, that any consideration of his
humanity is ignored. Both natures, however, were important if Jesus was to accomplish the task the New Testament represents him as having accomplished. As it was
necessary that he be a member of the Godhead if his life
and death were to have any eternal significance for man,
it was necessary that he be man if he was to take man's
place.

His ability to take man's place is found in the fact that
he lived a perfect life and fulfilled in his person the
demands of the law. Paul states this expressly: "For our
sake he [God] made him [Jesus] to be sin who knew no
sin, so that in him we might become the righteousness of
God" (II Cor. 5:21). It is not sufficient merely to speak
of the humanity of Jesus. That humanity must always be
qualified by the adjectives "perfect" and "sinless." As
Wallace has observed, "Besides this emphasis on his true
humanity, there is nevertheless always an emphasis on the
fact that even in his humanity he is sinless and also
utterly different from other men and that his significance
must not be sought by ranking him alongside the greatest
or wisest or holiest of all other men."[30]

While we shall emphasize the title "Son of Man" as of
primary importance as it relates to his human nature, we
shall in addition refer to two other names or titles that
are ascribed to him and are of special importance as they

[30] Ronald S. Wallace, "Christology," *Baker's Dictionary of
Theology*, ed. Everett F. Harrison (Grand Rapids: Baker, 1960), p.
117.

relate to his humanity. His given name, "Jesus," was the Greek equivalent of the Hebrew name that we transliterate "Joshua." It was characteristic of the Hebrews to use names that bore a religious significance, as for example Joshua or Jesus—"Yahweh is salvation." That this name had special significance as attached to Jesus, however, is demonstrated in the annunciation to Joseph: "You shall call his name Jesus, for he will save his people from their sins" (Mt. 1:21).

While Jesus does not specifically call himself "Servant" in the Gospels, he is so designated in the preaching of the early Church in the book of Acts (Acts 3:13, 26; 4:27, 30). That the servant motif pervades his thought, however, cannot be denied. He doubtlessly insisted on the servant nature of his role for at least two reasons: (1) He found it necessary to counteract the militant, politically conceived ideas of the Messiah which his disciples harbored; and (2) he looked upon his task as being primarily that of a servant as illustrated most clearly in the suffering servant of Isaiah. It is against this background that passages like the following must be interpreted: "The Son of man also came not to be served but to serve, and to give his life as a ransom for many" (Mk. 10:45).

The title "Son of Man" is perhaps the most intriguing title that has been given to Jesus. This is true for a variety of reasons. In the first place, this is the only title that Jesus used of himself, and he used it frequently. In contrast, the disciples never refer to him directly by that title.

The development of the title is another factor that makes it of great interest to us. The customary use of the expression "Son of Man" in the Old Testament is equivalent to "man." In the book of Ezekiel, for example, the expression is used about ninety times when the prophet refers to himself. In the book of Daniel, however, the Son of Man is a heavenly figure who would come at the close of the age as a Judge. It thus appears that in Judaism the term had these two almost diametrically opposite meanings: (1) an earthly man, and (2) a heavenly pre-existent man.

Why did Jesus prefer this as a self-designation? We can

arrive at some probable reasons for his having done so. In the first place, it was the only term that Jesus could have used that was free of the possibility of being misinterpreted by his followers. The term "Messiah," as we have seen, was subject to a very materialistic interpretation. It also would have thrown him open to prosecution as a political pretender. The title "Son of God" may have opened him to the same limitations as the title "Messiah" on the one hand, and to the charge of blasphemy on the other. The very indefiniteness of the title "Son of Man" was what commended it to Jesus' use during his lifetime. On the one hand, it allowed him to identify himself with man; and on the other, it enabled him to pour into the term such content as he desired. This significance would be realized fully only after his death and resurrection. Thus, while the term is not one that expresses exclusively the significance of Jesus' humanity, it does to a very important degree give expression to that ideal and perfect humanity. Jesus is set opposite Adam as the new representative of the race: "Both Adam and Christ have the representative relationship to the whole of mankind that is involved in the conception 'Son of man.' But Christ is regarded as One whose identification with all mankind is far more deep and complete than that of Adam."[31]

The double significance of this title is summarized by Cullmann: "We conclude that, apart from one or two passages in which the term may designate all men, Jesus used the title Son of Man to express his consciousness of having to fulfill the work of the Heavenly Man in two ways: (1) in glory at the end of time—a thought familiar to the expectation of the Son of Man in certain Jewish circles; (2) in the humiliation of the incarnation among sinful men—a thought foreign to all earlier conceptions of the Son of Man."[32]

One question remains for us: Why did not the title "Son of Man" attain a place of importance among the disciples and in the early Church as a designation for

31 *Ibid.*, p. 118.
32 Cullmann, *The Christology of the New Testament*, p. 164.

Jesus? There is no simple answer to this question, but the comments of Vos are perhaps as suggestive as any:

> By calling Himself the Son of man Jesus imparted to the Messiahship His own heaven-centered spirit. And the height to which He thus lifted His Person and His work may well have had something to do with the hesitancy of His early followers to name Him this greatest and most celestial of all titles. As a matter of fact, we can still test this by ourselves. Neither in the language of private piety, nor in that of common worship, hymnodic or otherwise, has the title Son of man ever become thoroughly domesticated. And it is perhaps good that this should be so.[33]

We have thus expressed in the two titles, "Son of God" and "Son of Man," the significance of Jesus as it relates respectively to his deity and his humanity, although, as we have seen, neither title is to be regarded as referring exclusively to one facet of his person.

Relation of the two natures. The union of two natures in one person has been a source of endless difficulty in the history of the Church. It would appear that there are two primary sources of such difficulty. One of these is an emphasis on a part of the New Testament record to the exclusion of another part. A second is the inability of the finite human mind to comprehend the infinite. We list here four kinds of errors to be avoided: (1) Sometimes the two natures have been confused so that the resultant personality was neither human nor divine. This error first rose to prominence in the fifth century and was then known as Eutychianism. (2) Sometimes the two natures are so separated as to give Jesus a double or split personality. This error also arose in the fifth century when it was known as Nestorianism. (3) Sometimes his deity is emphasized to the exclusion of his humanity. The ancient and modern heresy of Docetism is a case in point here. (4) Sometimes his humanity is emphasized to the exclusion of his deity. In some respects the early Ebionites were representative of this error, and there have been many advocates of it in modern times.

[33] Vos, p. 254.

The present writer likes the way in which the relation of the two natures has been described by Boettner:

> Throughout the whole study of the relationship which exists between the two natures we are, of course, face to face with impenetrable mystery. It is one of those mysteries which the Scriptures reveal but which they make no effort to explain. Christ is an absolutely unique person; and although in every age much study has been expended upon His personality it remains a profound mystery, in some respects as baffling as the Trinity itself. All we can know are the simple facts which are revealed to us in Scripture, and beyond these it is not necessary to go. As a matter of fact we do not understand the mysterious union of the spiritual and physical in our own natures; nor do we understand the attributes of God. But the essential facts are clear and understandable by the average Christian. These are that the Second Person of the Trinity added to His own nature a perfectly normal human nature, that His life on earth was passed as far as was fitting within the limits of this humanity, that His life remained at all times the life of God manifest in the flesh, that His action in the flesh never escaped beyond the boundary of that which was suitable for incarnate Deity, and that all of this was done in order that in man's nature and as man's Substitute He might assume man's obligation before the law, suffer the penalty which was due to him for sin, and so accomplish his redemption.[34]

Death

If one takes the New Testament documents at face value, there are two features of the death of Jesus that are self-evident: (1) He fully expected to meet death and looked upon its occurrence as an accomplishment; and (2) the death of Jesus is looked upon as a part of the eternal plan of the Godhead.

From the time of the Transfiguration, Jesus spoke of his death openly to his disciples. One of the purposes of the Transfiguration was apparently to show the disciples the glory that would follow the hour of trial. Thus we are told that Moses and Elijah "appeared in glory and spoke of his departure, which he was to accomplish at Jeru-

[34] Boettner, pp. 202-03.

salem" (Lk. 9:31). In the weeks that followed, Jesus
spoke to his disciples repeatedly about his death (see in
particular Mk. 9:30-32; cf. Mt. 17:22-23; Lk. 9:43-45;
Lk. 12:50; Mk. 10:32-34; cf. Mt. 20:17-19; Lk. 18:
31-34).

That the death of Jesus was in the eternal plan of God
is emphasized particularly in the book of Acts. On three
occasions in the sermons contained there (Acts 2:23;
3:18; 13:27-29), the death of Jesus is referred to in
connection with words like "foreknowledge," "foretold,"
"fulfilled." And in an early prayer of the Church, the
event of Jesus' death is referred to as that which was
"predestined to take place" (Acts 4:28).

The death of Jesus is therefore looked at from the New
Testament point of view as an accomplishment. The
significance of that death is indicated in a number of New
Testament words which we shall notice briefly. The word
that has received the largest share of theological attention
is atonement. This idea goes back into the Old Testament
and the sacrificial system. There God appointed animal
sacrifice as the means to atonement. The efficacy of this
means of atonement was seen not as something inhering
in the blood of the animal, but rather as the divinely
appointed means for procuring atonement. While the
Greek word used to translate the Hebrew *kipper* (atonement) in the Septuagint does not appear in the New
Testament, the equivalent idea is expressed in other terminology.

The idea behind the death of Jesus, therefore, as it
relates to the atonement, is that Jesus is the perfect
sacrifice. A large literature has developed on the idea of
the atonement in the New Testament. The subject increasingly demanded the attention of the Church. From
the period of the Middle Ages onward theories of the
atonement were developed by Church scholars. A consideration of these theories is beyond the scope of our
study here, but the writer feels that the theory that best
accounts for the New Testament data is the penal substitutionary theory.[35] This is clearly the idea of Peter as he

35 For a good treatment see Berkhof, pp. 373-83.

writes, "He himself bore our sins in his body on the tree, that we might die to sin and live to righteousness" (I Pet. 2:24).

The words used in the New Testament to carry the idea of atonement are a group of related words that have been translated either as "expiation" or as "propitiation." Expiation carries the connotation of the cancellation of sin, while propitiation carries the connotation of the turning away of God's wrath. There is some division among scholars as to which of these words most adequately translates the New Testament idea. Some feel that expiation is the proper word.[36] Others feel that the idea of propitiation must be given the primary place.[37] It is perhaps safest to say that both ideas are contained in these words. "In this is love, not that we loved God but that he loved us and sent his Son to be the expiation [and propitiation] for our sins" (I Jn. 4:10).

While the terms we have discussed so far have dealt primarily with the *means* by which God's eternal plan was accomplished, the word "reconciliation" tells us *what* was accomplished in the death of Jesus. It tells us that through the death of Jesus two parties (God and man) who had formerly been cut off from fellowship with one another now have the possibility of the renewal of that fellowship. Paul writes, "Therefore, if any one is in Christ, he is a new creation; the old has passed away, behold, the new has come. All this is from God, who through Christ reconciled us to himself and gave us the ministry of reconciliation" (II Cor. 5:17-18).

Though none of the titles that are applied to Jesus in the New Testament may be properly understood apart from his death, there is no New Testament title that speaks of his significance primarily in his death. The most significant title we could give him in this respect would be the title "Redeemer." God is spoken of as Israel's Redeemer in the Old Testament, and it is certain that

[36] C. H. Dodd, *The Bible and the Greeks* (London: Hodder and Stoughton, 1935), pp. 82-95.

[37] Leon Morris, *The Apostolic Preaching of the Cross* (Grand Rapids: Eerdmans, 1956).

Jesus is thought of in the same relation to the Christians in the New Testament. Redemption in biblical thought is the deliverance from some evil by the payment of a ransom. Jesus, the Redeemer, is thus looked upon as the one who paid that price in his death. Paul points this out to the Galatians: "But when the time had fully come, God sent forth his Son, born of woman, born under the law, to redeem those who were under the law, so that we might receive adoption as sons" (Gal. 4:4-5).

We make here one final observation in connection with the death of Jesus. No theory of the atonement, or of any of the other terms that we have discussed in connection with the death of Jesus, is adequate which does not hold a delicate balance between the love and justice of God. If one puts undue emphasis on the love of God to the exclusion of his justice, he is in danger of making God less than God. If one puts undue emphasis on the justice of God to the exclusion of his love, he is in danger of making him a vindictive tyrant.

Resurrection

We have already devoted a chapter to the resurrection of Jesus, so our treatment here can be comparatively brief. We shall look briefly at its significance. While one would be in error if he were to say that atonement was due only to the death of Jesus, and that justification was due only to his resurrection, there is a certain sense in which justification is more closely attached to Jesus' resurrection.

Justification means that one is pronounced, accepted, and treated as just. It signifies, on the one hand, that one is not penally liable for breaking the law, and on the other, that one is entitled to all the privileges of one who has kept the law.

Justification thus has a legal flavoring. It is often viewed as being a result of the entire work of Jesus, but Paul in particular attaches it more specifically on occasion to his resurrection: "It [faith] will be reckoned to us who believe in him that raised from the dead Jesus our

Lord, who was put to death for our trespasses and raised for our justification" (Rom. 4:24-25).

The title that gives us the significance of Jesus at the time of his resurrection more clearly than any other is that of "Christ," the promised Messiah of the Old Testament. We have noticed in an earlier chapter that during his lifetime Jesus used this title with a great deal of hesitancy. This was due primarily to the crass, materialistic ideas that had gathered themselves about the term "Messiah." When, however, the realization of his resurrection dawned upon the Church, it became apparent to them all that he was the promised deliverer. Now the term could be used freely, because it would be understood in connection with what Jesus had actually accomplished rather than in connection with a vague deliverer who was to appear in the future.

It is little wonder that this became the most frequent designation for Jesus in the Church. It was the title that linked Jesus most definitely with the expected one of the Old Testament era. As such it was well suited to designate Jesus as the central figure of all human history. It was the primary concern of Paul to proclaim Jesus as the promised Christ. We read of his dialogue with the Jews in the synagogue in Thessalonica, and this is only typical of what he did in every Jewish community: "And Paul went in, as was his custom, and for three weeks he argued with them from the scriptures, explaining and proving that it was necessary for the Christ to suffer and to rise from the dead and saying, 'This Jesus, whom I proclaim to you, is the Christ' " (Acts 17:2-3).

Ascension

Forty days after his resurrection Jesus ascended into heaven (Acts 1:1-11). He had accomplished what he had come to do. He had lived a perfect life. He had revealed, as fully as man needed to know, the nature and requirements of God. He had suffered abuse at the hands of wicked men that eventuated in his crucifixion. God had accepted his perfect sacrifice and raised him up three days later. He had spent a period of time with his followers. Now he returned to the Father.

It would seem that the title that would most adequately suggest the significance of Jesus in his ascended majesty would be "Lord." The Greek word for Lord, *kyrios*, had a wide variety of usages in the New Testament era. It was used as a polite form of address, much as we in contemporary English use the word "sir." It had a deeper religious significance in that it was used for the numerous cult deities of the Roman world. In this spirit it was also applied to the Roman emperors.

This title was used in a far more profound sense to translate the name for God in the Septuagint. As such it passed into the New Testament as a regular designation for God.

Two of these usages are primary in the New Testament. When the disciples refer to Jesus as "Lord" in the Gospels, it is usually in the form of a polite address to the authoritative teacher. After Jesus' resurrection and ascension, however, it is applied to him in the latter sense, as God. It is the latter of these two usages, of course, that primarily interests us here.

In his Pentecost sermon Peter proclaimed, "Let all the house of Israel therefore know assuredly that God has made him both Lord and Christ, this Jesus whom you crucified" (Acts 2:36). Paul makes reference to the same thing when he writes in that lofty christological passage to the Philippians, "Therefore God has highly exalted him and bestowed on him the name which is above every name, that at the name of Jesus every knee should bow, in heaven and on earth and under the earth, and every tongue confess that Jesus Christ is Lord, to the glory of God the Father" (Phil. 2:9-11).

This is a fitting conclusion to the list of titles that we have considered as they are applied to Jesus in relation to the incarnation. He who first left his splendor with the Father to come into our world and was designated as "Emmanuel," "God with us," now returns to his heavenly splendor to resume his place as the Second Person of the Trinity. But his return is far more glorious than was his exit; for now he has procured, through his death, burial, and resurrection, the means whereby man may be reunited with the Godhead.

Return

The New Testament does not restrict its attention to the past. The events of the past give meaning to the present, but the events of the past also give certainty to the future. Jesus in his first advent stands at the center of human history. Jesus in his second advent will initiate a series of events that will mark the end of human history. The biblical record sheds a great deal of light on that consummation of human history, but not enough for us to set up a neat chronology of the events. Of this much, however, we may be certain. Christ will return. The dead will be raised. All mankind will be judged. The basis of the judgment will be men's relationship to God in Jesus Christ. As a result, men shall either spend an eternity in fellowship with Christ, or they shall be eternally banished from his presence.

At the end of human history Jesus stands as "Judge." We have already noticed that the title "Son of Man" has in part this idea of an eschatological Judge. To this one could add a number of New Testament passages that designate Jesus as Judge. In Paul's final letter he gives Timothy instructions for his ministry in light of the return of Christ: "I charge you in the presence of God and of Christ Jesus who is to judge the living and the dead, and by his appearing and his kingdom: preach the word, be urgent in season and out of season, convince, rebuke, and exhort, be unfailing in patience and in teaching" (II Tim. 4:1-2).

In early Christian art the fish was used as a symbol of faith in Christ. This was legitimate because the Greek letters for "fish," *ichthus*, could be used acrostically to designate a confession that we would translate "Jesus Christ God's Son (our) Savior." In light of the investigation we have conducted in this chapter relative to Jesus' significance, and the various titles applied particularly to him at various stages of his self-revelation, it can be seen how completely appropriate that symbol was.

In view of the study we have conducted in this chapter, it would be impossible for us to overestimate the significance of Jesus for mankind. He brought human history into being as a result of his creative action in his eternal pre-existence with the Father. He entered our world at the center of human history to reveal more fully God's nature to man and to provide the means for man's redemption. He will return to terminate human history and to take into his fellowship those who by his grace have entered into a redeeming relationship with him. Paul's ascription of praise should be the sentiment of every believer: "O the depth of the riches and wisdom and knowledge of God! How unsearchable are his judgments and how inscrutable his ways! 'For who has known the mind of the Lord, or who has been his counselor?' 'Or who has given a gift to him that he might be repaid?' For from him and through him and to him are all things. To him be glory forever. Amen" (Rom. 11:33-36).

The Weaknesses of Critical Theories

As we have seen the weaknesses of critical attempts in the study of the Jesus of history at other points in our investigation, we must examine here some of the shortcomings of this kind of investigation as it relates to Jesus' significance. One such weakness is found on the part of those who accept only a part of the biblical record concerning Jesus. One must not approach the New Testament as he would a piece of mythology. One must first decide what kind of literature he has in hand and then interpret it in accordance with that investigation. The contention we have made in this study is that the New Testament is sober history. Therefore, one is not justified in accepting the golden rule as an authentic utterance of Jesus and rejecting statements in which he claims for himself a metaphysical relationship to the Father, nor is he justified in accepting Jesus' teaching and rejecting his miracles. In other words, one is not justified in accepting that part of the record which identifies Jesus simply as a man and rejecting that part of the record which identifies him as the God-man.

There are grave difficulties that beset such an attempt. Why has this magnificence been displayed in only this man? Why has not this magnificence been displayed in others since his time? Via this kind of approach Jesus becomes a kind of all-time ideal man without giving one an adequate explanation of why this should be so.

Often attending this arbitrary process of selection has been the raising of an item of subsidiary importance to the place of supreme importance. Such, for example, was the mistake of liberal theologians who raised the ethics of Jesus to the place of supreme importance. The New Testament ideas of atonement and redemption were repulsive to them. But it has become self-evident in our century that one cannot apply the ethics of the New Testament to unregenerate man, for he lacks both the desire and the ability to use them in a meaningful way.

This leads us to comment on a further weakness of many modern attempts in the study of the life of Jesus. There is often accompanying such study too high an estimate of modern man. Man is looked upon as being in a position of moral continuity with God. This weakness stands out particularly in the liberal treatments of Jesus' life and among critics to the left of Bultmann. Here we are returned to the subject with which we began this study. If man is fallen, then he needs to know more about God than he can find by the unaided use of his intellect. Special revelation is necessary. Man needs to be restored to fellowship with God before he can do anything of significance with his life. It is the New Testament contention that such a life becomes possible only when one relates himself meaningfully to Christ in the light of the redemption he has accomplished.

If, on the other hand, there is nothing basically wrong with man, then general revelation is all that is necessary. In spite of all the literature that has been penned in recent years on the subject of modern man, one needs to be reminded of the similarities of modern and ancient man as well as the differences. When it comes to his relationship to God, it must be seriously questioned whether there is any significant difference at all. Schniewind has keenly observed, "The real point at issue between Christianity and modern man is not mythology but the *krisis:* it is man's rebellion against God."[38] As a matter of fact modern man's basic condition as it relates to this rebellion may be even worse than that of ancient man, for his achievements in some areas, primarily in those related to science, have inflated his ego beyond that of ancient man. The twentieth century, however, has done much to demonstrate the futility of human actions apart from their proper relationship to God. In this kind of context the question of Schniewind gets to the heart of the matter: "Will the modern man believe us when we tell him that the Christian revelation gives us a better understanding of his own predicament than he has himself?"[39]

As modern man has been estimated too high morally, the moral estimate of God has been too low. There is, for example, no adequate definition of sin. God is looked upon as a magnificent benefactor who overlooks man's sin and rebellion. It is the thrust of the New Testament that God is holy *and* loving. In his holiness he cannot tolerate sin. In his love he provided the means for redemption. The doctrine of the atonement is thus central to the New Testament. Any portrayal of the life of Jesus that tries either to avoid or dismiss this point makes of God less than the New Testament makes of him.

There is one other weakness that we need to notice in our criticism of modern approaches to the Jesus of history. Often ideas and concepts that are foreign to biblical faith are introduced into a theological system, and then called Christian. The theologies we have in mind here are those which have become wedded to existentialism. This kind of dominance of philosophy over theology has beset the Church from its beginning. We have singled out existentialism because it is currently the most popular one. The great plea for "authentic existence" is basically a plea that is not related to faith in Jesus Christ. In

[38] Julius Schniewind, "A Reply to Bultmann," *Kerygma and Myth*, I, ed. Hans Werner Bartsch, trans. Reginald H. Fuller (London: S. P. C. K., 1964), p. 100.

[39] *Ibid.*

existentialism authentic existence is viewed as man's achievement. In Christianity authenticity results from a proper relationship to God in Christ.

But even beyond this, there is a serious question whether authentic existence, however achieved, can be the goal of the Christian. The words of Williams summarize this objection:

> Christian faith holds that the goal of life is not man's own authentic existence, not his own self-affirmation, not his own freedom, not his own salvation; rather the end for which man is made can be none other than God: His glory, His kingdom, His will. God would indeed have all men live "authentically" (e.g., the Parable of the Talents: Matthew 25:14-30), but this is impossible if such living is viewed as the goal. For those who seek to save their lives (and does not existentialism make this search primary?) can only lose them; but those who lose their lives for the sake of Christ and the kingdom of God will surely find them (e.g., Matthew 6:33, 16:25).[40]

It is not by accident that the New Testament represents faith in Christ as the necessary condition for entrance into the world of the spirit. For that reason the expressions "new birth," "regeneration," etc. are particularly appropriate to describe that experience. The Christian must always remember the source of his new life, and he must make his daily experience a vital demonstration of gratitude for that life.

[40] Williams, *Contemporary Existentialism and Christian Faith*, pp. 173-74.

Bibliography

Abrahams, Israel. *Studies in Pharisaism and the Gospels*. Vol. I. Cambridge: The University Press, 1917.

Albright, William Foxwell. *From the Stone Age to Christianity*. Baltimore: Johns Hopkins, 1957.

American Revision Committee. *An Introduction to the Revised Standard Version of the New Testament*. New York: Nelson, 1946.

Anderson, Hugh. *Jesus and Christian Origins*. New York: Oxford University Press, 1964.

Baillie, D. M. *God Was in Christ*. New York: Scribner, 1948.

Barr, James. *Biblical Words for Time*. Naperville: Allenson, 1962.

Bartels, Robert A. *Kerygma or Gospel Tradition . . . Which Came First?* Minneapolis: Augsburg, 1961.

Barth, Karl. "Rudolf Bultmann—an Attempt to Understand Him," *Kerygma and Myth*. Vol. II. Ed. Hans Werner Bartsch. Trans. Reginald H. Fuller. London: S. P. C. K., 1962. Pp. 83-132.

————. *The Word of God and the Word of Man*. Trans. Douglas Horton. New York: Harper, 1957.

Berkhof, Louis. *Systematic Theology*. Grand Rapids: Eerdmans, 1959.

Bettenson, Henry (ed.). *Documents of the Christian Church*. London: Oxford University Press, 1967.

Black, M. *An Aramaic Approach to the Gospels and Acts*. Oxford: Clarendon, 1967.

Boettner, Loraine. *Studies in Theology*. Grand Rapids: Eerdmans, 1947.

Bornkamm, Günther. *Jesus of Nazareth*. Trans. Irene and Fraser McLuskey and James M. Robinson. New York: Harper, 1960.

————. "Myth and Gospel: A Discussion of the Problem of Demythologizing the New Testament Message," *Kerygma and*

History. Ed. and trans. Carl E. Braaten and Roy A. Harrisville. Nashville: Abingdon, 1962. Pp. 172-96.

Bornkamm, G., Barth, G., and Held, H. J. *Tradition and Interpretation in Matthew*. Trans. Percy Scott. Philadelphia: Westminster, 1963.

Bruce, F. F. *The New Testament Documents: Are They Reliable?* Grand Rapids: Eerdmans, 1960.

————. *The Spreading Flame*. Grand Rapids: Eerdmans, 1961.

Bultmann, Rudolf. "Bultmann Replies to His Critics," *Kerygma and Myth*. Vol. I. Ed. Hans Werner Bartsch. Trans. Reginald H. Fuller. London: S. P. C. K., 1964. Pp. 191-211.

————. *Existence and Faith: Shorter Writings of Rudolf Bultmann*. Trans. Schubert M. Ogden. New York: Meridian, 1960.

————. *The History of the Synoptic Tradition*. Trans. John Marsh. New York: Harper, 1963.

————. "New Testament and Mythology," *Kerygma and Myth*. Vol. I. Ed. Hans Werner Bartsch. Trans. Reginald H. Fuller. London: S. P. C. K., 1964. Pp. 1-44.

————. "A Reply to the Theses of J. Schniewind," *Kerygma and Myth*. Vol. I. Ed. Hans Werner Bartsch. Trans. Reginald H. Fuller. London: S. P. C. K., 1964. Pp. 102-23.

————. *Theology of the New Testament*. Trans. Kendrick Groebel. New York: Scribner, 1955.

Cairns, David. *A Gospel Without Myth?* London: S.C.M., 1960.

Carnell, Edward John. *An Introduction to Christian Apologetics*. Grand Rapids: Eerdmans, 1948.

Clarke, William Newton. *An Outline of Christian Theology*. New York: Scribner, 1917.

Conzelmann, H. *The Theology of St. Luke*. Trans. G. Buswell. New York: Harper, 1960.

Creed, J. M. *The Gospel According to St. Luke*. London: Macmillan, 1930.

Cullmann, Oscar. *Christ and Time*. Trans. Floyd V. Filson. Philadelphia: Westminster, 1951.

————. *The Christology of the New Testament*. Trans. Shirley C. Guthrie and Charles A. M. Hall. Philadelphia: Westminster, 1959.

Davies, W. D. *Christian Origins and Judaism*. Philadelphia: Westminster, 1962.

Dibelius, Martin. *Studies in the Acts of the Apostles*. Trans. Mary Ling. New York: Scribner, 1956.

Dodd, C. H. *The Bible and the Greeks*. London: Hodder and Stoughton, 1935.

————. *The Apostolic Preaching and Its Developments*. New York: Harper, 1936.

Dods, Marcus. *The Bible: Its Origin and Nature.* New York: Scribner, 1910.

Ebeling, Gerhard. *The Nature of Faith.* Trans. Ronald Gregor Smith. Philadelphia: Fortress, 1961.

Ellwein, Edward. "Rudolf Bultmann's Interpretation of the Kerygma," *Kerygma and History.* Ed. and trans. Carl E. Braaten and Roy A. Harrisville. Nashville: Abingdon, 1962. Pp. 25-54.

Farrer, Austin. "An English Appreciation," *Kerygma and Myth.* Vol. I. Ed. Hans Werner Bartsch. Trans. Reginald H. Fuller. London: S. P. C. K., 1964. Pp. 212-23.

Fuchs, Ernst. *Studies of the Historical Jesus.* Trans. Andrew Scobie. Naperville: Allenson, 1964.

Fuller, Daniel P. *Easter Faith and History.* Grand Rapids: Eerdmans, 1965.

Fuller, Reginald H. *The New Testament in Current Study.* London: S.C.M., 1963.

Geldenhuys, Norval. *Commentary on the Gospel of Luke* ("The New International Commentary on the New Testament"). Grand Rapids: Eerdmans, 1960.

Gerhardsson, Birger. *Memory and Manuscript.* Trans. Eric J. Sharpe. Uppsala: Gleerup, 1961.

Goodenough, Erwin R. "John, a Primitive Gospel," *Journal of Biblical Literature,* LXIV (June 1945), 145-82.

Grant, Robert M. *A Historical Introduction to the New Testament.* New York: Harper, 1963.

Guthrie, Donald. *New Testament Introduction: The Gospels and Acts.* Chicago: Inter-Varsity, 1965.

Harrison, Everett F. *Introduction to the New Testament.* Grand Rapids: Eerdmans, 1946.

————. "The Phenomena of Scripture," *Revelation and the Bible.* Ed. Carl F. H. Henry. Grand Rapids: Baker, 1958. Pp. 235-50.

Hepburn, R. W. *Christianity and Paradox.* London: Watts, 1958.

Hodge, Charles. *Systematic Theology.* Grand Rapids: Eerdmans, 1952.

Howard, Wilbert F., and Gossip, Arthur John. "The Gospel According to St. John," *The Interpreter's Bible,* VIII (1952), 435-811.

Hughes, Philip Edgcumbe. "Myth," *Baker's Dictionary of Theology.* Ed. Everett F. Harrison. Grand Rapids: Baker, 1960. Pp. 368-71.

Hunter, Archibald M. *Interpreting the New Testament 1900-1950.* Philadelphia: Westminster, 1951.

————. *Teaching and Preaching the New Testament.* Philadelphia: Westminster, 1963.

————. *The Work and Words of Jesus*. Philadelphia: Westminster, 1950.

Jaspers, Karl, and Bultmann, Rudolf. *Myth and Christianity*. New York: Noonday, 1958.

Jaubert, Annie. *The Date of the Last Supper*. Trans. Isaac Rafferty. New York: Alba, 1965.

Jeremias, Joachim. *Die Wiederentdeckung von Bethesda*. Göttingen: Vandenhoeck und Ruprecht, 1949.

Kähler, Martin. *The So-Called Historical Jesus and the Historic Biblical Christ*. Trans. Carl E. Braaten. Philadelphia: Fortress, 1964.

Käsemann, Ernst. *Essays on New Testament Themes*. Trans. W. J. Montague. Naperville: Allenson, 1964.

Kee, Howard Clark, and Young, Franklin W. *Understanding the New Testament*. Englewood Cliffs, N.J.: Prentice-Hall, 1960.

Kenyon, Frederic. *Our Bible and the Ancient Manuscripts*. Rev. A. W. Adams. New York: Harper, 1962.

Kinder, Ernst. "Historical Criticism and Demythologizing," *Kerygma and History*. Ed. and trans. Carl E. Braaten and Roy A. Harrisville. Nashville: Abingdon, 1962. Pp. 55-85.

Kittel, Gerhard. "The Jesus of History," *Mysterium Christi*. Ed. G. K. A. Bell and G. A. Deissmann. London: Longmans, Green, 1930. Pp. 31-49.

Künneth, Walter. "Bultmann's Philosophy and the Reality of Salvation," *Kerygma and History*. Ed. and trans. Carl E. Braaten and Roy A. Harrisville. Nashville: Abingdon, 1962. Pp. 86-119.

Ladd, George E. "The Resurrection of Christ," *Christian Faith and Modern Theology*. Ed. Carl F. H. Henry. New York: Channel, 1964. Pp. 261-84.

Langton, Edward. *Essentials of Demonology*. London: Epworth, 1949.

Mackinnon, James. *The Historic Jesus*. New York: Longmans, Green, 1931.

Macquarrie, John. *The Scope of Demythologizing*. New York: Harper, 1962.

Marxsen, W. *Mark the Evangelist*. Trans. Roy A. Harrisville. Nashville: Abingdon, 1969.

Mickelsen, A. Berkeley. *Interpreting the Bible*. Grand Rapids: Eerdmans, 1963.

Morris, Leon. *The Apostolic Preaching of the Cross*. Grand Rapids: Eerdmans, 1956.

Mullins, Edgar Young. *The Christian Religion in Its Doctrinal Expression*. Philadelphia: Williams, 1917.

Munck, Johannes. "The New Testament and Gnosticism," *Current Issues in New Testament Interpretation*. Ed. William Klassen and Graydon F. Snyder. New York: Harper, 1962. Pp. 224-38.

Oesterley, W. O. E. "Demon, Demonical Possession, Demoniacs," *A Dictionary of Christ and the Gospels.* Ed. James Hastings. I (1909), 438-43.

Ogden, Schubert M. *Christ Without Myth.* New York: Harper, 1961.

Ogletree, Thomas W. *Christian Faith and History.* Nashville: Abingdon, 1965.

Olmstead, A. T. *Jesus in the Light of History.* New York: Scribner, 1942.

Orr, James. *The Christian View of God and the World.* Grand Rapids: Eerdmans, 1947.

————. *Revelation and Inspiration.* New York: Scribner, 1910.

Price, Ira Maurice. *The Ancestry of Our English Bible.* Rev. William A. Irwin and Allen P. Wikgren. New York: Harper, 1956.

Ramm, Bernard. *The Christian View of Science and Scripture.* Grand Rapids: Eerdmans, 1954.

————. "The Evidence of Prophecy and Miracle," *Revelation and the Bible.* Ed. Carl F. H. Henry. Grand Rapids: Baker, 1958. Pp. 251-63.

————. *Protestant Biblical Interpretation.* Boston: Wilde, 1956.

————. *Protestant Christian Evidences.* Chicago: Moody, 1957.

————. *Special Revelation and the Word of God.* Grand Rapids: Eerdmans, 1961.

Reid, J. K. S. *The Authority of Scripture.* New York: Harper, 1957.

Riesenfeld, Harald. *The Gospel Tradition and Its Beginnings.* London: Mowbray, 1961.

Roberts, C. H. *An Unpublished Fragment of the Fourth Gospel in the John Rylands Library.* Manchester: Manchester University Press, 1935.

Robinson, James M. *A New Quest of the Historical Jesus.* London: S.C.M., 1959.

Rohde, Joachim. *Rediscovering the Teaching of the Evangelists.* Trans. Dorothea M. Barton. Philadelphia: Westminster, 1968.

Schniewind, Julius. "A Reply to Bultmann," *Kerygma and Myth.* Vol. I. Ed. Hans Werner Bartsch. Trans. Reginald H. Fuller. London: S. P. C. K., 1964. Pp. 45-101.

Schweitzer, Albert. *The Quest of the Historical Jesus.* Trans. W. Montgomery. New York: Macmillan, 1910.

Scott, Ernest Findlay. *The Validity of the Gospel Record.* New York: Scribner, 1938.

Stauffer, Ethelbert. *Jesus and His Story.* Trans. Richard and Clara Winston. New York: Knopf, 1960.

Stewart, James S. *A Faith to Proclaim.* New York: Scribner, 1953.

Strong, Augustus Hopkins. *Systematic Theology*. New York: Armstrong, 1902.

Tasker, R. V. G. *The Gospel According to St. John* ("The Tyndale New Testament Commentaries"). Grand Rapids: Eerdmans, 1960.

Taylor, J. B. "Word," *The New Bible Dictionary*. Ed. J. D. Douglas. Grand Rapids: Eerdmans, 1962. P. 1337.

Taylor, Vincent. *The Formation of the Gospel Tradition*. New York: Macmillan, 1933.

Tenney, Merrill C. "Reversals of New Testament Criticism," *Revelation and the Bible*. Ed. Carl F. H. Henry. Grand Rapids: Baker, 1958. Pp. 351-67.

Thielicke, Helmut. "The Restatement of New Testament Mythology," *Kerygma and Myth*. Vol. I. Ed. Hans Werner Bartsch. Trans. Reginald H. Fuller. London: S. P. C. K., 1964. Pp. 138-74.

Thompson, Claude H. *Theology of the Kerygma*. Englewood Cliffs, N.J.: Prentice-Hall, 1962.

Vos, Geerhardus. *The Self-Disclosure of Jesus*. Grand Rapids: Eerdmans, 1953.

Wallace, Ronald S. "Christology," *Baker's Dictionary of Theology*. Ed. Everett F. Harrison. Grand Rapids: Baker, 1960. Pp. 117-23.

Warfield, Benjamin Breckinridge. *The Inspiration and Authority of the Bible*. Philadelphia: Presbyterian and Reformed, 1948.

Weatherhead, Leslie D. *Psychology, Religion and Healing*. Nashville: Abingdon, 1952.

White, Victor. *God and the Unconscious*. London: Harvill, 1952.

Williams, J. Rodman. *Contemporary Existentialism and Christian Faith*. Englewood Cliffs, N.J.: Prentice-Hall, 1965.

Windisch, H. *Johannes und die Synoptiker*. Leipzig: Hinrichs, 1926.

Wright, G. Ernest. *God Who Acts*. London: S.C.M., 1952.

Index of Subjects

Index of Authors